THE POWER OF RACE IN CUBA

TRANSGRESSING BOUNDARIES

Studies in Black Politics and Black Communities
Cathy Cohen and Fredrick Harris, Series Editors

The Politics of Public Housing: Black Women's Struggles Against Urban Inequality
Rhonda Y. Williams

Keepin' It Real: School Success Beyond Black and White
Prudence L. Carter

Double Trouble: Black Mayors, Black Communities, and the Call for a Deep Democracy
J. Phillip Thompson, III

Party/Politics: Horizons in Black Political Thought
Michael Hanchard

In Search of the Black Fantastic: Politics and Popular Culture in the Post-Civil Rights Era
Richard Iton

Race and the Politics of Solidarity
Juliet Hooker

I Am Your Sister: Collected and Unpublished Writings of Audre Lorde
Rudolph P. Byrd, Johnnetta Betsch Cole, and Beverly Guy-Sheftall, Editors

Democracy Remixed: Black Youth and the Future of American Politics
Cathy J. Cohen

Democracy's Reconstruction: Thinking Politically with W.E.B. DuBois
Lawrie Balfour

The Price of the Ticket: Barack Obama and the Rise and Decline of Black Politics
Fredrick Harris

Malcolm X at Oxford Union: Racial Politics in a Global Era
Saladin Ambar

Race and Real Estate
Edited by Adrienne Brown and Valerie Smith

Despite the Best Intentions: How Racial Inequality Thrives in Good Schools
Amanda Lewis and John Diamond

London is the Place for Me: Black Britons, Citizenship, and the Politics of Race
Kennetta Hammond Perry

Black Rights/White Wrongs: The Critique of Racial Liberalism
Charles W. Mills

The Power of Race in Cuba: Racial Ideology and Black Consciousness During the Revolution
Danielle Pilar Clealand

THE POWER OF RACE IN CUBA

Racial Ideology and Black
Consciousness During the Revolution

Danielle Pilar Clealand

OXFORD
UNIVERSITY PRESS

OXFORD
UNIVERSITY PRESS

Oxford University Press is a department of the University of Oxford. It furthers
the University's objective of excellence in research, scholarship, and education
by publishing worldwide. Oxford is a registered trade mark of Oxford University
Press in the UK and certain other countries.

Published in the United States of America by Oxford University Press
198 Madison Avenue, New York, NY 10016, United States of America.

© Oxford University Press 2017

Library of Congress Cataloging-in-Publication Data
Names: Clealand, Danielle Pilar, 1978– author.
Title: The power of race in Cuba : racial ideology and Black consciousness
     during the Revolution / Danielle Pilar Clealand.
Description: New York, NY, United States of America : Oxford University Press, [2017] |
     Series: Transgressing boundries : studies in Black politics and Black communities |
     Includes bibliographical references and index.
Identifiers: LCCN 2017006337 | ISBN 9780190632298 (hardcover : alk. paper) |
     ISBN 9780190632304 (pbk. : alk. paper) | ISBN 9780190632335 (online course content) |
     ISBN 9780190632311 (UPDF) | ISBN 9780190632328 (EPUB)
Subjects: LCSH: Blacks—Cuba—Politics and government—20th century. |
     Cuba—Race relations—Political aspects—History—20th century. |
     Blacks—Cuba—History—20th century. | Cuba—History—Revolution, 1959.
Classification: LCC F1789.N3 C55 2017 | DDC 305.80097291/0904—dc23
LC record available at https://lccn.loc.gov/2017006337

In loving memory of my mother, Ida Vega, whose light and love continue to shine within me and my grandmother, Dea Clealand.

Both of these incomparable women brought me to this project and gave lovingly and generously to the foundation that I stand upon.

CONTENTS

ACKNOWLEDGMENTS

I am truly grateful for all those that supported this very special project. I am indebted to the many, friends, colleagues, mentors and spirits who contributed to this book.

The research for this book was the most rewarding part of this process. Thank you to my many sisters and brothers in Cuba who were just as passionate about this project as I am. I must thank my "tio" Tomás Fernández Robaina, who has been my friend, cheerleader, and kindred spirit. I hope that this book adds to your lifelong mission of uncovering the story and power of black Cuba. To those who helped me to reach the many voices included in this book, thank you. I never could have done this without you. To Maikel Colón, thank you for your solidarity and your commitment to the project. You were indispensable to the success of this research! Thank you to the many Cuban scholars who lent their thoughts, time, and support, especially to Lourdes Serrano, Roberto Zurbano, Gisela Arandia, and Rafael Robaina. Rafael, I wish that you could have seen this project come to fruition. Many of its insights came from our memorable conversations and your *sabiduría* is present in these pages. To my friends who supported my research and made my time in La Habana one of the best of my life, thank you: Ana, Alexei, Aliam, Isnay, Ernesto, Damian, and Balesy. To Alexey and Magia—you are the true messengers of black consciousness in Cuba and I thank you for your friendship and for the work that you do. To Norma and Lorenzo "Papacho," although you may never read this, I would never have made it through without you. My love for the both of you is eternal! To the Cuban institutions that gave their support to the research, although the finished product likely leaps over many of your boundaries, I thank you for being willing to support a project about racism and blackness in Cuba. Finally, to all of those in Cuba who gave their time, this book is for you. There is a particular magic about Cuba where you can call someone on their home phone and they will not know who you are, but they will come to your house or invite you to theirs and sit down with you for an hour or more to talk to you about personal experiences with racism on their island. The "data" in this book is so rich because of the generosity of all of the people with whom I visited, shared ideas, and drank coffee and rum.

Thank you to the amazing group of scholars in Chapel Hill and Durham that contributed to this project. To the members of my dissertation committee, Jonathan Hartlyn, Evelyn Huber, Lars Shoultz, Eduardo Bonilla-Silva, and Paula McClain, thank you for your insight and for your mentorship. Jonathan, you made me improve as a writer and researcher—thank you for going through every page of the original project to make it better. To Eduardo, my fellow Afro-Boricua, you may not know this, but you are the voice in my head when I write. Thank you for taking the time when you had no time to give, and, most importantly, for guiding my intellectual journey as a graduate student. To Sandy Darity, thank you for your mentorship and for always being in my corner. I am among many scholars that you have supported and guided and for this I am grateful. Thank you to Cathy Zimmer and the Odum Institute for helping this qualitative researcher to think quantitatively too. Cathy, you were vital to this project. Thank you to the University of North Carolina at Chapel Hill, particularly the Graduate School, for the research support. Finally, my thanks to the Department of Political Science , particularly to Frank Baumgartner and Isaac Unah, who gave me critical guidance and support.

To the African American Studies Department at Princeton University, your belief in me and this project was so significant. The dissertation was transformed during my time there and I benefited immensely from being able to write (and laugh and share) in such a special place in the midst of such brilliant scholars of black studies. My year at Princeton fortified my resolve as a scholar. To Eddie Glaude, Angel Harris, and Imani Perry in particular, thank you for everything that you contributed to this book, to my conviction, and to my scholarship. Thank you, also, for the important work that you do. A special thank you also goes to my partner at Princeton, Emily Lutenski.

To my colleagues at Florida International University, thank you for the support. Thank you in particular to my colleagues in the Department of Politics and International Relations as well as the Latin American and Caribbean Studies Department and the Cuban Research Institute. To my colleagues in the African and African Diaspora Studies Program, you have been a wonderful resource not only for scholarship, but also for solidarity and encouragement.

This project has benefited immensely from the many scholars that have read through all or a portion of this work: Michael Hanchard, Ollie Johnson, Mark Sawyer, Imani Perry, Angel Harris, Paul Frymer, Andrea Queeley, Edward Telles, Jean Rahier, Chantalle Verna, Caroline Faria, Iqbal Ashtar, Carlos Moore, Sandy Darity, and Tukufu Zuberi. Many of the people on this list have been vital to my personal journey in academia and I thank you. Andrea Queeley, thank you for your friendship and for pushing me to toot my own horn. Michael Hanchard, you are also one of the voices in my head when I write and I am grateful for your solidarity. You are challenging me even when you do not know it. Ollie Johnson, thank you for always cheering me on and highlighting the work that we all do on black politics in Latin America.

To those at Oxford University Press, thank you for your support of this project, in particular David McBride and Kathleen Weaver. To Cathy Cohen, I am proud to be among so many remarkable scholars in this series and I owe that to you, thank you. To my anonymous readers, the close reads that you gave to this text were immeasurable. Your suggestions furthered the text in exactly the ways that I had hoped for and I am so appreciative of your generosity and insight.

The family and friends that surround me are the ones that provide the energy and love needed to push forward. To Kendra Cotton, you are the consummate friend and sister. Thank you for all that you have done—I am forever grateful that our paths began in political science at the same time and in the same place. I am happy to serve in the future as your progressive (radical) conscience when you are elected to office. To Melissa Colón, thank you for your immense friendship through the years—the next book will be yours! To my sisters, Jada, Rachel, Zenda, Isis and Yvette: love you always. To my extended family, thank you for your support not just for this book, but for my journey. To my brother Evan, thank you for always believing in me—I love you. To my father, Mark Clealand, there is not a day that goes by that I do not know how proud of me you are and that means everything. To my two daughters, Naima and Savannah, I am so lucky to be your mom. You two make this life wonderful. Naima, you traveled through La Habana with me both in the womb and as a newborn and the energy, resolve, and strength you gave me has made this project such a cherished one. To my beautiful mother, Ida Vega, this book is dedicated to you because every step that led me to write my first book was guided by your spirit and love. You are untouchable and I miss you every single day. To my husband, Michael, I love you more than words can say. Thank you for the support and excitement about this project and what I do. Here's to many years together, side by side, as partners in the struggle.

INTRODUCTION

During the 2008 US presidential campaign, I was in La Habana listening to Cubans of all races tell me a black man could never be elected president of the United States of America. The prediction was no doubt couched in decades of government rhetoric that proclaims the United States to be the prime example of racism and marginalization of blacks. Racism is designated as a problem that resides outside of the island's borders, thus negating the significance of race in Cuba. Despite the skepticism concerning the United States electing a black president and the dominant discourse that denies the implications of racial identity in Cuba, many *black* Cubans were heavily invested in the election. When I returned in 2009, there was a palpable sense of pride among them in President Obama's accomplishment and position. Black people felt connected to his victory and the possibilities it symbolized for racial progress in a country where blacks are marginalized. The reactions to the 2008 election indicate that black Cubans occupy an alternative position with regard to the dominant discourse: a position that affirms the relevance of race. This book is about the influence of racial ideology and the blueprint it etches in people's everyday lives, thoughts and actions, but it is also about (and inspired by) black struggle and affirmation that transcend the dominant discourse and its professed truths.

In 1961, two years after the revolution came into power, Fidel Castro declared that the government eradicated racism and racial discrimination. His declaration portrayed the key elements of race talk in Cuba that still exist today: 1) Cuban citizens enjoy harmonious race relations; and 2) through policies and persuasion, Cuba was able to eliminate structural racism from society. The importance of this characterization is the consequence: with racial harmony achieved, the need to address race or racism was rejected. After the first few years of the revolution, race ceased to be an issue open to critical discussion or public debate.[1] Racial difference was deemed irrelevant with regard to national identity, and thus racial affirmation and racial consciousness among nonwhites was believed to be unnecessary and incompatible with the revolution. The act of racism was defined as an aberration, only present as a function of individual prejudice among a small portion of the population. The vision the government put forth was one of equality and national unity.

Today, while leaders within the government admit that nearly sixty years of revolution did not eradicate racism completely, the relative insignificance of race due to the presence of equal opportunity and access and the absence of structural and state-sponsored racism remain at the center of Cuba's racial narrative. In March of 2016, Fidel Castro wrote an open letter to President Barack Obama in response to his historic visit to the island and accompanying address to the nation. The letter was published in the state newspaper, *Granma*, where Castro decries the US president's characterization of Cuba and states,

> Nor does he say that the Revolution swept away racial discrimination, or that pensions and salaries for all Cubans were decreed by it before Mr. Barack Obama was 10 years old. The hateful, racist bourgeois custom of hiring strongmen to expel black citizens from recreational centers were swept away by the Cuban Revolution.[2]

The mention of racial discrimination was mostly likely in response to President Obama's short but crucial commentary pushing for more black rights in Cuba as both countries, he stated, work to fight racism. Although Fidel Castro is no longer at the helm of the Communist Party's leadership, his letter, published in *Granma*, still represents the ideological message of the revolution and the racial paternalism that has characterized the government's rhetoric and policies.[3] This message continues to be guided by the idea that racial discrimination was eradicated early on by the revolution's government and rejects the narrative that black Cubans still have reason to pursue civil rights and racial

---

1. It should be noted that during the Special Period beginning in the mid-1990s there was a resurgence of racial scholarship and during the past decade government leaders have slightly altered their rhetoric to discuss some aspects of racial inequality (primarily housing and representation) that has legacies before the revolution. The structure of racism within the revolution, however, continues to be a silenced topic.

2. The letter, published in the March 28, 2016 issue of *Granma* is titled "El hermano Obama."

3. Robinson 2000.

equality. Thus, the revolution continues to reject substantive policy measures to address racism based on integrationist policies that are now more than fifty years old.

Although I discuss the uniqueness of the Cuban case in this book, the negation of the presence of racism is part of a broader ideological framework that exists throughout Latin America and the Caribbean.[4] The racial ideology or racially based frameworks[5] that I identify as racial democracy argue that 1) racial identity is not a relevant social cleavage and is deemphasized through a unifying national identity; 2) there is an absence of racial hierarchies such that race is not connected to life chances or socioeconomic status; 3) individual prejudice may still exist, but only as isolated incidents; and 4) racism and discrimination are foreign problems (primarily within the United States). Racial democracy in Cuba was not born in 1959.[6] The ideology has roots that can be traced back to the period of independence, but the revolutionary regime's success in creating higher levels of equality during the first years of the 1960s brought the ideology a legitimacy it did not previously possess.

Indeed, the regime was able to increase opportunities for blacks at its inception by weakening formal and informal barriers to social inclusion and professional and educational advancement. These initial advances diminished racial inequality in important sectors and allowed the regime to make a formidable claim of solving the problem of racial discrimination. However, if the presence of racism in revolutionary Cuba was in fact miniscule and did not create a disparate experience for blacks, *mulatos*,[7] and whites, Fidel Castro's speech in 1961 would be the end of the story. This is not the case, as racial

4. Moreover, the United States shares ideological rhetoric with the region as leaders increasingly paint a picture of the country as postracial. The irony of Barack Obama's mention of black rights in his 2016 speech in Havana was not lost on many who note that he has been unwilling (or unable, depending on who is making the argument) to substantively address racism during his own administration. The potential for a robust racial politics throughout the Americas continues to be limited through colorblind or racial harmony ideologies that maintain racial inequality and confine the perceived possibilities of change among various citizenries. The lack of will in the leadership of Cuba, the United States, and beyond further solidifies the skepticism of the potential for achieving racial justice.

5. See Bonilla-Silva 2014 for his definition of racial ideology, which is used here.

6. "Racial democracy" is a term first used in Brazil; however, it has come to refer to similar colorblind ideologies throughout the region of Latin America. Other terms that are used are "racial harmony" and "Latin American exceptionalism," depending on the country and the authors' choice of terms. I will use both racial democracy and racial harmony throughout this book to refer to the racial ideology in Cuba, and Latin America as a whole.

7. I use the terms *mulato* and *mulata* in Spanish throughout the book as a term for those of mixed race. This is the term that is used in Cuba and may also be replaced with mestizo, which also represents someone of mixed race and is the terminology used on the census.

inequality remains a reality in contemporary Cuba and the persistence of racist practices supports inequality and contradicts the sustained assertion of its absence by the government. This book examines the relationship between rhetoric and reality, highlighting the intricacies and complexities of racial attitudes in Cuba, illustrating the ways in which they both align with and challenge the government's rhetoric regarding race.

Many who have done work on race in Cuba agree that racism on the island exists, but remains difficult to quantify. Scholars have pointed to racial disparities within the government and certain employment sectors as well as the marginalization of Afro-Cuban culture.[8] Due to the inability to analyze national data, we do not know the degree to which racism affects opportunity for nonwhites. One of the major contributions of this work is to show empirically, using original survey and interview data, that experiences with discrimination are quite common for blacks and there is awareness within this group of differing opportunities for whites, blacks, and *mulatos*. My data on experiences with discrimination as well as interviews with elites and tourism workers provide more insight toward what kinds of racist practices exist in Cuba at the institutional level to exclude blacks from certain sectors, in addition to evidence of racist attitudes among whites. I demonstrate that despite the argument made by the Cuban leadership that racism can only be found in the form of prejudice among a few individuals, present-day racism must also be attributed to structural mechanisms that compound historical patterns of exclusion. The decision by the revolutionary government to suppress dialogue on racism and to ignore its relevance politically, prevented its ability to build on the initial advances made toward racial equality and ultimately preserved the presence of racism in Cuban society.

Cuba and other Latin American countries have claimed to be racial democracies since the period of nation building. Consequently, the literature on the ideology in Latin America is extensive and many authors have pointed to the use of the ideology as a political tool to disguise racism. Although this book does argue that racial democracy is used by the revolutionary government as a political tool and is in fact a myth, I go beyond this well-argued point in much of the literature to outline precisely *how* racial democracy functions and is so effective in Cuba. Even amidst acknowledgment of racism, the foundational elements of racial democracy continue to be credible to everyday citizens. Through a detailed investigation and analysis of the racial

---

8. Moore 1988; de la Fuente 2001a; Adams 2004; Sawyer 2006.

norms that racial democracy in Cuba has created, this study reveals why it is so intractable, thereby contributing to understanding its power not only in Cuba, but throughout Latin America.

My research also examines what effect this racial ideology has on black perceptions of racism in Cuba. By conducting the first survey sample of only black Cubans, I uncover the ways in which racism affects blacks in Cuba and how they perceive, discuss, and act on both racism and feelings of black consciousness. This allows me to answer critical questions that are missing from contemporary debates about race in the region, such as: how does the way race is situated in the national image and discourse influence the ways in which subordinate groups 1) view the importance of racial identity in their lives, and 2) perceive racism and their own experiences with racial discrimination?

While the context in each country is vastly different, the rhetoric of racial democracy—or the idea that a country has achieved enough racial progress to deem race no longer consequential for a person's opportunity—has similar consequences. Racism remains embedded in each country's institutions and the call to erase it from the policy agenda and social imaginary leaves racism unaddressed in both realms, and thus preserves the status quo of racial inequality. In essence, racial democracy protects racism and anti-black stereotypes by denying their power, influence, and even their existence. The ideology of racial democracy is used as a signal of racial progress, yet declarations of the defeat of racism are arguments that stunt racial progress.[9] It is from this contention that I begin this book on racial politics in Cuba, arguing for increased attention to racial ideology in the study of racial inequality. The way governments and citizens frame race is crucial in determining policy outcomes and public opinion in any society. A particular racial ideology shapes the attention that race and racism receives by the state, elites, the media, and the citizenry. The following section discusses how racial democracy remains so entrenched in people's perceptions of racism in Cuba, which are discussed in greater detail in the chapters of the book.

Racial Norms in Cuba

There are three primary components to racial democracy in Cuba that work as mechanisms to maintain racial inequality and racist practices and language. The first is the policy of silence regarding racism. The elimination of black

---

9. For treatment of the effects of postracialism or the "raceless state" see Goldberg 2009, Brown et al. 2003, and Bonilla-Silva 2014.

civil society coupled with the decision by the Cuban government to eliminate any public discussion of racism helped to solidify a national silence on the topic. Although racial democracy in other Latin American and Caribbean countries created a similar norm in which racism was often negated and seldom discussed, Cuba, in effect, legislated this silence. While there was of course no law that proclaimed it illegal to discuss issues of race, by eliminating black organizations the government legislated the end of racial discourse and discourse that was specific to the black experience. In addition, claims regarding the presence of racism were deemed counterrevolutionary and came with consequences. The inability to critique the government, particularly in the early decades of the revolution, and the notion that racism had been eliminated, removed the subject from the public sphere.[10] Consequently, the subject was erased from many private circles as well, producing the national silence. I show throughout the book that the norm of silence has an effect on public opinion and how people perceive the role of racial identity and racism in Cuban society. It keeps discussions of the subject minimal and hides awareness of the presence of racial inequality and a racist culture, both of which maintain black subordination.

The marriage of racial democracy and socialism is unique to Cuba and cannot be applied to the rest of Latin America. The joining of these two ideologies, coupled with the institutionalization of silence, have made racial democracy in Cuba acutely effective and credible among Cuba's citizens, but mainly for supporters of the revolution who connect their belief in the revolution to their belief in the absence of racism. Thus, socialism strengthens the power of racial democracy in Cuba. The absence of racism, or the perception of its absence, supposedly achieved through socialist policies that increase class equality, strengthens the regime's relationship to social justice and its legitimacy (especially for those groups previously marginalized). While this was particularly true at the start of the revolution, the strategy of racial democracy produces an image of Cuba today that places the country at the forefront of racial justice, an image many continue to believe and promote. The Cuban government has explicitly stated throughout the revolution's history that it is, in fact, socialism that has brought about racial equality, while pointing to capitalist countries that have been unable to achieve this. Within

---

10. The next chapter discusses the ways in which artists and activists in the early decades of the revolution attempted to bring the subject of racism to the public sphere and were repressed and silenced (Guerra 2012).

this context, citizens believe in the silence as part of their belief in the revolution; they practice it, and it has been passed on to the next generation.

As the government sought to legitimate the silence by ridding the country of overt forms of racism through economic and social policy, citizens were in turn asked to cleanse their personal attitudes. Revolutionaries in the new Cuba were expected to be free of racism. This ethos of anti-racialism, the second mechanism, not only treated racism as an historical matter that the country overcame, but it sought to make racial identity irrelevant.[11] It removes the category of race as a cleavage that can produce unique social, economic, and political consequences and sides with the logic that race is irrelevant because racism has disappeared. The use of anti-racialism by both the government and the citizenry in Cuba serves to deny the presence of racism while simultaneously preserving negative black stereotypes and the belief in black inferiority.[12] The idea that no one is racist means that racist language and practices are acceptable and are often regarded as humorous or trivial, because anti-racialism protects acts of racism from being defined as such.[13]

The third mechanism is the definition of racism as attitudinal, rather than structural. This mechanism is the most significant in that it allows for people to acknowledge racism and trivialize it simultaneously. Furthermore, the definition of racism as attitudinal has been employed by various governments throughout the Western Hemisphere and continues to be the primary ideological tool to deny systemic racism and tout racial equality. The way in which racism is framed as racial prejudice is an undertheorized concept in the study of racial democracy and its staying power throughout Latin America.

The Cuban government has defined racism as a set of prejudiced attitudes since the start of the regime. The revolution's commitment to social justice, desegregation, and the removal of formal barriers toward advancement for nonwhites provided tangible examples of the end of structural racism in Cuba. The government released itself from any accountability regarding racism not

---

11. Anti-racialism should not be confused with anti-racism. As David Theo Goldberg argues (2009), anti-racialism refers to a stand against categorizing race, but not against the conditions that racism creates. Anti-racialism puts the concept to bed, while ignoring (and thus retaining) the negative effects of the concept.

12. Chapter 5 discusses the presence of anti-black humor and terminology in everyday language as well as anti-black attitudes among whites and *mulatos* that are expressed freely alongside the belief that none of these expressions or ideas constitute racism.

13. In my own experience, when I reacted to anti-black jokes with offense, I was met with surprise. These jokes are seldom challenged and those that speak out are often told not to take such language so seriously.

only through these policies, but because it was beyond the purview of lawmakers to solve issues of racist attitudes among individuals, they could only discourage them. I show that this way of defining racism also became pervasive among the citizenry and today holds great influence over the ways in which Cubans perceive racism in their country. As I discuss in chapter 6, the majority of those interviewed for this project viewed racism as a measure of individual prejudice and not something that could be connected to systemic patterns and policies. Racism, then, can only diminish with the progression of time and consequently, is accepted as the status quo.

The way that race is framed ideologically is integral to its analysis. Racial ideology shapes the way we see race and the way we interpret our own experiences, and it influences our decisions to organize and act. Moreover, definitions of racism that rely only on an individual-level analysis cannot offer explanations of the structural and ideological mechanisms that reinforce racial hierarchies. If racism is defined as only an individual phenomenon by the Cuban government, it would follow that data that would identify systemic racist practices and structures are not available. Through this book I explain how racial democracy affects not only public opinion at an individual level, but how it also reinforces racism on a structural level.

Uncovering Black Consciousness

Despite the power and attractiveness of the racial harmony rhetoric, racism continues to adversely affect blacks in Cuba. Racial difference determines modes of access and influences everyday social interactions, creating a space for black consciousness. Race matters in Cuba for individuals' commonsense notions of identity, so that racial consciousness among many blacks is indeed both present and relevant. During a book presentation in Havana in 2008, a Cuban scholar stood up and said,

> We are in the midst of the beginning of a black movement in Cuba. Our education must reflect that by representing both parts of history, white *and* black. Our history is incomplete if only one part is taught in our schools. Our government must represent our black citizens as well. But I do not care about the number of blacks in government if these blacks do not think like blacks. If they are not conscious, then what is the point? If they think like whites, if they are Uncle Toms that wish to perpetuate white privilege and say that racism is no longer a problem, then I can do without that black representation in government.

Black civil society has begun to grow again after the political opening in the 1990s and as a result, conversations and positions such as the one above are being given a (limited) space.

One of the key aims of this project is to identify what constitutes black public opinion in Cuba and how racial ideology influences racial attitudes. In other words, how does a black Cuban view and experience their social relations, life chances, and their position in the Cuba's racial hierarchy? This work gives a nuanced portrait of black attitudes in Cuba and argues that while spaces of black consciousness do exist, even among those that are the most vocal regarding racism in Cuba, elements of the dominant ideology are infused in their framework. Rather than offer a dichotomous concept of black consciousness (those that are conscious reject racial democracy and those who are not embrace it), the data in this book allow for a much more comprehensive analysis. Through survey data and interviews with formal organizers, hip-hop artists, and everyday citizens, this book draws from the many black spaces, both formal and informal, to highlight what black attitudes and experiences look like in Cuba.

One of the seminal works on black identity as it relates to racial politics is Michael Dawson's 1994 book *Behind the Mule*, where he analyzes whether race continues to be a "major social, and political force in American society and a major shaper of African-American lives."[14] My contention, as it relates to Cuba, uses Dawson's point of departure to say that race matters to many black Cubans and does indeed shape their lives. I demonstrate that although race matters, racial ideology creates complexities in the *way* that it matters for black Cubans. I do not apply his argument in the same way for black Cubans,[15] but race is a social and political force in Cuba. This is partially due to the changes following the economic crisis in Cuba, during which racial inequality increased and blacks began to experience discrimination more visibly and more often. Not only do many blacks identify with blackness as something separate from whites and *mulatos*, but this phenomenon has been further solidified and strengthened by the advent of the economic crisis, tourism, and dollarization where race plays a more visible role. Nonetheless, racial disparities and a visible lack of black representation in various sectors and media have existed since the start of the revolution and figure prominently into Cubans' notions of consciousness and racism.

---

14. Dawson 1994 (7).

15. As Michael Hanchard argues (2006), blacks living in different areas of the world cannot experience blackness in the same way.

In *Making Race and Nation*, Anthony Marx offers a state-centered analysis of racial politics that comprehensively argues why states reinforce racial distinctions or not and what effect this has on racial mobilization.[16] The study of racial mobilization is indeed an important component of the study of racial politics and identity. This book coincides with Marx's contention that states make race and that racial ideology is a strategic enterprise that has a significant effect on notions of racial solidarity. Similarly, scholars have highlighted the lack of racial mobilization in many countries in Latin America as part of the power of the ideology of racial democracy. This book employs a different way to look at racial consciousness outside of movements. In chapter 2, I identify two forms of racial critique that are significant to the study of black consciousness. These forms, underground critique (private conversations regarding racism in Cuba) and above-ground critique (activism, scholarship, art, and music) together give us a complete picture of what black consciousness looks like in Cuba. I place a high importance on underground or private conversations and collectives because I find that informal networks also reproduce messages of group identity that are salient, but are not necessarily expressed through mobilization. These networks communicate similar information regarding the black experience and ways in which race has everyday significance for blacks. Despite a raceless rhetoric produced from above, race, assigned by the state on each citizen's identification card, determines how many nonwhite Cubans view their country, their opportunities, and their personal relationships. Racial identity has still been consolidated through the state's imposition of racial categories, the tolerance of anti-black stereotypes, and the visible and lived racial inequalities.

The critique of the national narrative on race that occurs above-ground benefits from the political opening following the economic crisis, which allowed for more expression in the public sphere beginning in the mid 1990s. Scholarship, journalism, music, and artistic expression have taken on the subject of racism and racial identity since this period and have opened up a critical dialogue in Cuba. The limited reach of this activity to elite circles (with the exception of hip-hop) makes the underground or hidden expressions regarding race in Cuba a crucial part of black political thought. Through everyday conversation, ideas about blackness and racism in Cuba are shared in private spaces. The informality of these collectives does not discount their importance in producing and reinforcing black group consciousness. These underground conversations are the foundation of racial micropolitics and black public

---

16. Marx 1998.

opinion in Cuba. Discussions regarding racial profiling, black representation within the government, black visibility on television, and experiences with discrimination all serve as testimony to the black experience (decidedly different from the white or even *mulato* experience) and are brought out in later chapters. I argue that the analysis of experience expressed through private conversation is an alternative way to examine group consciousness.

The economic crisis of the 1990s created a context for nonwhite Cubans that was far different from the previous decades of the revolution. As tourists flowed into Cuba, surveillance of Cubans increased in places designated for tourists and police began to target nonwhite Cubans as persons that did not have any business in tourist areas. Even beyond these specific areas, particularly in central areas of Havana, police stop nonwhites at much higher rates than whites, asking for their identification. As a result, the experience of being black in Cuba now includes being racially profiled by the police and being kept out of privileged spaces. In addition, employment in tourist areas is reserved almost exclusively for whites, and uneven access to dollars (necessary for survival in the new dual economy after 1994) created racial inequalities that did not exist prior to this period. The experiences and inequalities that arose produced new realities for nonwhites where discrimination became more obvious and more prevalent in everyday terms. The conversations and collectives, both in private and in public, that build racial consciousness are often centered on these changes. This project explores the connection between experience and solidarity. Discrimination heightens the saliency of race and has a direct relationship to how blacks view their own identity and their connection to other blacks.

In addition to providing a way to understand how racial democracy remains so entrenched in Cuba, the data that I use in this book provide critical information about how racial ideology can both influence and be debunked by black racial attitudes, black consciousness, and racist practices that reinforce racial inequality in Cuba. Thus, I build a complete story about the interactions between racial ideology, racism, and racial consciousness. My study of Cuba also highlights the ways marginalized groups both create and are discouraged from creating racial discourse and counterideologies in a society that promotes a colorblind interpretation of race. This kind of inquiry can be applied to the United States, Brazil, and Puerto Rico, among others.[17] We can look at the ideological currents on race in any particular country

---

17. The study shows that while there are certainly contextual differences among each country in Latin America and even throughout the Diaspora, racial ideology often produces similar results regarding racial progress.

and examine how those currents affect black agency, either directly or indirectly, and find that a colorblind approach retards racial progress. What is unique about Cuba is that black consciousness and activism exist in response to Marxism's inability to bring about black liberation. As Cedric Robinson argues, "Western Marxism . . . has proven insufficiently radical to expose and root out the racialist order that contaminates its analytic and philosophic applications."[18] That racialist order became more visible with the Special Period, but was always embedded within Cuban society, culture, and politics throughout the revolution.

Nevertheless, the revolution places a special emphasis on producing a society of racial harmony through socialist policies that increased economic equality and equality of opportunity for blacks at the start of the revolution, making Cuba an optimal case study of racial democracy. The dominant discourse promoted by the government represents the purest form of a colorblind approach to race in the region. Thus Cuba is generalizable, but also unique in its combination of socialist ideology and racial democracy that connects attitudes about race to political attitudes about the revolution. Finally, because of the limits in collecting data on the island, the original data in this book are crucial to providing a comprehensive contribution to the study of racial politics on the island.

Methodology

The data for this project consist of a survey taken from March to October of 2008 and in April and May of 2009 in the city of Havana, as well as forty-two in-depth interviews conducted during the same time period. I conducted the surveys in the city of Havana with assistance from two black Cuban colleagues.[19] The survey was conducted among black Cubans to analyze the components of black identity and black consciousness, and is the first of its kind conducted in Cuba. We surveyed 409 respondents ranging in age from fourteen to seventy-eight, and in educational levels from the completion of primary school to postgraduates. Sample sizes for each question ranged from 393 to 409. Forty-two interviews were conducted with twenty-one blacks, eleven *mulatos*, and ten whites. Interviews were conducted by myself only

---

18. Robinson 2000, 317.

19. Although the survey data and coversations include people from outside of Havana, the majority of the data come from the capital. There is more work to be done on racial politics throughout the island, particularly to be able to compare notions of black consciousness in different provinces in Cuba. See Andrea Queeley (2015) for important work on blackness, identity formation and racism in Santiago de Cuba.

and ranged in length from twenty minutes to two hours. The interviewees ranged in age from nineteen to eighty-three, and interviews were conducted in various neighborhoods in Havana differing in socioeconomic levels. When one is in the field conducting research every experience, conversation, and observation helps to inform the project. Moreover, I observed that the study of race was seen as something quite controversial, while informal discussions, jokes, and preferences regarding race were seen as completely normal. Many of the insights and even some of the quotes and anecdotes included in this work were born out of my everyday interactions and were not always part of an interview. The ethnographic work done in addition to the surveys and interviews are a sizeable part of my findings and constitute the bulk of the knowledge that I have gathered regarding racial politics in Cuba since 2003.[20]

Despite the sensitivity of the subject of race, most of my interviewees spoke about the topic with surprising candor. My position as both an American and a *mulata* allowed me to gain interesting insight into people's racial attitudes. As an American, I was perceived to be outside of Cuban racial categorizations and as a person of mixed race, I was able to navigate racial lines in a way that made white interviewees feel comfortable expressing their views of blacks, and black interviewees similarly comfortable expressing their attitudes regarding whites. Similarly, *mulatos* would consider me to be one of them, and often would say phrases such as "we *mulatos*," referring to me in their racial conceptions. While various studies on the race of interviewers have pointed to the limitations of blacks interviewing whites and vice versa,[21] there have not been similar studies on the effects of being a foreigner or a member of a mixed-race category in a country that does not have a dichotomous racial classification scheme. In my experience, being of mixed race did not place me in the black or white category, and thus did not usually limit people from expressing their genuine views about these two groups. As a foreigner I would often be considered by Cubans to be excluded from racial meanings on the island, which seemed to allow people to be candid about race as well.

The respondents for the survey were all black Cubans identified by a dual process. First, they were identified by myself and my colleague by phenotype and according to the Cuban racial schema, and then after we approached them, they were self-identified. My colleague and I discussed each respondent before approaching them to ensure that we were in

---

20. The ethnographic research was amassed during my time in Cuba, which consists of one month in 2003 and 2005, ten months in 2008, one month in 2009, and one month in 2010.

21. See Finkel et al. 1991 and Davis 1997.

agreement about whether the person would be considered black by Cuban racial standards.[22] Although *mulatos* are also Afro descendants, this survey focuses only on those that identify as black and are considered black in Cuba and not *mulato*. Using Cuba's racial classification system, *mulato* represents a separate racial category, both formally and informally, and was not subsumed into the black category, as would be the case in the United States. Each respondent was asked if they identified as black before completing the survey. The questions in the survey used the term "black" in the first person and thus could not be filled out by someone who did not identify as such.[23]

The survey is a convenience sample but with dispersion in that data were collected in neighborhoods, workplaces, and a university. The neighborhoods were chosen for their diversity in both racial make-up and socioeconomic conditions. This was done to ensure diversity in the sample, and based on these methods, no subpopulation should have a sampling probability of zero. The surveys were conducted in person, and survey respondents were chosen randomly. Under such a restrictive political environment, this sample represents the best methods available and has succeeded in capturing the opinions of a large variety of black Cubans.

Although the inability to access racial data from the Cuban census makes this dataset invaluable, it also means that it is impossible to know the extent to which indicators for factors such as education, age, and occupation among blacks differ from overall census numbers for Havana that include all races. Data for the 2002 census are not made available for black Cubans alone, and thus the demographics in my sample have to be compared with census data

---

22. I use the term "black" to describe persons that would be considered black or in some cases *mulato* by Cuban standards. The category of *mulato* includes both those of very light skin and those of darker skin, and there is not a definitive line separating dark *mulatos* and blacks of lighter brown skin. Thus, while someone may be considered *mulato* or *moro*, a term to describe dark-skinned *mulatos*, they are likely to identify with blackness as well. While the respondents we approached are considered black in Cuba, we did survey those of mixed-race heritage, who may be considered *mulato* with darker skin, who confirmed that they identified as black.

23. Research in other Latin American countries has found that often racial self-identification does not match with interviewer identification primarily due to nonwhites identifying as lighter than they may be identified by others (Telles 2004). My finding in Cuba is that there is a high level of agreement with self-identification and interviewer identification in that those considered to be black in Cuba self-identify as such. In my implementation of the survey we only received four denials to complete the survey, because someone who we identified as black identified as *mulato*. Moreover, Mark Sawyer (2006) found in his study of racial identification in Cuba that there was significant agreement with both interviewer and self-identification not only among blacks, but all races.

of all races.[24] Gender and levels of schooling are reported for all of Cuba, and age distribution is reported for Havana only. The gender distribution of my sample closely matches that of the 2002 census. My survey oversamples university students, which leads to a higher level of education when compared to national education levels and a younger sample when compared to statistics on age in Havana.[25]

According to the 2002 census, the racial make-up in Cuba is 65 percent white, 24 percent *mulato* or *mestizo*, 10 percent black, and 1 percent other.[26] Several authors have called into question the accuracy of the census numbers on race, suggesting that the black and *mestizo* population is much higher than 35 percent.[27] During a trip to Cuba in 2005, I came upon many conversations among scholars and activists regarding what they considered a whitening of Cuba's racial make-up by the census collectors. A person's race is determined by the data collector and not by self-identification, which may account for a whitening of the population. The same is true for identification cards, where a person's race is also listed. While it cannot be determined if the census is a project that is purposefully whitening the national racial make-up, just from observation throughout the island, it is doubtful that 65 percent of the population is white.

A survey conducted by someone from the United States, particularly on a politically sensitive issue, has the potential to affect survey respondents' answers. Respondents may be less candid or even wary of answering certain questions. Moreover, Cubans may be less likely to consider filling out a survey if they know that it is being conducted by a scholar from the United States. Contact with someone from the United States, especially in an official capacity, can bring negative repercussions to Cubans. To avoid this issue, when conducting surveys my Cuban colleague would approach all respondents with me but would be the only person who would conduct initial communication. Although I appear to be Cuban, my accent may have suggested that I am a foreigner and could have affected both our response rates and the actual

---

24. See Appendix A for a comparison of survey respondents and Cuban census data.

25. Education levels for Havana only were not available, and thus national statistics were used. There may be reason to believe that education levels may be higher for residents in the capital than they would be in the country as a whole.

26. See Appendix.

27. Both Carlos Moore (1988) and Henley Adams (2004) discuss what they perceive to be discrepancies between the census reporting of racial identity and the actual racial make-up of the population.

answers in the survey. Once the survey was completed and respondents had questions, both my colleague and I talked freely to them. As a result, we had only five people that did not want to fill out the survey and another nine who filled it out but chose "neutral" as all of their answers. These nine surveys are not included in the sample. Four out of the five who chose not to participate in the survey said that they did not want to, and one said that they were not educated enough to fill it out.

Although the survey data examined black identity on its own, I conducted the interviews with Cubans of all races. The interviews are used to examine racial attitudes and discuss how the dominant discourse regarding race and racism influence whites, blacks, and *mulatos*. The interviews serve as a complement to the survey data in that they provide a more nuanced view of how people view race, and they also serve to explain in more detail areas that the survey instruments cannot cover. This is not a random sample in a conventional sense, though on occasion I provide aggregated replies or broad trends in the interviews to reinforce the evidence provided by the survey data in the previous chapter. While the questions in the survey can give insight into questions of black identity and consciousness, the interviews are able to address the meanings, thoughts, and reasons for many of the survey results. In addition, it is necessary to understand how members of different races view the same topics and whether perceptions may differ according to race. Finally, interviews are able to make up for some of the limitations that arise from survey respondents answering what may be socially preferable answers as opposed to their true positions on racial matters. In one of my interviews, for example, an interviewee shared that she had no problem socially mixing with nonwhite Cubans and had many friends who were black. As the interview progressed, she began to tell a story that indicated she had racist views of blacks. Through people's stories, opinions, and feelings we can get a far more comprehensive idea of what their racial attitudes are than the answers given on a questionnaire.

Organization

The organization for this book follows a two-part model that examines racial politics in Cuba from the point of view of both structure and agency. My treatment of racial ideology does not only consider how the dominant ideology promoted by the state is communicated and then received by those on the ground. It also examines how the realities that do not coincide with these ideological frames create a unique black experience through which new

currents of thought are created. Those currents pass along racial commonalities and build solidarity as they contradict the dominant ideology and its
claim of equal opportunity. These spaces of communication and solidarity
have reached their highest level in Cuba since the start of the revolution, and
are largely due to an increase in racism that opened up these conversations
and the strengthening of counterideologies. In this way my model not only
probes the dominant, but emphasizes the subordinate, making a contention
that it is the subordinate that not only completes the picture but speaks to the
future of racial politics, both in Cuba and throughout the African Diaspora.

The top portion of the model, as shown in Figure 0.1, argues that racial
ideology in Cuba, a combination of racial democracy and socialism, creates
social norms with regard to race that support the racial status quo of black
subordination. These norms are silence regarding racism; anti-racialism; and
the perception that racism only manifests as prejudice among individuals,
rather than as a structural phenomenon. These norms allow for race to appear
less salient, and thus nonwhites are less likely to connect their life chances
and opportunities to racial identity. Each norm and its effect on racial attitudes and the presence of racism are discussed in a separate chapter. The
bottom portion of the model argues that the presence of racism in Cuban
society can create a break with these norms and allows for the development
of counterideologies that support black consciousness, dialogue on racism
among blacks, and the recognition of racism as a structural phenomenon. The
presence of black consciousness and increased dialogue and activism against
racism seeks to create a break with the racial status quo of inequality (represented by the dotted line). The development of black consciousness is the
principal way to challenge racial inequality. For that to flourish, the ideology

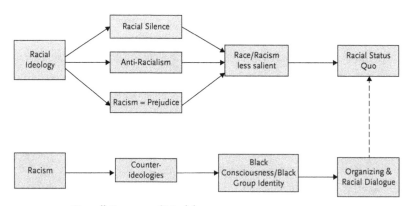

FIGURE 0.1 Overall Conceptual Model

of racial democracy must be confronted and eventually dismantled. Racial disparities, experiences of racism, and differences in life chances and opportunity between blacks and whites allow for this space.

Chapters 1 and 2 present the theoretical framework that is represented in the above model. Chapter 1 examines racial ideology and how racial democracy works in Cuba. This chapter engages in a discussion of how ideology creates norms and shapes people's perceptions and interpretations of social realities. The ideology of racial democracy or racial harmony serves to legitimate the racial status quo by trivializing racial hierarchies or refuting them completely. Consequently, the ideology has created, over time, standard ways of perceiving race, or racial norms.

Chapter 2 is a theoretical examination of black consciousness in Cuba and the dialogue that comes out of black communities, which often contradicts dominant ideologies. The two forms of ideological critique, underground and above-ground, are discussed as equally important to the study of black consciousness in Cuba. Despite the lack of institutions and networks that support dialogue and agency, blacks have managed, both formally and informally, to challenge the rhetoric from above and sustain a crucial narrative about racism in Cuba from the black perspective. There is an element of solidarity and group identity that stems from blacks' marginal position not only in Cuba, but also throughout the Americas.

In chapter 3, I discuss racial democracy and black activism prior to 1959, during the Cuban Republic. The historical foundations of racial ideology in Cuba offer critical information about how the revolution developed its racial discourse. Racial ideology during this period was a dominant narrative, but was not institutionalized to prohibit discussion of racism. Consequently, this period saw the development of an above-ground black voice represented through associations, clubs, press, and a black political party. These voices were silenced by the revolution, and the chapter chronicles an important history of black activism and expression that was relegated to the private sphere after 1959.

Chapter 4 demonstrates how racial ideology has operated in Cuba during the revolutionary period. The unification of two ideologies—racial democracy and socialism—creates a racial ideology that is distinct from other Latin American countries. By supporting racial democracy with policy measures at the start of the revolution and officially declaring the end of racism, the government has ensured that the influence of racial democracy in Cuba is particularly strong up until the present. Moreover, the initial advances that the revolution was able to make by dismantling segregation and increasing equality of opportunity for nonwhites provided a formidable claim by the government that race was no longer relevant in Cuba. The economic crisis that followed the fall of the Soviet Union, termed the Special Period, marked the first serious challenge to racial ideology in Cuba as inequalities increased with significant racial dimensions. I examine the change in rhetoric among the leadership and how ideological discourse was adjusted during this time. The chapter outlines the various theoretical components of racial ideology in Cuba and how it interacts with the socialist system and its nationalist rhetoric. Finally, I include interviews that show how support for the revolution is tied to racial attitudes and belief in Cuban racial democracy.

One of the major components of Cuban racial ideology is the notion of anti-racialism. The start of the revolution created such an ethos by condemning the presence of racism among people's set of beliefs: beliefs that were expected to change and progress in concert with the new government. The phrases "there is no racism here" or "I am not racist" are the common responses when asked about racism or discussing one's own beliefs. Consequently, the revolution's noble declaration and goal of creating a racism-free country has created a norm in which racism is an external concept. It either resides in another country or another, less enlightened person's mindset, but it is never present or accounted for on a personal or national level. I argue in chapter 5 that this norm has hindered any discussion or reflection on race and racism in Cuba such that its presence goes ignored (we do not have it, so it must be something else). Additionally, the act of ignoring racism allows for negative racial stereotypes to continue to be expressed with little challenge. The chapter examines my interviews with whites on their opinions regarding racism in Cuba as well as their own connection to anti-black attitudes. I also use survey data to highlight blacks' position on race relations in Cuba, particularly in their individual relations with whites.

Chapter 6 explores the framing of racism in Cuba both from above and below. Although it cannot be denied that there are instances of discrimination that whites still practice against nonwhites, often admissions of such treatment are, at worst, linked to individual prejudice that is uncontrollable by government or society and, at best, viewed as mere aberrations that do not represent the national attitude toward race.[28] This view of racism as personal

---

28. Part of the rhetoric common among whites is that blacks are in fact racist against themselves or even worse, racist against other whites. This notion is often communicated by whites to both deny the existence of white privilege and to suggest instead that maybe the problem of racism is not with whites, but with blacks. The historical belief of black racial inferiority by members of that same group is not attributed to white supremacy but rather is reinterpreted as intraracism among blacks. This argument is part of the framework of racial democracy in that racism can be deflected not only to individual attitudes and prejudice, but away from whites as well.

rather than structural represents a standard way of perceiving race that is supported by racial democracy and obscures any correlation between race and opportunity. Through interviews and survey data on the nature of experiences with discrimination, I examine 1) how pervasive this way of characterizing racism in Cuba is among the citizenry, and 2) whether discrimination is indeed experienced and perceived by blacks as something between individuals or on a structural level.

Chapter 7 is an examination of racist practices in Cuba, and explores the commonality and nature of racial discrimination. This chapter begins the discussion of the bottom portion of the model to show how racism operates on the island. The economic crisis of the 1990s marked the first serious challenge to racial ideology in Cuba as inequalities increased with significant racial dimensions. Racism and discrimination became much more visible, particularly to nonwhites. I outline some of the practices that have taken place to limit nonwhites' opportunities in the emergent sector and how anti-black stereotypes have informed policy and practice. Using survey data, I demonstrate who is most likely to experience discrimination in Cuba and how.

Chapter 8 analyzes how components of Cuban racial ideology influence black consciousness and identity formation. The data in this chapter add to the information we have about what underground racial consciousness and dialogue looks like among blacks. I argue that although racial democracy has been successful in creating a perception of equality and decreased saliency of race, black consciousness continues to exist and racial identity is quite significant to blacks in their daily lives. The experience of discrimination, the presence of racism, and perceptions of being undervalued in Cuban society heighten the saliency of race and have a direct relationship to how blacks view their own identity and their connection to other blacks. At the same time, the dominant racial ideology promoted by the state is paramount to how blacks view social and political realities and their racial implications.

The last chapter of the book, chapter 9, takes a look at formal or aboveground expressions of racial consciousness in Cuba and the development of a space, albeit a small one, for racial dialogue on the island. The chapter looks at organizations that were created after the political opening in the 1990s to address issues of discrimination, and how their focus and influence affect the debate that is beginning to circulate around race. I also highlight how the hip-hop movement, one of the most important and far-reaching messengers of black consciousness in Cuba, uses music to insert a new racial rhetoric into the public sphere that has not been heard prior to this period. Finally, I join the under- and above-ground components of black consciousness to show that black public opinion regarding organization and activism often aligns with what scholars and activists are pushing for and writing about in the public sphere.

This project comes during a period in Cuba where we can observe the racial consequences of the economic crisis and its recovery measures. Pockets of organizing and expression have arisen, and we see for the first time since the start of the revolution black consciousness coming to the surface. It is an extremely timely point in history to examine the changing racial politics in Cuba and people's notions of identity and racial consciousness. In the conclusion, I discuss the future of racial politics in Cuba in the current context of change both within Cuba and between the United States and Cuban governments.

My aim for this project is to be one of the first studies of black politics in Cuba that will eventually be part of a larger conversation about the intersection of ideology and black political thought, both in Cuba and throughout Latin America. As I was conducting my interviews and surveys throughout Havana, many respondents expressed surprising curiosity and excitement about where this work would be published. Many thanked me for approaching such a topic and asking questions that no one had asked them before, but that they clearly wanted to answer and continue to ponder. In this way, my small project became part of a conversation that would endure beyond the time spent filling out a survey. I hope that this book brings a voice to those Cubans and is part of the process of reducing black invisibility.

1 TODOS SOMOS CUBANOS

HOW RACIAL DEMOCRACY WORKS IN CUBA

The work of racial ideology is to shape people's common sense notions of race and its effects. How people perceive race in their individual lives and within the larger society is influenced by racial ideology and rhetoric, both from above and below. The framework that guides how racism is defined and discussed is supported by institutions, state policy, and the mass media, and holds tremendous influence on how we interpret both structural phenomena and our own personal experiences within and surrounding these structures. Whether or not people think that race plays a role in their social relationships, economic opportunities, levels of access, and everyday experiences has much to do with the way that race and racism are framed and the social norms that racial ideology produces. These norms become part of a nation's identity and because they are historically embedded, they have represented a particular way of thinking, talking and doing with regard to race for generations.

The revolution, throughout its decades, has reinforced the ideology of racial democracy and in doing so, has created a set of norms that guide attitudes about race and racism in Cuba. These norms are silence regarding racism; anti-racialism; and an understanding of racism as racial prejudice, rather than systemic racism embedded in the country's institutions. The norms are part of a purposeful program that sought to define racism after the revolution and rid the island of its existence and any discussion of its existence. This chapter discusses racial ideology during the Cuban Revolution and the ways in which the state has developed a racial ideology that negates racism and the importance of race, while race has remained a powerful and ever relevant cleavage among Cubans.

The ability of ideologies to create norms and thus influence citizens' interpretations of everyday occurrences and phenomena lies in their discourse. Anti-racist ideology has engaging rhetoric that describes an ideal society without the problem of racism. The power of racial ideology to create an illusion lies in its relationship to values that are attractive to citizens. Discourse surrounding anti-racism, integration, and a humanistic ethos that does not divide a nation's citizens is more appealing than discourse that refers to racial difference and unsettling topics such as racism and white privilege. Discussion of racist actions or beliefs can consequently be viewed as unpatriotic and against the national image of equality.[1] Under an ideology where race is no longer important, nonwhites can feel certain that their opportunity will never be affected by their race and that they are equal to whites. Whites can claim that neither race nor white privilege are a part of society and thus can be free of accountability. An anti-racist ethos is produced whereby whites can characterize themselves as being nonracist regardless of their actions or beliefs. Thus, both whites and nonwhites have reason to preserve racial democracy both within and outside of Cuba and their support is crucial to the ideology's maintenance and survival.[2]

The racial ideology promoted by the Cuban government serves dominant interests by negating the presence of racial inequality and preventing a sustained challenge to the racial status quo of white supremacy. Notwithstanding, racial ideology could not produce any level of consent if it did not look to include subordinates as well.[3] As Mary Jackman argues, ideologies support dominant actors, but are designed to soothe subordinates about the existing power relationship.[4] The assertion that each individual was equal under the law by the country's first leaders during independence sought to placate racial tensions and assure blacks and *mulatos* that race should not be a consideration in matters of opportunity and equality. The revolution of 1959 sought to do the same by declaring that racism was eradicated. The desegregation efforts at the start of the revolution to support this assertion, combined with the notion of equal opportunity and equality among racial groups, served to include subordinates and avoid dissent. Subordinates were not only "soothed"

---

1. Robin Sheriff (2001) calls the discussion of racism and racial difference in Brazil as being "unBrazilian." Also see Skidmore 1993.

2. See Bonilla-Silva 2001.

3. In *The German Ideology*, Marx (1970) argues that the ruling class aims, "to represent its interest as the common interest of all the members of society, that is, expressed in ideal form: it has to give its ideas the form of universality, and represent them as the only rational, universally valid ones" (61).

4. Jackman 1994.

regarding the power relationship between whites and nonwhites, but the racial discourse also communicated a message that there was in fact no power relationship at all with regard to race.

Racial Ideology

The debate on ideology (both in definition and intent) is expansive,[5] but ideological projects regarding race stand separate from this debate. My concept of racial ideology uses Eduardo Bonilla-Silva's definition where racial ideologies are the "racially based frameworks used by actors to explain and justify (dominant race) or challenge (subordinate race or races) the racial status quo."[6] Racial ideologies are belief systems that not only serve to legitimate or bury racial hierarchies, but also provide the lens through which to understand everyday occurrences and realities that can be connected to race. They produce dominant societal views about race, which can then be transferred to individual beliefs.[7] Racial ideologies seek to provide a framework for how we might interpret a particular set of conditions—the relationship between race and opportunity, the presence of a racial hierarchy in which whites occupy the highest positions, the presence of structural racism and how we view our social position and experiences vis-à-vis racial identity (or if we should at all). The ways in which these various conditions are framed within different contexts and countries differ in their relationship to truth, but all racial ideologies serve to interpret and often justify the racial status quo.

With this in mind, racial ideology cannot take on a neutral or benign characteristic, a possibility that scholars have argued for when defining ideology

---

5. The study of ideology has produced many varying definitions of the concept, most of which agree that it is a system of beliefs around which people cohere. Ideologies form the framework through which individuals perceive, interpret and make sense of their own realities (Bonilla-Silva 2001). Scholars differ considerably on how ideology should be conceived: its relationship to truth, whether it is historically situated, or whether ideology is motivated by the interests of rulers and elites. Some authors have developed neutral conceptions of the term without connotations of truth, illusion, or political intent (Williams 1977). Mannheim (1991) distinguishes between the particular and total conception of ideology, marking the particular version as one that is created by individuals and, in turn, one of which we can be skeptical. Particular ideologies are often used to consciously obscure reality whereas the total conception of ideology refers to the thoughts of an era or group. Much of the later work on ideology, specifically in the Marxist tradition, uses this conception of particular ideologies in order to link ideological production to domination and false consciousness (Horkheimer 1972; Rorty 1994), using power and illusion to promote consent (Jackman 1994).

6. Bonilla-Silva 2014, 9.

7. See Neville et al. 2005.

in the general sense. Racial ideology, particularly when promoted by the state or elites, furthers an illusion, whether the biological inferiority of a race, or the professed equality of all races amidst inequality. The system of ideas and beliefs created with regard to race carries strategic and political intent.[8] In Latin America and the Caribbean, these ideas were constructed by elites following abolition of slavery in order to create a stable racial order without racial divisions, amidst a racial status quo of inequality.[9] Nonwhites, in many cases remained excluded from opportunity, employment and rights while rhetoric of racial equality served to assuage the discontented. The Cuban Revolution did not invent racial democracy or discourses promoting racelessness; these discourses were always present throughout Cuba and the surrounding region in an effort to create a picture of racial harmony, despite the reality that blacks were continually at the bottom of the social hierarchy. Today, the lack of congruence between the racial rhetoric promoted by the Cuban government and the realities of racism on the ground demonstrate that there is political intent in the promotion of a racial harmony. Chapter 7 discusses specifically the commonality of racial discrimination experienced by blacks as well as the high levels of awareness of racism within Cuban society. While blacks and *mulatos* are barred from employment opportunities and experience racial profiling by the police, the dominant discourse continues to promote a society without systematic racism.

Scholars have argued that racial democracy in Latin America emerged as—and continues to be—a politically driven tool.[10] Many racial scholars have presented the argument that racial democracy acts as a mask rather than

---

8. The nature of racial ideology takes on what Eagleton (1994) describes as ideas that are "granted an active political force, rather than being grasped as mere reflections of their world" (6).

9. During the 1930s and 1940s, Latin America experienced a surge of intellectual thought on race that served to solidify the legitimacy of harmonious race relations and contributed to the institutionalization of racial democracy. Racial discourse was often a product of elite exchanges throughout the Caribbean and Latin America (Blanco 1942; Torres 1998). Tomas Blanco first presented his work *Racial Prejudice in Puerto Rico* in Havana in 1937, after being invited by La Institución Hispanocubana de Cultura y por la Sociedad de Estudios Afro-Cubanos. Blanco subsequently dedicated his book to Fernando Ortiz, a prominent Cuban scholar who promoted similar ideologies on race in Cuba. Moreover, Puerto Rican scholar Juan Manuel Carrión used Ortiz's conception of the Cuban identity as a stew or *ajiaco*, to discuss national identity in Puerto Rico as a mix of cultures, rather than being racially based (Torres 1998).

10. This argument has been made for various countries in Latin America. Elisa Nascimento (2007) makes the argument for Brazil that racial democracy "transforms a social system composed of profound racial inequalities into a supposed paradise of racial harmony" (73). Scholars focusing on Cuba both in the contemporary period and the prerevolutionary period also point

a prescriptive ideal.[11] These arguments do not deny the reach or the popular attractiveness of the ideology, but in fact recognize these elements as part of the power to create an illusion of racial equality.[12] Citizens want to believe that their country does not suffer from systematic racism, and nonwhites in particular want to believe that advancement is achieved through merit and thus opportunity is not limited for them as individuals. The appeal of this message at the start of the revolution in Cuba drew from these desires for equality.

In Cuba, the perception of political intent tends to vary among citizens.[13] While many would argue in Cuba that racism does exist in a form more entrenched than the government suggests, my research shows that few would say that the revolutionary government strategically glossed over this problem. In other words, racial democracy in Cuba is a political project of the revolution that has managed to convince citizens, perhaps not of its truth, but of the genuine desire of the government to make it true. This is quite an accomplishment by the government, and signals that after five decades, many still believe in the revolution as an anti-racist movement that sought to eradicate racial inequality even while silencing the subject. The narrative that runs through Cuba on the ground is in fact quite similar to the government's current narrative regarding intent:[14] at the start of the revolution, the government thought

---

to the clear strategic characteristics of racial ideology to foment unity and suppress black activism. See Aline Helg (1995) and Melina Pappademos's (2011) work for the Republican period, and Mark Sawyer (2006) for a contemporary argument. Moreover, as colorblind ideology in the United States becomes more pervasive, scholars have examined how racial ideology serves to conceal racial hierarchy and inequality (Bonilla-Silva 2014; Forman 2004; Brown et al. 2003). Also see Dulitsky 2005.

11. See Hanchard (1994), Caldwell (2007), and Vargas (2004).

12. In his seminal work on Brazilian racial politics, Hanchard (1994) points to the strategic nature of racial democracy by arguing that state policy "sought to mask or downplay racial differences" (47). Elisa Larkin Nascimento (2007) similarly argues that the national popular consciousness is infused with what she refers to as the myth of racial democracy and the sorcery of color, which replaces race with color. She discusses racial democracy as a "scheme" that serves to erase racism both from history and from present day society in an effort to highlight color, which disguises the "racial content of hierarchies that are, in fact, based on white supremacy" (18). Several scholars have pointed to the role of ideology in justifying or obscuring racial hierarchies which in turn places the blame of lower socioeconomic positions on subordinates rather than elites (Sidanius et al. 1997; Bobo 2004; Bonilla-Silva 2001).

13. What is significant for this book is not whether or not racial ideology has political intent, but how this political tool guides public opinion, identity formation, and racial attitudes and norms.

14. The widespread support that racial democracy receives among ordinary citizens can bolster arguments that the ideology is not just the work of elites. In her book on race in urban Brazil,

it would be able to rid society of the ills of racism, but after fifty years, it was not able to.[15] In an interview, a young male Cuban thought that Fidel Castro's decision to declare racism solved was an error, but not a strategy:

> I don't see it as a strategy. Fidel thought that the problem would be solved without having to promote it. He thought that if he created this way of thinking, everyone would follow him and his line of politics. But it didn't happen that way because everyone doesn't think equally.

Here the interviewee displays a cognizance of racism in Cuban society, but views the problem as a measure of people's belief systems rather than an issue that needs to be tackled from a structural or policy standpoint. Thus, the Cuban government did not fail in eradicating racism systemically; the failure lies in the assumption that a revolution can alter people's belief systems with regard to racial difference. It would follow, then, that the declaration of the end of racism and the presence of racial harmony was not a strategy to quell nonwhite discontent, but an underestimation of the extent of individual racism.

The removal of dialogue regarding race during the first three decades of the revolution, coupled with the prohibition of organizations and scholarship that might debate the matter, meant that race was to be silenced without any inquiry into what was actually being solved or eradicated. Other arenas to which the government professed dedication (illiteracy, health care, sexism) were tackled at the start of the revolution through a process of comprehensive activism and organization. The race issue, however, was dismissed as a something that would simply disappear through desegregation, higher levels of economic equality, and adherence to anti-racist, revolutionary ideals.

Robin E. Sheriff argues that racial democracy, while emanating from the power center, operates as more than just an elite conspiracy. The ideology has been able to reach those far beyond this power center and continues to win over adherents through its idealistic features. As Sheriff argues, the ideology "organizes sentiments as well as public discourses" (7). The ideal of racial democracy continues to be supported throughout Latin America, even as it is challenged on a national level. There have been many critiques of the components of racial democracy throughout Latin America, yet it continues to be an ideal to which many at the very least aspire to and at most, believe to be true. The very maintenance of racial democracy requires an acceptance of the masses and would have to reach beyond those in power in order to possess the character of an ideology. Nonetheless, the reach of its rhetoric does not discount its character as an elite driven framework to define race relations as something contrary to what they are.

15. This admission only coming after the economic crisis revealed and exacerbated racial inequalities that had always existed, but remained concealed.

Attempts to raise the issue of racism in the late 1960s were met by repressive acts by the government revealing the intention of the government to silence and ignore the problem.[16] One of my interviewees argued:

> In '59 we declared racism solved and we repressed it and we repressed people that wanted to talk about it. We couldn't talk about racial differences because that was negative and would divide us. And it would be against official policy. It sounds ridiculous but it's not, you have to understand what the environment was then.

The need for national unity at the start of the Cuban revolution is often used as a justification for the silence. While national unity was one of the focal points of the revolutionary rhetoric in 1959, history suggests that unity or the threat of the United States was not the only reason that dialogue regarding racism was silenced. The negation of racism in Cuba has worked to suppress black activism since the beginning of the Republic. Chapter 3 points to this history arguing that the revolution sought to eradicate dissent and racial activism, rather than racism.

In addition to the suppression of black activism, racial democracy has been argued to conceal both the presence and effects of institutional racism.[17] In Cuba, desegregation and the opening of opportunity for nonwhites in certain sectors changed race relations and access for nonwhites. Although nonwhites remain underrepresented in particular sectors, a new group of black and *mulato* professionals arose, particularly in medicine and primary and secondary education. The gains that the revolution brought for nonwhites and for racial equality as a whole cannot be denied. In fact, the successes allowed for the claim that racism had been solved to hold legitimacy among the populace during that time. As many of my interviewees born before the revolution opined, racism went away because of the revolution. Many of these interviewees referred not only to the programs of desegregation, but to the changes in economic policy that brought on high levels of class equality. Despite these

---

16. See Guerra 2012.

17. Literature on ideology has pointed to the duality of the concept in that it can both present an illusion, but have some relationship with truth as well. Both Althusser (1994) and Eagleton (1991) discuss the relationship between ideology and illusion, arguing that while there may be falsehoods contained within ideological rhetoric, it still has some link to reality. Eagleton (1994) in particular argues that focusing only on the characteristic of illusion denies ideology's materiality. It would be difficult for rhetoric that supports a particular set of beliefs to acquire popular support without reflecting any part of people's everyday experiences.

changes, racism (separate from class inequality) was not tackled directly outside of these desegregation efforts, which left institutional sediment that continued to privilege white Cubans.

The Cuba of the twenty-first century can no longer point to these early gains so easily, especially to younger generations that have seen access for blacks decrease with the economic reforms of the 1990s. Institutional racism remains an obstacle to black economic and social advancement (particularly in lucrative sectors such as tourism) and the declarations by the government of a Cuba without structural racism leans heavily toward illusion and has lost many of the previous connections to reality. Nonetheless, the claims still enjoy a great deal of support. Scholars have argued that the ideology of racial democracy in Latin America and the Caribbean has little resemblance to racial realities but enjoys wide popular support and credence.[18] In the United States as well, an ideology of colorblindness has begun to enjoy similar support particularly among whites despite the continued presence of institutional racism.[19] Racial ideology that touts the end of race in exchange for a colorblind or harmonious way of looking at society seems to have wide support regardless of its connection with reality. The notion of being colorblind and living in a society that has progressed beyond the evils of racism carries a great amount of popularity, irrespective of one's actual views on race.

Some scholars argue that the lack of congruence between discourse and reality is benign since racial democracy acts as only an ideal. Therefore the link between rhetoric and reality is represented in what citizens want their society to be and not what it actually is.[20] Most often, and particularly in Cuba, racial democracy or colorblind ideology is not framed as an ideal, but as the present state of affairs and thus cannot be benign. It serves as a denial of racism rather than a model to strive for and in this way obscures realities of racial exclusion that as a result, remain largely unchallenged. The subtle or covert practice of racial exclusion does not make it any less systemic and the established channels by which racial discrimination is carried out bars access

---

18. For scholarship on racial democracy and its support among the populace in Latin America see Hanchard 1994, Widdance Twine 1998, Daniel 2005, and Nascimento 2007.

19. See the 2006 edited volume by Krysan and Lewis for a discussion of colorblindness in the United States.

20. While Robin Sheriff has argued that racial democracy serves as an ideal as well as a myth (2001), Stanley Bailey (2009) contends that its characterization as a myth or politically driven discourse is conflated with its intent to be an ideal for citizens.

for blacks in many sectors despite the ideology of racial democracy. The government's unwillingness to recognize such discriminatory practices maintains them, leaving nonwhites with little room to manipulate their position or challenge the practices.

Racial Norms

Racial ideology remains legitimate to citizens largely through the social norms that it creates, which shape how citizens think about race and how they act and react as well. The products of racial ideology in Cuba are the following racial norms: silence regarding racism, an ethos of anti-racialism, and the perception of racism as individual prejudice rather than racism of a structural or institutional nature. These norms are outlined in the top portion of Figure 0.1, drawn out in the previous chapter. Social norms are argued to provide the mechanism through which members of a society create beliefs about their social reality.[21] These norms then produce explanations about experiences and influence people's ways of thinking, in this case about race.[22] As a collective set of interpretations or beliefs, norms suggest conformity, perhaps not universally, but if they are able to guide behavior and attitudes, they then produce a level of pervasiveness. When race disappeared from the public sphere and institutional racism was declared solved, for example, many stopped talking about it—and even, as my field research suggests, thinking about it as well. Public discussions of racism were known to be taboo and these discussions were thus relegated to the private sphere, or they disappeared all together.

The racial norms in my model have been inscribed into society through political rhetoric, media, organizational activities, literature and scholarly work, cultural expression, and so on. The state-owned media in particular have been silent regarding racism in Cuba throughout the decades of the revolution. The break in the silence among small circles following the Special Period includes a smattering of newspaper columns and television programs on prejudice; however, the silence regarding institutional racism has remained. The small number of changes that have arisen both on television

---

21. See Glynn 1996, Hogg and Reid 2006.

22. Much of the scholarship on norms focuses on their characteristic as something that is a shared or group perception, rather than an individual notion of society (Sherif 1936). These authors argue that norms are collective interpretations of the social world that influence social behavior, attitudes, and our way of thinking (Glynn 1996; Moscovici 1976).

and in print are loyal to the conception of racism as individual prejudice that require individual efforts to combat.[23]

The first norm, silence regarding racism, was legislated by the revolutionary government, an act which had tremendous influence on how people view racism and racial identity. The prohibition of racial organizations as well as the policy that declared such organizations divisive or even racist converted anti-racist or civil rights groups, press, dialogue, and so on into counterrevolutionary projects. Alongside the silence was the idea that to move beyond or to leave race behind indicated progress, and to discuss or address it demonstrated societal regression. The silence around race does not just exist because of governmental pressure, but has in fact become the type of norm that people instinctively follow. In other words, not talking about racism (particularly institutional racism) has become something that everyone is doing.[24] This is partly due to the belief that it is in fact divisive, but also because the declaration of the end of racism on a structural level is something that is widely embraced even after several decades. Racism and the power of race within Cuban society continue to exist without reflection while at the same time, racial difference remains ingrained both institutionally and colloquially (which is discussed later in the chapter).

The social norm of silence is closely connected with the norm of anti-racialism. Anti-racialism in fact functions because of the silence on racism in that citizens do not talk about race and in turn do not imagine themselves to be racist. The subject has left the island as well as people's thoughts. Anti-racialism also has the quality of being what ought to be, but also what most people are—nonracist. The third social norm, the attitudinal conception of race, shapes people's opinions about how to define racism, where to find it (in just a few people's homes), and thus why not to take it seriously. A society's attention to a particular social issue is based on the collective perception of its importance and whether certain problems become public issues.[25] If people are not talking about institutional racism, the belief that racism resides only in the minds of some remains commonplace.

---

23. Two articles that appeared in the Cuban newspapers during my time there in 2005 and 2008 (Ronquillo Bello 2008 and Perera Robbio et al. 2005) discussed racial prejudice in new ways, but did not address its systemic nature.

24. See Cialdini, Kallgren, and Reno's (1991) discussion of descriptive and injunctive norms where descriptive norms consist of what most people are doing or thinking while injunctive norms constitute what is socially desirable or what ought to be done.

25. Glynn et al. 2004.

While several authors have focused on how norms affect behavior, my conception of norms is tied to how they affect public opinion and racial attitudes. Public opinion on racism certainly has much to do with whether people wish to act, organize, or debate around the subject, but in a country where such acts are prohibited, I place primary importance on Cubans' thoughts and beliefs about race and racism.

Racial Categories

While racial democracy does indeed negate the importance of race as a social cleavage and discourages discussion regarding racism, it should be emphasized that it does not generate popular silence on racial difference. Racial categories are part of racial ideologies (even those that profess colorblindness) as they provide the rules for perceiving the other while reinforcing racial notions and stereotypes.[26] Racial categories throughout the Americas are often well defined and are used to describe, emphasize, valorize, and denigrate physical and cultural difference. The multiple categories that exist in the Latin American color schema are commonly used by all races to denote differences in phenotype as well as other racial markers such as hair, nose, and lips. Racial descriptions are often the first mode used to describe someone, most often when referring to nonwhites. While racial difference is clearly catalogued and unambiguous, the effects of one's race on their life chances remain murky and often denied or ignored.

In Cuba, race is listed on each person's identification card (*el carné de identidad*) and is counted in the census as well. The Cuban government uses three categories to count skin color in Cuba: white, mixed race (*mestizo*), and black.[27] A person's racial designation, both on the official identification and the census, is chosen by a state official. When I was in Cuba as a temporary resident, for example, an official wrote my race on my identification card as *mestiza* without asking how I personally identify. The state, by including race on the identification cards and the census, regulates race, assigns racial identity, and maintains the importance of such an identity despite the rhetoric that claims it is of little to no relevance.[28] In 2005 in Havana, I came upon a conversation

---

26. See Bonilla-Silva 2001.

27. The question on the census does not refer to race, but asks, "Cual es su color de piel?" or "What is your skin color?"

28. It is in this way that the state is "capillary" as Comaroff (1998) argues: "It stretches, autonomically and unseen, into the very construction of the subjects, into their bodily routines and

between academics outside of a meeting who were comparing how the state identified them in the census versus how they self identify. In almost all of the cases in this group the state had whitened them, placing them in a category closer to white than they—and society—would consider them. Those that would be racialized in Cuban society as black reported being assigned the *mulato* category, and lighter *mulatos* reported being marked as white by the officials.[29]

The Cuban government has been argued to whiten its population based on census figures available since 1981.[30] The calculation in the 2012 census that only 9.3 percent of Cubans are black and 26.6 percent are *mulato* or of mixed race lends doubt to the accuracy of the statistic, even if we can only rely on visual assessments. One of the racial activists that I interviewed suggested that the government produces inaccurate numbers regarding the census in an attempt to whiten the discourse. She discussed the treatment of race by the government referencing the census results of 2002.

> How do the people of the census see the racial problem? The government doesn't provide racial data because they say no one has asked for it. These are arguments that are so petty. They present a census where 65 percent of the Cuban population is white, 10 percent black, and 24 percent *mestizo*. I have to raise my hand and say, *Where are you?*? You are presenting a point of view that says the nonwhite population is a minority. A minority?!? There must be other methods they can use. If you design a census where you come to my house, you look at me and you say I'm white because it's clear to *you*, what validity does that have? I don't want to throw the census on the floor and create chaos in Cuban society but this is a serious question. Simply observing as you walk in the street, you see that 65 to 70 percent of the population is nonwhite. I don't care about conflictive terms like *mestizo, mulato*; I put everyone in a nonwhite sack. But the discourse is always whitened.

---

of self-regulation" (9). The state "imposes order on its citizenry," but this social control remains largely invisible because it is embedded into people's everyday social practices.

29. I do not suggest here that everyone that is counted by the Cuban government is whitened. The designation that I was given was indeed the way that Cuban society would classify me as well. It is to say that there does seem to be a whitening process that is occurring, both evidenced by ethnographic research as well as the official census numbers, which do not correspond to the observed racial make-up in Cuba.

30. See Moore 1988.

She offers a critique that does not only question the validity of the census, but the intent as well. Instead of pointing to the government's lack of attention to race because it is not salient, she contends that the government in fact is purposely creating a picture of race that does not exist.

Despite the government's argued tendency to whiten, racial categories in the census do correspond with the categories that Cubans use among each other to self-identify and identify others as well. This is a different reality than what we often find in other countries in Latin America. There is significant scholarship discussing the confusion about accurate categorization on Latin American censuses and surveys because of the varied societal interpretations of racial identification and categories.[31] What is clear in Cuba is that society generally puts people into one of the three categories.[32] I do not want to suggest that race is without complexity or that different races do not view these categories differently depending on their racial positionality. Although there are various racial terms that are used beyond white, *mulato*, and black, the various labels used to mark race all fall within these larger categories.

It is critical to state that not only do citizens use white, black, and *mulato* to describe other Cubans, but who belongs within these categories in Cuba is generally agreed upon by the population. In Cuba, there is little confusion among the citizenry about who is black, white, or *mulato*, despite the debates that exist regarding how the government officials make such decisions. In fact, much of the wonder regarding why government officials tend to whiten is based on the understanding that race is universally understood in Cuba. There is indeed fluidity in the ways in which racial categories are interpreted, but who belongs to which designation is most often consistent. At different points throughout the book I demonstrate this point through interview and ethnographic evidence.[33]

The origins of this clarity may be located in the historical organization of civil society in Cuba. Social and political organization in Cuba prior to the revolution were separated by race such that white, *mulato*, and black organizations operated independently from each other and membership was based on

31. Various census tools have been used (for example, in the Latin American poll, AmericasBarometer) to try to administer surveys that coincide with everyday racial understandings, a concept that is often elusive in Latin America. See Telles 2004, Godreau 2015.

32. See Godreau et al. 2010 for an example of census categories and colloquial categorization that do not correspond.

33. In my field research, I only encountered four people that did not want to complete the survey because they did not identify as black, as discussed in the introduction. Moreover, my designation as *mulata* in Cuba was consistent regardless of geography, the person's race, or context.

racial designation. The genesis of these categories carries its own history, but the creation of the black organizations came out of exclusion from membership in white organizations. Moreover, *mulatos*, who were also excluded from white organizations but wanted to separate themselves from black Cubans, created their own associations as well.[34] Thus, the revolutionary government certainly did not impose the racial categories that are present on identification cards in Cuba as these designations have origins prior to the revolution. The inclusion of race on the identification cards, however, demonstrates that racial categories are indeed enforced and reinforced by the government.

Racial designations are used not only as mere description, but to indicate one's closeness to whiteness. They are a marker of race for nonwhites. It is common, for example, to hear someone call another person *mulato* or *negro*, but rare to hear someone refer to another as *blanco*. In my own experience, I was always referred to as *mulata*, both by strangers on the street as well as people that I knew. Whites are not assigned race; this practice is reserved for those that are racialized, and thus nonwhite.[35] It should be noted that labels that denote color and hair gradations among *mulatos* and blacks are often most significant among these groups; those that occupy these many shades of blackness may be viewed similarly by whites as a nonwhite collective. In his study of Brazilian racial politics, Michael Hanchard writes that "racial identity assumes the form of resemblance between individuals of similar, not necessarily identical color, through their contradistinction from white Brazilians."[36] Yet also important in this contradistinction between whites and nonwhites is the fact that the racial identity of nonwhites is determined by whites. A *mulato* can call himself nonblack if he or she wishes, but many whites would just consider *mulatos* to be nonwhite and thus racialized as black. Through her interviews in Brazil, Francis Winddance Twine finds that upper and middle class whites hold a binary view of race where light and dark-sinned Afro-Brazilians are lumped into one category, all undesirable for marriage.[37] Therefore, self-identification matters little when those in power (whites) are assigning race. It is blacks and not whites who have to buy into racial democracy to justify their social position.[38] The ideology of racial

---

34. See Montejo 2004.

35. Brodkin 1998; Frankenburg 1993; Twine 1998.

36. Hanchard 1994, 79.

37. Twine 1998.

38. See Marx 1998.

democracy relies on nonwhite support more than white support in maintaining social order and needs nonwhites to continue to operate within its realm.

Although whites in Cuba may perceive blacks and *mulatos* as nonwhite, both occupants of a lower position, *mulatos* can participate in a different process of racialization. This process inferiorizes blacks in relation to *mulatos* whereby they would sometimes exhibit the same racism that whites would toward their own group. When walking down the street in Havana with a T-shirt that read "negrita," several people stopped me asking why I would want to claim blackness when I didn't have to. A security guard at a bank said, "You are a beautiful *mulata*, why would you want to wear that shirt?"[39] There is a position of privilege associated with being *mulato* with regard to blackness, and it is seen as a middle category in the white-black hierarchy that places blacks on the bottom and whites at the top. Any discussion of race in Latin America and the Caribbean must take into account how those of mixed race are categorized as well as what effect lighter skin has on one's life chances. Although my survey research focuses on black Cubans, throughout the book I point to the ways in which *mulatos* fit into the Cuban racial hierarchy, both through my own experiences and my interviews.

The existence of the *mulato* category is also used as evidence for the so-called fluidity of race in contrast to the United States, where a separate mixed category does not exist. Multiple color categories in Latin America have been argued by proponents of racial democracy to confirm the lack of racial hierarchies and racial intolerance. A closer look at this color continuum shows that the existence of multiple color categories is connected to racial hegemony and the various racial terms constitute clear hierarchies. Rather than multiple racial categories serving as evidence of a lack of racial sensibility, societies tend to place a significant emphasis on race in their everyday language and when ascribing individual attributes to one another. The multitude of ways to describe someone racially evidences a strong racial sensibility as each slight difference in skin tone or hair texture can designate a different racial description.[40] Similar to João H. Costa Vargas's argument in the case of Brazil, Cuba can be identified as a society that is "hyperconscious" about race and despite the anti-racialist ethos that accompanies racial democracy, citizens are "deeply immersed in racialized understandings of the social world."[41]

---

39. Implicit in this comment, of course, was the reference to *mulatez* as more beautiful than blackness.

40. For a discussion of the various racial categories, see Guanche 1996.

41. Vargas 2004, 446.

This immersion must be understood within the context of the social norm of silence: the public is quite vocal about assigning race and its accompanying characteristics, but silent about the societal consequences of the racial assignments and their significance for individual outcomes.

Various analyses of racial ideology in Latin America have supported the view that a dichotomous racial classification scheme reflects a higher sensitivity to race as opposed to societies that place racial identity on a continuum. Others have highlighted the hierarchical significance of multiple color categories, discarding the notion that as opposed to a dichotomous racial system such as the United States, systems that boast a color continuum have a less rigid notion of race.[42] Kia Lilly Caldwell argues that "the color continua found in many Latin American societies are as ideologically overdetermined as bipolar racial categories are in other national contexts (i.e., the United States)."[43] The number of racial categories or the use of a racial continuum do not have a positive correlation with anti-racialism, and in fact I argue the contrary. The use of various color categories along a continuum, the classification that is employed in Latin America, is merely a way of being more specific about race. The presence of mixed categories or multiple color gradations do not connote the existence of nondiscrete racial groups, but rather suggest a colloquial and fine-tuned method of categorization.[44]

There are several authors who liken the use of race in the United States to a rigid classification system that supports an equally rigid notion of identity and race relations. In *Legacies of Race*, Stanley Bailey argues that the racial discourse in Brazil celebrates the fact that there is no clear cut criterion for race.[45] Bailey outlines a contrast between the United States and Brazil, where Brazil's color continuum gives evidence of a more fluid way of marking race. Brazil and Cuba, as well as many other Latin American countries, do indeed have a clear cut criterion for classifying race and that criterion has been enforced by the state, much like the United States.[46] When examined comparatively

---

42. See Vargas 2004; Caldwell 2007.

43. Caldwell 2007, 36.

44. My designation in Cuba was a *mulata*, due to my light brown skin and curly hair, but someone slightly lighter than me with the same hair could be designated as a *mulato claro* (or a lighter *mulato*). The categories went farther, calling someone with curly hair and whiter skin a *mulato blanconazo* and someone with darker brown skin *moro*. These are all ways to determine how close to whiteness someone is.

45. Bailey 2009.

46. See Marx 1998 and Nobles 2000.

to the United States, the classification based on the assignment of extra racial categories on the basis of color and other physical traits in Latin America is different, but not unclear. The racial classification systems of Latin America and the United States should not be analyzed according to levels, but instead according to difference. Color or racial categories are significant and connected to a racial hierarchy that prefers whiteness over blackness in both contexts.[47]

The idea that race is fluid does not, as the myth suggests, signify the absence of racism or racial recognition, but rather signals the ability to move up these fluid racial lines toward whiteness. In other words, while it is true that the myth of racial democracy boasts a racial fluidity or a color continuum, which seems to be more tolerant than the United States' dichotomous and static categorization, in fact, in supporting an easier road toward whiteness, it also facilitates anti-black sentiment.[48] While this argument is often made for Brazil and its various color categories, the same can be said for any racial continuum that uses a mixed category and promotes or touts racial mixing, particularly Cuba. These color gradations, or just the presence of a middle category, are framed with the idea that a family can gradually move up the color ladder through racial mixing.[49] Wishes of whiteness can thus become not only an idea, but a strategy.[50] The saying *mejorar la raza* or "improving the race" is one that is prevalent in Cuba as well as many Latin American countries, and denotes the ability to improve the black race by intermarriage with someone who occupies a higher (and lighter) place in the racial hierarchy. It is important to note that while there are those who realize the problems associated with the notion of *mejorar la raza*, it is still believed to be true by many. This can be expressed in a sentiment by one of my interviewees: "I know I should love my race, but I'd rather not have a child with bad hair." There is often consciousness about the sentiment being anti-black, but it is not strong enough to dismantle beliefs that white traits are more aesthetically pleasing than black traits. The phenomenon of being obsessed with race, but silent regarding racism creates a clear irony. Furthermore, the absence of

---

47. See Torres 1998.

48. See Fernandez 2001.

49. It is also part of a discourse that claims that everyone is of mixed race, and thus racism is irrelevant.

50. See Vargas 2004.

dialogue regarding anti-black sentiment allows for these practices to continue without reflection or debate.

Conclusion

Racial ideologies are used to justify social realities. Racial democracy, in particular, works to do that by denying the presence of racism or attributing it only to individual attitudes. In this way, racial democracy works as a political tool to 1) influence how citizens perceive racial disparities and experiences of discrimination, and 2) decrease the saliency of race for individuals' notions of identity. Although racial democracy is an ideology that is not unique to Cuba and continues to find support in many Latin American countries, the Cuban government is unique in its official policies that prohibited organization based on race and public dialogue on racism on the island. Cuba's racial ideology was thus institutionalized and continues to be supported through various norms that I outline in the chapter. These norms—silence regarding racism, anti-racialism, and the practice of defining racism as individual prejudice—help to obscure both the intent of the Cuban government in promoting their racial ideology as well as the government's ability to tackle racism through policies and actions. The policies to institutionalize racial democracy meant that the government effectively determined what was deemed enough effort toward combating racial inequality and removed this right from its citizens. As racism left the public sphere, the power of race in shaping society was negated. Public reflection on what racism is, whether more struggle is required, and whether the black contribution is sufficiently and formally recognized were also unnecessary. Racial democracy in Cuba works to influence the way that citizens view race in their present lives, and thus cannot be seen as a mere ideal or as benign rhetoric. Moreover, the consequences of rhetoric that negates the presence of racism and the effect of race on one's opportunities are far more important than its intent. The ideology succeeds in creating a lens that inhibits racial explanations of phenomena that are often connected to race and racism.

The move to leave racism behind was not accompanied by a policy that stopped counting race and racial markers continue to be a principal way of identification. The Cuban government assigns each citizen a racial categorization, yet ironically asserts that these categorizations have no meaning. Cuba places a high importance on racial markers and racial difference and the various ways of characterizing someone racially are in fact part of a highly sensitive and meticulous way of marking blackness. Racial systems throughout the Americas place a high emphasis on phenotype and ways in which one can get closer to whiteness. Cuba does not escape from this phenomenon because of the national silence on racism and racial inequality. Moreover, the silence and negation of the presence of racism supports the prominence of racial difference and the racialization of the people by disallowing any dialogue on it. Finally, by indicating race on identification cards, Cuba represents a clear racial order where one's racial group is seen as an official way to identify someone, equal to their address, birthdate, and name. While racial categories continue to carry significant social meaning, an ideology that denies that reality is implicit in reinforcing it.

2 *DE AQUÍ PA'L CIELO*

BLACK CONSCIOUSNESS AND RACIAL CRITIQUE

The effort to search for the meaning of blackness seems like a daunting task for which there can be no definitive answer. Even within a single case study, it still would be impossible to produce a definition that includes each individual experience, each personal reality, and each set of beliefs about the social and political significance of race. This chapter's goal, then, is not to define blackness in Cuba, but to locate it and identify its potential for collectivity and the development of a black counterideology. I will discuss its varied meanings and interpretations among those that matter most to its definition: black people. Moreover, I want to attach these meanings and interpretations to their political importance as I consider race and identification to be a political stance that cannot be relegated only to the personal or separated from the political. The political importance of both blackness and dialogue that comes out of black communities can also be found in their ability to contradict dominant ideologies. There is a strong link between black consciousness and power in Cuba. Discourse that speaks to the black experience in Cuba and the possibility of action based on this discourse can not only challenge racial ideology that seeks to silence the black voice, but can create a new movement in Cuba. This chapter represents the second part of my theoretical framework, where I examine black consciousness as a counterideology that serves as an ongoing response to the rhetoric and norms discussed in the previous chapter.

By grouping blacks into one concept of black consciousness I do not wish to suggest that all blacks have the same opinions or beliefs on what it means to be black in Cuba. Nor do I wish to argue that all black Cubans possess group consciousness and solidarity. There are many different ideas among blacks about the causes and solutions to blacks' social position and even what that social position is. What remains true to many blacks is the acknowledgment of the experience of being black in Cuba.[1] It is this particular reality that produces difference in experience among whites and nonwhites. As one of the leaders of racial activism in Cuba said in an interview, "Yes, there is discrimination toward black Cubans that occurs in hotels, restaurants, etc. That is our experience, any black person will tell you that." The political reality in Cuba is clear to many blacks: discrimination exists. There is a shared position that is acknowledged by many, yet how does the awareness of positionality manifest politically and socially, if at all? The varied ways in which blacks view, discuss, and act on their commonality constitute black consciousness.

In the case of Cuba, we must analyze black consciousness in the context of silence. At the start of the revolution, when the government eliminated all existing societies, organizations, and media that were associated with race or created to address black concerns regarding rights and representation, blacks could no longer organize on the basis of race. The topic was silenced as racism was declared to no longer be a societal problem. Despite the lack of black institutions and networks that support black dialogue and agency, blacks have, both formally and informally, challenged the rhetoric from above and communicated the relevance of race based on racial democracy's visible (and sometimes not so visible) fallacies. Above all, I argue not only that black consciousness exists in Cuba and that race matters to black people, but that we must look beyond the public sphere to identify how race matters.

There are two forms of critique occurring in Cuba that challenge the official ideology and serve as a testament to the presence of black consciousness. The first consists of above-ground political activity led primarily by academics, writers and artists that have opened a space for expression regarding race in Cuba through art, scholarship, and debate. This above-ground movement has benefited from the political opening created during the economic crisis that followed the fall of the Soviet Union and has introduced art, music, scholarship, and even some journalism that talks candidly about black identity, anti-black racism and stereotypes, and discrimination in Cuba. Bounded by the confines of what the Cuban state will allow, these expressions and works do not have complete freedom, but they do highlight issues that have previously been silenced. Their role is critical as the beginnings of a racially consciousness movement, but their reach outside of their own circles

---

1. See Banks 2000 for a discussion regarding black women's consciousness as the recognition of a set of historical and political realities, rather than an essentialist conception.

is limited. Academics and other activists do not command a nonelite audience, but their work is vital to the conversation and is also commanding the attention of government officials. Hip-hop in Cuba has garnered the largest following within the above-ground movement and some of its musicians have become the primary messengers of black expression in Cuba. Many of their songs exhibit consciousness, solidarity, pride, and, can also be accompanied by pro-revolutionary rhetoric. I discuss the above-ground movement in more depth in chapter 9.

The second form of critique is primarily underground and is the forum that those outside of artistic and academic circles utilize to express what it means to be black in Cuba and the common experiences among them. What occurs underground is an unorganized, informal, and often unintentional group of collectives that create and reinforce their own ideas about blackness and its political implications in their everyday lives through conversation. My discussion of underground critique follows James Scott's concept of hidden transcripts,[2] which is particularly relevant for Cuba as an authoritarian regime where political critiques are largely forbidden. Knowledge of these hidden transcripts in addition to dominant ideologies is necessary to understand power relations in their entirety.[3] Through familiar talk, blacks can create their own intimate networks of information about race. These conversations vary and include discussions on the lack of black representation on television, stories of experiences with discrimination, complaints about obstacles that impede black progress, and many other issues that uniquely face black Cubans. They remain under the radar yet the informality of this form of expression does not undercut its importance. These underground conversations are the focus of this chapter as they are the foundation of racial micropolitics and black public opinion in Cuba. A study of black politics in Cuba that only analyzes the public challenges to racial discrimination would indeed be incomplete. Private discourse coupled with the arena—albeit small—of public discourse together make up black political thought in Cuba and both serve, in different ways, to challenge the status quo.[4] These two modes of

---

2. As Scott argues, "subordinates in large-scale structures of domination . . . have a fairly extensive social existence outside the immediate control of the dominant. It is in such sequestered settings where, in principle, a shared critique of domination may develop" (Scott 1992, xi).

3. Ibid.

4. The anti-racism and pro-black expressions that have been introduced during the last fifteen years or so have had an influence on the government's willingness to address the race question, but it should be noted that these elite efforts are virtually unknown by those that do not seek out these circles and information. Thus, while elite activity coupled with the private activity of

discourse serve to maintain and reinforce black consciousness among a racial group that is not afforded the proper institutions or networks to do so in the public sphere.

Group Consciousness

Much of the work on group consciousness refer to the 1980 article by Gurin et al., which delineates the difference between consciousness and identification. They define identification as the relationship to others within a stratum, whereas consciousness is "an action orientation, the view that collective action is the best means to realize the stratum's interest."[5] My definition of black consciousness uses Gurin et al.'s conceptualization of both identification and consciousness in that black consciousness represents an awareness of the position of blacks as a group in relation to others, namely whites and *mulatos*, creating a politicized identity. Consciousness is not just one's social condition, but how one perceives and evaluates that social condition. Those at the bottom of the social hierarchy, for example, may perceive that position as a result of inequities and use the group's status as a marker for their own opportunities as a member of that group, relative to other groups.

It is on the point of collective action that I depart from the bulk of the literature on group consciousness.[6] Black consciousness is most useful as a political tool through participation, voting, and activism seeking to combat racial inequalities, but it is important not to conflate consciousness with political action. Political action can be a product of group consciousness, which can facilitate organization, but group consciousness does not always lead to agency. I would agree that a distinction between identification and group consciousness needs to be made in order to understand the set of beliefs associated with one's relative position as well as the potential for political action. The same distinction should be made between consciousness and action. Group consciousness represents cognizance of group position relative to other groups and a feeling of identification and solidarity with members of

the majority of blacks constitute black political thought in Cuba, the latter, more often than not, operates without knowledge of the existence of the former. Certainly this fact is not accidental, as elites are allowed by the state to create this debate within their own circles and not on a mass level that could lead to any kind of widespread movement or challenge to the state's policies on race.

5. Gurin et al. 1980.

6. See Miller et al. 1981 and Tajfel 1974 as other seminal works on group consciousness that identify the concept as group action.

your group. Group members can display this viewpoint and even express it to other members of the group without acting on it, for various reasons. Inaction does not discount their group consciousness, but action can often be product of group consciousness. The authoritarian nature of Cuba's political system impedes the opportunity for most political activism as well as the exercise of vote choice. Thus, if we equate group consciousness with political activity or collective action, we would exclude the possibility of black consciousness among all Cubans.[7] I do not omit political action from the definition of group consciousness with only Cuba in mind. Even in democratic societies, there are those that display markers of black consciousness without engaging in political activity.[8]

There is a clear difference between racial consciousness that remains within the individual and that which is expressed and acted upon. Michael Hanchard, in his work on Afro-Brazilian racial consciousness, develops a distinction between apolitical, identity-based similarities and an identity-based collective with clear political goals, naming them faint and strong resemblances, respectively. In his definition of faint resemblances he discusses an ephemeral bonding that is based on attitudes or emotion, but does not possess any strategic component. Strong resemblances lie in the ability of a group to place race as a primary and overriding foundation for organization with a stated political agenda or objective. The distinction that Hanchard makes is a critical one, whereby those that simply identify with being black do not possess the same ideas or conceptualization as those who turn this identification into political strategy.[9]

What I put forth is a crucial third category in between the above two categories that tends to get lost in the study of tangible examples of racial politics, such as black movements. A study of Cuba in particular requires such a category, as political activism around race and racism remains prohibited. The category is rooted in my argument that group consciousness does not equate political action, nor do its members have to possess any commitment to political action. Those that possess an acute awareness for their racial group's hierarchical position due to distributional inequities as well as

---

7. As I've stated earlier, there is a degree of political activity among elites in Cuba aimed toward eradicating anti-black racism and its accompanying stereotypes. This space is only open to academics and other elite activists, and a public space such as this is not afforded to nonelites.

8. See Sellers et al. 1998 and Shelby 2005 for discussions of black consciousness and its various manifestations.

9. Hanchard 1994.

the ways in which racism and even individual prejudice can hinder their own progress, do not always possess the desire for political involvement. While those among this group may indeed believe that political organization is necessary to further their group's advancement and combat inequality, they may never join any such organization nor express their ideas publicly. Their ideas are politicized, but their actions are not so that one can display solidarity outside of a political realm and be race conscious without ever transferring that into a political act.

Group consciousness can lead to collective action, yet political action may also have to do with certain characteristics that are not tied to strong feelings of group consciousness. In their 1981 article, Miller et al. define collective action through voting, participation in group organizations, lobbying, demonstrations, or engaging in other pressure tactics on behalf of the group.[10] With the exception of voting, these activities are not necessarily common activities of the average citizen, but are activities that political activists may take part in. A definition of black consciousness should go beyond the set of beliefs among those most active in the community. In Katherine Tate's study of black political participation in the 1984 and 1988 elections in the United States, she highlights the characteristics that would lead people toward political participation.[11] Psychological attributes that favor political participation, Tate argues, include civic duty, a sense of efficacy, and having a general interest in politics. It is possible for someone to possess group consciousness but not possess the attributes that would make them likely to engage in political activity. In Cuba in particular, a sense of efficacy is particularly significant as citizens do not possess freedom of association and are not presented with candidates from multiple parties at the voting booth. If racism is a subject that is deemed taboo, it will not be addressed by any Cuban candidates, as all of their platforms are in line with the Communist Party's position. In addition, citizens know that any political act that would be considered counterrevolutionary carries serious consequences. It is not hard to imagine that without free elections, freedom of association, or free speech that any challenge to such an entrenched policy would be imagined as futile by most. Factors such as political efficacy are presented here for definitional purposes for the group consciousness concept, as it is beyond the scope of this project to test the sources of political

10. Miller et al. 1981.

11. Tate 1991.

action. My goal is to expand the definition of black consciousness or black group identity to include those who do not act politically, but think and speak this way, albeit in a private space.

The Politics of Everyday Conversations

The foundation for black solidarity and consciousness lies in the common experience of blackness. From the experience, dialogue grows that reinforces consciousness through collective recognition. While it is true that consciousness lies in individuals' ideas that become politicized, these ideas must be shared in order to gain recognition as common experience and reinforce the solidarity among the group members. In a society where there is very little freedom of expression and a genuine fear of speaking out in public spaces regarding issues that are taboo, how then do you build racial solidarity and reinforce consciousness?

The role of underground expression regarding race is one of the most significant ways in which solidarity is built. In his book *Race Rebels*, Robin Kelley provides us with a way to redefine politics among oppressed groups by emphasizing the politics of the everyday that originate not from above, but from below. He cites James C. Scott in his conception of a hidden transcript as a "dissident political culture that manifests itself in daily conversations, folklore, jokes, songs, and other cultural practices."[12] Despite a public display of consent of the official transcript by subordinated groups, the hidden transcript tells the true political ideologies of these groups, but remains buried in private, everyday conversations. What Scott terms *infrapolitics*, I argue are the building blocks of black solidarity in Cuba, especially in the absence of black institutions or public spaces. These everyday forms of resistance are purposely hidden and designed to remain outside of the public sphere, but are of no less importance to Cuban politics. I move beyond the traditional definition of what is political, where when traditional activism is barred, it is replaced by political talk. This talk may not always be deliberately political, but it speaks to the lived experience of black people. Talk couched in race that relays what it means to be black in Cuba is always political. As Kelley aptly writes, "politics is not separate from the lived experience of the imaginary world of what is possible; to the contrary, politics is about these things."[13]

---

12. Kelley 1994, 8. See Scott 1992 for the reference to the hidden transcript.
13. Kelley 1994, 9.

The effect of infrapolitics on power relations is of supreme importance. Everyday resistance to the dominant ideology affects those that perpetuate the ideology, just as the dominant ideology affects identity formation and racial norms. The younger generations in particular, who grew up during the Special Period and after, are talking more about race and experiencing its meaning and weight in their everyday interactions. This generation will take part in a new way of viewing society, one much different than what the generations that were raised during the early years of the revolution experienced. In this sense, the hidden transcript has the potential to affect the social order and become part of the public transcript. One of the university students that I interviewed shared with me his practice of conducting informal, underground surveys within his classrooms regarding politics, race, and the future of the revolution. In classrooms through mass media, music, and resistance to everyday manifestations of discrimination, the newer generation continually shapes the dominant ideology and challenges its legitimacy.

A crucial component to black consciousness-building is the sharing and distribution of information. While continuous contact with the dominant ideological rhetoric has the power to influence how one may view their own social realities, counterideologies possess this same power. Those that may be exposed to racial democracy's counterideologies may alter their approach of analyzing race and viewing their own experiences. The spaces that elites have been afforded to explore racial issues are an example of the conscious distribution of information about race, albeit on a small scale. Those who gain access to these spaces and are exposed to things such as academic workshops and debate in the classroom are part of the current shift in racial thinking among blacks. This in turn can create a cycle of information, or a network that circulates these ideologies to a different, or even larger black audience. In an interview with a popular hip-hop group in Havana, Obsesión, they expressed to me that much of their consciousness had come from workshops that they attended by a well-known race scholar.[14] Considering that hip-hop is one of the primary vehicles of race talk and the celebration of black identity, I asked them if they entered into the hip-hop movement with a racial consciousness.

No, that came later. In fact, it's incredible because my first song talked about racism but it wasn't really what you would call a conscious treatment of race—it was because the hip-hop movement in the United

---

14. The scholar referred to in the interview is Tomás Fernández Robaina, author of many books in Cuba on race and one of the foremost scholars on black Cuban history on the island.

States talked about those things. They talked about being discriminated against and so did I until I said, hold on a minute, this applies to me too. Tomás had a lot to do with our learning process also; he accelerated the process. We had a lot of unconscious lyrics dealing with the racial issue but they became more conscious after a workshop that we attended with him. From there, we were able to explain many things to ourselves and it made us continue to look at race in more depth. We have many more questions, more doubts that we still have not answered, but we've advanced on quite a few.

The group in turn hosts an annual hip-hop symposium that includes workshops and discussions on racism in Cuba. The influence of the African Diaspora is present in many hip-hop movements, and throughout Latin America there are many similarities in the connections that hip-hop has to activism and in turn, black affirmation.[15] Through their music, the group presents strong messages of black consciousness to their audience who are then made to look at racial issues with more depth. They also provide a much needed space for the expression of black pride.[16]

Other scholars have made use of James Scott's theoretical work on infrapolitics, and Michael Dawson introduces a construct in between infrapolitics and the public sphere known as the black counterpublic.[17] The black counterpublic is a concept used to define the space for black political thought and debate, created because of historical exclusion from the mainstream public sphere. Dawson discusses the counterpublic among blacks in the United States, but the counterpublic among black Cubans manifests itself much differently. Without black institutions or public spaces that allow for debate that stands counter to the dominant racial ideology, would-be public spaces are private and less formal, only among friends and family.

---

15. See Pardue 2008.

16. These expressions of black pride were present throughout the symposium that I attended in 2008. One of the members of the audience gave a thought provoking comment regarding the common saying "we are all equal" during the workshop on race. She shared that the saying is often used as a tool of discrimination that reinforces the image of white beauty. If we are all equal, then we are all aspiring to whiteness. Thus, being equal means that black women perm their hair to match the beauty image of whites. The equality discourse, she argued, never includes a discourse of black pride that says, black is beautiful. She ended her commentary by sharing that rather than saying, we are all equal, we need to find harmony among the unequal and embrace our difference.

17. See Helg 1995; Harris-Lacewell 2004; Hanchard 2006; Sawyer 2006; Dawson 2001.

Melissa Harris Perry offers critical theoretical work on the significance of everyday political talk in black politics. She argues that everyday talk, while often not purposely political, tackles issues central to racial politics and its driving mechanisms.[18] Many conversations that center on race try to avoid the political and just concentrate on the everyday. In Cuba there is a tendency among nonelites to avoid discussion of anything political (both due to the sensitivity of freedoms of expression and the barrage of politics presented in state-owned media), yet these informal conversations about inequalities, race, and opportunities are not only political but, as Harris-Perry argues as well, vital in the creation of black political ideologies. The space where black political expression takes place in Cuba is more often an informal one, particularly among those that are not part of the group of above-ground activists that are afforded recognition. Harris-Perry puts forth a definition that states, "the hidden transcript is a collective enterprise that must be created within a public sphere that operates beneath the surveillance of dominant classes."[19] These spaces do not necessarily have to be public: the creation of political thought and ideology can occur in everyday conversations in private spaces as well. Thus, I want to expand this definition to include private spaces that are away from the gaze of the government as well, but are not necessarily official spaces.

The only spaces in Cuba insulated from control and surveillance from above are private, and thus are places for the creation of hidden resistance and debate. A *mulata* woman who worked at the front desk in a large hotel in Miramar noted that there are hardly any nonwhites working in positions visible to tourists. She was the only nonwhite person that worked in the lobby area of the hotel. I asked her if other nonwhite workers in the hotel talk about the racial exclusivity of hiring practices in the tourism sector.

> The issue of racism is talked about in particular groups, but not in public. Just in select groups. Here whites are always nice in front of you, behind your back I don't know, it could be different. So there is solidarity, but not that much because we can't always be talking amongst ourselves in little groups at work. People stop working and they go home. It's in the house or with friends that you talk about those things.

18. Harris-Lacewell 2004.

19. Ibid., 7.

It should also be noted that the informal and private character of black dialogue in Cuba undercuts its diffusion into black communities and its effect on the dominant ideology. Hanchard and Dawson discuss the upward diffusion of black ideological discourse and idea clusters that can significantly influence black discourse, thought, and cultural production.[20] The silence on race and the elimination of racially based organizations in Cuba produced not only an informality of black politics relegated to private spheres or spaces, but it prevented this upward diffusion of black political thought so that the state-produced ideology faces few challenges in any formal or public way. While social structures and hierarchies can serve to challenge the dominant ideology, those that occupy the upper positions in these structures are not obligated to separate practice from theory or reality from ideology.

Amidst a state that does not recognize the existence of racism or the societal relevance of race, blacks need a space where they can discuss how blackness affects their lives. In addition, these conversations can also help to frame the interpretation of inequality and obstacles toward black advancement. If one adheres to the doctrine of racial democracy it is possible to attribute an experience of discrimination to something else. In other words, if you do not believe that blacks are disadvantaged in Cuba, you do not possess the necessary information or framework to identify that disadvantage when it affects you personally. During my time in Cuba, conversations regarding racism often centered on the media. Discussion regarding the lack of blacks as major characters in Cuban programs arose often, particularly when juxtaposed with movies and shows from the United States where black actors are more visible. Among black residents of Havana, discriminatory treatment by the police also sparked complaints by black males. Conversations about race are not only present, but they are important and can reinforce blacks' views on race and inequalities within a society that does not discuss such phenomena.

While I do argue that private spaces are often the site of black political talk, I also acknowledge that one of the major influences of racial ideology in Cuba has been to silence even these conversations. The silence on racism, although challenged by some, still persists for many, even in private spaces. As I was surveying Cubans in the neighborhoods of Havana and discussing the survey with them afterward, I found that the ideas expressed in the survey were issues that blacks were yearning to talk about, but they did not have the

---

20. Hanchard and Dawson 2006.

space to do so. I was uncovering latent feelings about race and racism that people were holding in because they are deemed inappropriate. Through this work, I was giving blacks a chance to express their opinions about concepts that no one had asked them about, but that they clearly had a strong opinion on. The censorship regarding racism remarkably succeeds in infusing racial norms like silence even into households and private conversations. Moreover, the norms do not only bury political conversations among blacks beneath the radar of whites and elites, they can also bury them within individuals without ever being expressed.

Conclusion

As I walked through the streets of Havana asking people to fill out a survey on black identity and consciousness in Cuba, it was clear that often political pressures controlled people's actions far more than their attitudes on race. Many times I was met with skepticism by Cubans who did not want to be involved in any study that had to do with race. Yet for all of those that agreed to fill out the survey despite their initial hesitation, at the end of the survey they were all extremely eager to continue to discuss the topic. The survey, for many, had opened a Pandora's box regarding an issue that holds critical importance to people, but is not brought into the open and is not welcome as a topic of discussion. Respondents wanted more space to express their opinions; most discussed the issue more in depth after filling out the survey, and many thanked me for doing this work and asking them questions about what race means to them as black people. One woman, at the end of the survey, smiled at me and my colleague and said, *"De aquí pa'l cielo."* We asked her to clarify what she meant and she said, *"Nosotros los negros, vamos de aquí pa'l cielo."*[21] Through not only the survey data, but the experience of how the survey was received by so many, it was clear to me that black consciousness has a strong presence in Cuba that cannot be discounted. The lack of political action and the seeming apathy for the subject stems not from a lack of salience of identity for blacks, but from government restrictions and ideology that has stymied the growth of black political thought in Cuba.

---

21. Her statement would be translated as, "We, black folks are going from here to the sky." When I first heard her say this in the context of the survey and our conversation about the racial obstacles she had encountered in her life, I interpreted this as a reference to black peo- ple achieving success without limits. When I gave this some more thought, I realized she was probably referring to heaven when she said, "cielo." Regardless of her intent, both translations display a notion of solidarity and pride that stayed with me well after our conversation.

This chapter challenges existent definitions of racial consciousness such that consciousness represents a politicized identity, but does not need collective action as evidence of its existence. I separate racial activism in Cuba into two categories: above-ground and underground. In doing so, I am able to emphasize that what I call the underground, private conversations and collectives, is vital to the definition of black consciousness and the analysis of racial politics. I argue that black consciousness and ideological production do not only develop in elite circles, but are present throughout black communities among ordinary citizens. While some elites may be better positioned to debate and address these issues among each other, the same attitudes and counterideologies that they debate run through private conversations among nonelites as well. As Melissa Harris-Perry argues, ideology should not be wrested from ordinary citizens.[22] The work of elites in public spaces and the expression of nonelites in private spaces together form to build black political thought in Cuba that often produces ideas and expresses experiences that directly challenge the dominant racial ideology in Cuba.

If given a space, private representations of black consciousness have the potential to come into the public and combat the dominant ideology that seeks to stifle them in order to bring attention to structural racism in Cuba. In his book *Racial Conditions*, Howard Winant writes that the "liberation of racial identity is as much a part of the struggle against racism as the elimination of racial discrimination and inequality. That liberation will involve a revisioning of racial politics and a transformation of racial difference."[23] The veil that was lifted at the onset of the Special Period in Cuba contributed to the revisioning of racial politics in Cuba, and as racial consciousness continues to develop and blacks are freed from the silence regarding racial expression, the importance of race will be difficult to ignore. There is an audience waiting to join the debates that many elites have put forth and if these elites are given a larger space to increase their visibility, many blacks will identify with the message of black consciousness and the need for solutions to the problem of racism in Cuba. Black consciousness in Cuba will serve as the starting point in assessing blacks' societal position and will determine the potential for change.

---

22. Harris-Lacewell 2004.

23. Winant 1994, 169.

3 MARTÍ'S CUBA

RACIAL IDEOLOGY AND BLACK
CONSCIOUSNESS BEFORE 1959

This chapter follows the state's historical role in framing racism and suppressing black activism. Through a discussion of the history of racial politics in Cuba, it demonstrates the development of racial discourse and understanding in Cuba that negated the effects of racism and the ways in which the state controlled (sometimes violently) the boundaries of racial activism and organization. It also highlights the various spaces in the form of societies, organizations, press, and arts that challenged the dominant discourse of racial harmony and sought to promote dialogue within the white dominated public sphere that pointed to racial inequality and supported black affirmation.[1] These spaces are significant for their role in challenging racial ideology during the period of the Republic, but also because they were silenced once the revolution came into power. Throughout the history of Cuba the rhetoric of a racial democracy has remained the same, but the boundaries of racial discourse and racial affirmation changed markedly after 1959. In this way the revolution strengthened the dominant view of race and racism and solidified the racial norms outlined in this book.

The ideology of racial harmony has been a part of Cuba's national image since the abolition of slavery and the wars of independence. Throughout Cuban history, the call for popular unity has been accompanied by a call for racial harmony in order to discourage

---

1. My description of a white dominated public sphere refers to a racial discourse not only dominated by white elites, but also by white interests such that nonwhite elites who participated in racial discourse and were given a privileged space contributed to the racial framework that served white supremacy and denied the importance of race in Cuba society. Melina Pappademos (2011) discusses this at length in her book on racial activism during the Republican period in Cuba.

racial divisions. One of the first and most famous articulations of the idea of racial harmony came from Cuba's national hero, José Martí, who spoke of the need for racial unity after abolition in order to fight for sovereignty as an integrated country. Martí's message of racial harmony became the foundation for Cuban racial politics and rhetoric throughout the Republican period and was the same rhetoric that Fidel Castro used to foment unity against US aggression at the start of the revolution. Throughout history, the declaration of racial problems as something of the past did not reflect an absence of racism, but the political needs of the governments at the time. Policy oriented remedies for racism in Cuba have never been seriously or adequately explored and instead of a significant problem, racism has continuously been treated as a political obstacle and thus disregarded. For this reason, popular belief in equal opportunity has largely been based on a falsehood.

Cuba as a Mixed Nation and the Erasure of Blackness

The ideal of a raceless nation was not an image or strategy that was born in 1959. The suppression of discourse regarding racial identity and racism began immediately following abolition and was an integral part of the nation building process in Cuba once independence was won in 1898. Following abolition in the late nineteenth century, leaders both within and outside of Cuba sought to diminish social tensions such as class and race in an effort to unify the nation for war against Spain. This call for unity depended on the participation of whites, blacks, and *mulatos* and in turn, a departure from the attention to racial difference and racial inferiority that characterized the slavery era. The building of a cohesive Cuban nation was aligned to the erasure of racial identity in exchange for national identity despite the recent abolition of slavery.[2] This strategy became part of Cuba's national discourse and was most popularly characterized by José Martí, who wrote in the late nineteenth century that the Cuban is more than white, more than *mulato*, and more than black.[3] The quote has become the ideal to which governments during the Cuban Republic and the revolution have ascribed, even if only in rhetoric and not application. Martí's words formed the ideological foundation for the supremacy of nationhood, aimed to unify Cubans under one singular national group that discarded racial categories. The silence was not representative of the disappearance of anti-black sentiment and race continued to be

---

2. See Ferrer 2000.

3. Martí 1963–1966.

a significant mode of exclusion. It was instead used politically to 1) inhibit racial divisions and conflict; 2) move the conversation away from race and racism; and 3) discourage black activism despite a racially unequal nation.[4] As Ada Ferrer argues, "The silence was active: it was an argument, a slogan, a fantasy."[5] As such, it represented the beginnings of racial ideology in Cuba.

In his writings on race, José Martí used the ideal of racial equality to unify blacks and whites, and to erase the importance of blackness. In his article, titled *Raza*, he wrote, "The black man who proclaims his race, when what he may only be proclaiming in this incorrect manner is the spiritual identity of all races, authorizes and provokes the racist white man."[6] Martí encouraged whites not to be racist, but he also encouraged blacks not to recognize or affirm their racial identity in order to not provoke white racism. The consequence to becoming part of the nation and the method to avoid being a victim of racism for blacks was the same—ignore blackness, both as it applied to one's own identity and to racial equality.[7] Martí is lauded in Cuba as the father of social justice and Cuban nationhood, and his ideology of nation over race has been used throughout the history as a way to dispel any racial conflict or division.

The idea of the Cuban being more than black, more than *mulato*, and more than white represented a solution to the struggle against racial divisions: Cubans were to look beyond race, rather than promote a struggle against racism. In this way Martí's writings built the foundation for anti-racialism that we find in racial thought in Cuba today. In an interview with a fifty-year-old male he said,

> Lately people have wanted to organize (against racial discrimination) but I do not really understand it. It's contradictory. If we are a country

---

4. During the period prior to independence the problem of racial divisions was perhaps more important than the discouragement of racial activism, although the possibility of the latter was recognized. During the period of the Republic, there was a higher awareness of the threat of black activism beyond the existence of black clubs and societies that often only pushed for racial equality through rhetoric and writings. Activism of a more popular nature was often stamped out, including the deadly massacre of 1912, or avoided alongside the promotion of racelessness as a more righteous endeavor.

5. Ferrer 2000, 62.

6. Martí 1963–1966.

7. This idea is not particular to Cuba, but common in race-less or colorblind ideologies throughout the black Diaspora. As Paul Gilroy argues in the case of Britain, the "price of admission to the colorblind form of citizenship . . . blacks are being invited to forsake all that marks them out as culturally distinct before real Britishness can be guaranteed" (1987, 59).

that isn't racist, if we are a country where the Martían principles, man is more than black more than white, are valid . . . it's sectarianism to me. You are calling the group Color Cubano,[8] but I am Cuban regardless. I know we have more work to do, especially with the media, but the project should be revolutionary.

In this interview, there is an admission of the existence of racism in some form, but the way in which Martí envisioned Cuban society is also intimately connected to the vision of race in the revolution: racial designations should be discarded in favor of national identity. This, as the interviewee argues, should be the case even in the struggle for racial equality in institutions such as the national media.

Perhaps one of the most famous writers who brought forth issues of race in Cuba is Afro-Cuban poet Nicolás Guillén. Guillén wrote that "the spirit of Cuba is *mulato*," and pushed for the fight against racism to include not just blacks, but all races.[9] Guillén's poetry and writings served as a challenge to the dominant ideas around racial mixture and poses an interesting case in thinking about how black Cubans view race. On the one hand, he wrote of the importance of Cuba as a mixed nation, but on the other hand, black Cubans often summon his works as one of the key writings affirming black pride.[10] Guillén represents black Cubans wanting to be a part of this Cuban mix that is a symbol of national pride while at the same time wanting to affirm their blackness. Throughout history, racial affirmation has often been perceived to be against the national project. Since its inception, the concept of the *mulato* nation has required its people to eschew race, and blackness in particular. The practice of a cultural homogeneity, even if this homogeneity consists of heterogeneous ancestry, neglects racial and cultural diversity. Today, voices such as Guillén's continue to push against the idea of racial mixture as a way to both unify and exclude. As Fernando Martínez Heredia writes, "There are Cubans who consider themselves Cuban above all . . . but also identify themselves as blacks and *mulatos*. We need for these identities and that consciousness to march together and to be the force of the socialist revolution and its project. And that . . . is very difficult in its practical

8. Color Cubano refers to an organization made up of writers, academics, and artists who hosted debates and events regarding the presence of racial discrimination in Cuba.

9. Morejón 1993; Fernández Robaina 2009.

10. See Fernandez 2001 and Morejón 1993.

realization."[11] Although Guillén continues to stand as one of Cuba's greatest poets, his call to celebrate individual black affirmation continues to be one of the challenges that the current regime has yet to tackle.

The characterization of Cuba as a mixed nation is an integral part of the silence on race. The racial framework focuses on the many degrees of racial mixture, rather than race,[12] to portray Cuba's people as many shades of the same ethnicity, the same national identity. The ideal has been a part of Cuba's representation of its national image since independence and is supported by black and white Cubans alike. The characterization is also used as a contrast to the United States. In many of my interviews, the presence of the one-drop rule in the United States, versus the mixed race category in Cuba, was presented as evidence that Cuba did not have the race problem that the United States does. Racial mixing is treated as evidence of harmonious race relations as well as a society that cares less about racial categories, putting Cuba in a morally superior position with regard to race and the United States. Despite the characterization of Cuba as a mixed nation with a rich culture of multiple origins,[13] the state does not glorify each origin equally. The cultural sameness acts as a political strategy for unity, but also serves as a dismissal of blackness. The cultural center to which all shades of Cubans should aspire to is a Eurocentric one that often characterizes black cultural expression as folklore.[14] Policies to reinforce this were instated from the onset of the Republic (the period after independence and before the revolution in 1959) and continued through the revolution.[15] While official discourse has consistently boasted a unified array of colors under a singular identity, the reality has historically

---

11. Martínez Heredia 2009, 323.

12. Martínez-Echazábal 1998; Moore 1988.

13. Cubans are often described as having a mix of Spanish and African blood.

14. Martínez-Echazábal 1998; Fernández Robaina 2007.

15. Shortly following independence, for example, policies were created to whiten the majority black population with European immigrants (de la Fuente 2001a). In the early 1900s Afro-Cuban drumming, music, and related activities were banned, an official measure enforced by Cuban police (Moore 1997). At the onset of the revolution, Afro-Cuban religious practices were banned and although all forms of religion were deemed incompatible with the new socialist system, Afro-Cuban religions in particular were officially deemed primitive, akin to witchcraft and often associated with criminal activity (de la Fuente 2001a). Despite the legalization of religious practice during the economic crisis of the early 1990s, Cuba has not seen the construction of an official place of worship for Afro-Cuban religions and they receive little to no attention in official spaces. The official cultural group that exists for the performance of Afro-Cuban dancing and music in Cuba is the Conjunto Folklorico Nacional de Cuba, or the National Cuban Folkloric Ensemble. This group receives significantly less attention than the

been not only a preference for the whiter cultural elements, but a blurring of Cuba's diverse elements, rather than their celebration.

The preference for Eurocentric values within the national imagery has been debated up until today and recently has been described as part of Cuba's problem with race.[16] In his critique of the dominance of whiteness, Cuban scholar Estéban Morales Domínguez calls not for a reconstruction of racial identities, but to resolve the national problem of respecting diversity by moving toward a recognition of African and nonwestern elements as well.[17] The racial rhetoric throughout the Americas claims to respect diversity, but diversity continues to be based on a racial (white) hegemony. Diversity and racial mixing are often used as evidence that racism does not exist, and thus preclude recognition of racial valuations. Today, the leadership describes Cuba as a racial mix where black ancestry is celebrated, but the historical contributions of black Cubans go largely unmentioned with the exception of a few historical figures. Activists, in conjunction with the government, have promoted events that serve to highlight the black historical contribution, but these measures have not been included in national campaigns or curriculums.

The continued use of the ideal of racial democracy coupled with the characterization of Cuba as a mixed nation by elites have not been able to stamp out the black voice throughout Cuban history. Black activism and organizations prior to 1959 flourished in Cuba and were able to communicate various black communities' goals and affirmations. The following section highlights this period of black activism in order to show not only the tradition of black expression, but the spaces that the revolution erased in 1959 and beyond. The revolutionary government dictated what would be the level of progress for black Cubans, silencing the voice that they previously possessed in the public sphere.

Racial Politics at the Start of Cuban Independence

Cuban racial history following abolition and prior to 1959 represents a unique period of black political activism. Before race-based organizing was

National Cuban Ballet. In addition, the National Cuban Ballet has received criticism for its low representation of nonwhite dancers (AFP, http://www.laprensagrafica.com/fama/espectaculos/111815-cubano-estrella-del-royal-ballet-llama-a-qerradicarq-racismo-en-la-danza; La Habana 2010).

16. See Fernández Robaina 2009; Morales Domínguez 2007.

17. Morales Domínguez 2007.

prohibited, blacks displayed varied yet clear commitments to racial progress, racial equality, and black political representation. Moreover, segregation and exclusion produced a separate black experience that often facilitated black solidarity and consciousness among black communities. Alongside the mainstream rhetoric of racelessness, black Cubans were affirming their racial identity through numerous mediums, demonstrating the importance of racial difference in Cuban society. While race has mattered in Cuba since the start of the slave trade up until the present, the Republic was the only period in history where blacks could legitimately and legally act on the significance of race and debate its meaning in their lives. This history of black activism 1) highlights the limitations of the racial harmony ideal and the challenges that nonwhites communicated during this time; 2) gives way to the state's historical suppression of black engagement; and 3) places the start of the revolution in context as we examine the ways in which active black voices were silenced following 1959.

Independence marked the beginning of the development of Cuban national identity. Leaders of the independence movement were looking to foment national unity and military unity in the face of nonwhite participation in the wars. Many of the soldiers had recently been freed from slavery and although blacks and *mulatos* represented one third of the population, they comprised half of the troops.[18] Black and *mulato* war heroes began to emerge among the senior ranks altering previous conceptions of Cuba as a white nation. The war from 1895 until 1898, in particular, was fought with approximately 70 percent Afro-Cuban soldiers.[19] It was during this time that José Martí spoke of racial equality, arguing that both blacks and whites had fought and died for the country and man should be judged for his defects and virtues rather than his color. He argued that fear of a race war was not a reality, and sought to build national unity by eschewing racial identity and declaring racism an evil that no longer belonged in Cuban society.

Despite Martí's thoughts on racial harmony and the overall rhetoric of national unity over racial divisions in the country, the beginning of the twentieth century was fraught with racial inequality and black subordination. For many of the former black and *mulato* soldiers, participation in the wars advanced their social position and served as a means to lay claim to their

---

18. See Saney 2004.

19. See Ferrer 1999.

rights as citizens.[20] Their military sacrifice raised hopes of a new post-war society that would grant Afro-Cubans equality and justice not only under the law, but in their everyday realities as well.[21] Following independence, these expectations were rejected with laws banning blacks from the political process along with other formal and informal segregation practices. During the US-controlled elections of 1902 Afro-Cubans, women, and those with less than $250 could not vote. Additionally, Afro-Cubans were banned from holding government posts and barred from ownership of private business. Blacks were also barred from holding various employment positions (including the police department), and finally, in spite of their service in the wars, were banned from high military positions.[22] Not only did blacks find themselves in a marginal position; black culture was publically denigrated.[23] Afro-Cuban culture and Afro-Cubans in general were deemed primitive and became a threat to Cuban identity, and many black cultural forms were prohibited by the state. Thus despite the rhetoric of inclusion, Cuban leaders during the Republic established a clear racial hierarchy with blacks on the bottom, holding little to no rights. Consequently, demands for inclusion and the development of black institutions and organizations began to flourish shortly after independence.

In response to the clear contradiction between official rhetoric and reality regarding racism came the largest challenge to the practice of black exclusion in Cuban history: the founding of the first black political party in Cuba. In the 1908 national election black candidates, who were only permitted to run for certain local positions, experienced losses for every position they contested. Political parties during this time, as Jorge Domínguez writes, did not reflect any ethnic cleavages and the parties were "alike in opposing black affirmations of identity as well as in courting their votes."[24] The sweeping losses that blacks experienced during this time triggered the Agrupación Independiente de Color to found the first black political party, El Partido Independiente de Color (the Independent Party of Color) or the PIC. The PIC viewed the Cuban government, led by President José Miguel Gómez, as racist and eager to exclude those of color from power and rights of citizenship. In turn, the PIC was seen as a threat to the dominant political parties, specifically

---

20. See Portuondo Linares 2002.

21. Pérez 2006.

22. Pérez 2006; Portuondo Linares 2002.

23. Moore 1997.

24. Domínguez 1978, 49.

to the Liberal Party, which had established a hold among the Afro-Cuban electorate.[25] They became the target of opposition from the Cuban government as they continued to remain vocal about civil and political rights for Afro-Cubans. Their platform in particular represented a clear, active stance toward the acquisition of civil rights for those of color: "Freedom is not asked or begged for, it is won; and rights are not handed out anywhere, rights are fought for and belong to all. If we go on asking for our rights, we will die waiting because we will have lost them."[26] The party stood as a direct challenge not only to the national rhetoric of racelessness, but to the established racial hierarchy based on white supremacy.

The party was accused by members of the government of promoting racial exclusion, yet much of their platform centered on social justice and equality for all Cubans, not just black Cubans. Moreover, party membership was not exclusive to black Cubans. Nevertheless, in 1910, in response to the party's continued existence and support, Martín Morúa Delgado, a conservative black senator, introduced the Morúa Amendment to the already established national electoral law, banning political parties on the basis of racial or class affiliation. The law passed, party leaders were incarcerated, and the party's publications were banned.[27] The role that nonwhite members of government needed to take with respect to race was one of assimilation, not affirmation. Reminiscent of Martí's warning to blacks about provoking white racism, Morúa's decision to introduce the amendment was motivated by a desire to ignore racial identity and its societal role in order to be included by the white power structure, thus adhering to the national ideal of racelessness. Morúa had long been a proponent of black elite unity not in the form of racial affirmation, but in order to distance educated blacks from poorer blacks who were not yet ready for assimilation or even full civil rights and might threaten the ascendance of black elites.[28] Morúa Delgado promoted conciliatory thought and maintained that organizing on the basis of race was detrimental to national unity and black progress. The implementation of the Morúa Amendment was emblematic of the usual rhetoric used to stifle black calls for rights and equality guised as protection against the threat of unwanted divisions in society.

---

25. Pérez 2006.

26. Portuondo Linares 2002.

27. De la Fuente 2001a.

28. Pappademos 2011.

Although the PIC made several attempts to fight the Morúa law, they were unable to be recognized as a party and organized a public protest in 1912. The armed demonstration by the PIC was quickly framed by the media as a race war against whites in order to justify the government's brutal response. In May and June of 1912 the Cuban government ruthlessly ordered soldiers to crush the rebellion, killing more than three thousand blacks irrespective of their involvement with the party.[29] More than solely a racial massacre, the government response to the PIC served as example to future associations looking to vocalize demands pertaining to racial discrimination in Cuba. It also reflected the position of the Cuban government to uphold white supremacy, as President José Miguel Gómez declared that the killings were done to "defend the civilization against barbarism."[30]

The massacre not only created a formidable deterrent to Afro-Cubans' ability to mobilize, but it was subsequently hidden from Cuba's written history. Consequently, President Gómez remained a celebrated figure in Cuba and in 1936, a monument of the president was erected in Havana. The black newspaper *Adelante* voiced its protest and indignation at the idea of the monument, naming Gomez responsible for the massacre of so many black lives in 1912. The silence continues today, where few are aware of the PIC or the violence in Santiago that resulted from their activism. The racial history has been concealed despite its potential after 1959 to produce a narrative much like the revolutionary racial narratives of today. The massacre is representative of the racial violence and injustice that the revolutionary leadership claims to have overcome, but it has remained veiled.[31]

The PIC represented one of very few breaks with the status quo of racial discourse in Cuban history and signaled that many blacks, both elite and working class, sought to challenge the rhetoric of racelessness and open up dialogue about blackness and inequality.[32] The government response to the PIC protest coupled with the Morúa Law were part of the consistent, state-sponsored policy, albeit informal, to suppress black activism throughout the

---

29. Portuondo Linares 2002.

30. Pérez 2006.

31. In 2008, to mark the centennial of the founding of the PIC, there were events held in Cuba to commemorate the party. The government sponsored these events, but the history of the PIC is still absent from official channels and curriculum; most Cubans are not aware of its existence.

32. Serafín Portuondo Linares, son of one of the members of the PIC, authored a book on the party in 1950. In Portuondo's critique of the PIC he remarks that because they were banned by the Morúa Law, by creating a popular entity rather than a racial one, they could have advanced while remaining under the legal auspices of the amendment to create a third

duration of the Republic. Despite varying political systems, the discouragement of black organization has been constant throughout Cuba's history and has provided the limits within which blacks can act and organize for over a century.

Racism and Organization

State suppression of black dialogue and association was not absolute. If activism remained within the informal boundaries dictated by the government, there was a certain freedom of association with regard to race. Despite official rhetoric that claimed the contrary, there was considerable dissent during the years of the Republic by those who did not believe that addressing the problems of race and affirming a nonwhite identity would lead to national division. There were also Cubans of color who wrote about the problem of racism in Cuba prior to the revolution.[33] Several black organizations and newspapers were created during the decades of the Republic. Sociedades de la Raza de Color, or Societies of Color, were created out of the exclusion of the black and *mulato* middle classes from white social clubs and represented various forms of organizing: religious practice, political discussion, athletic competition, and social clubs. These societies often received government subsidies and served as a primary way for blacks to advance socially and politically.[34] Alongside the organizational arm, a black press developed during this time that produced black publications that addressed racial issues in Cuba. These organizations served as a voice for nonwhite Cubans in all aspects of

party. This critique is not meant to suggest that Portuondo was not in favor of the racial basis of the PIC, but rather presents an alternative way that the party could have maintained its existence. Portuondo, in fact, was heavily criticized by the socialist party for advocating a place for racial discourse within the party and Marxist theory. Yet what was unprecedented about the party was its focus on race and its willingness to vocalize the needs of the Afro-Cuban population in particular. Championing the cause of a historically silenced community was necessary, and had the party conformed to a program that focused solely on social justice, the issues of racial exclusion and discrimination would have continued to be ignored. It is notable that the revolution has not taken Portuondo Linares as one of their heroes; he was a founder of the Local Workers Federation, Secretary General of the Communist Party, and a son of a veteran of the war of independence. In this case, the erasure of race and of blackness seems to have been more important than highlighting the injustices of past regimes.

33. It is for this reason that studies on racism in Cuba before 1959 abound among scholarly works when compared to contemporary studies on the subject; black political thought in Cuba was well documented before such writings and associations were banned.

34. De la Fuente 2001a.

society and were crucial in creating a public dialogue regarding race prior to the revolution.

Despite the existence of black societies and organizations along with the ascendance of a black and *mulato* elite, significant racial inequality remained during the years of the Republic. Illiteracy rates for black Cubans were significantly higher than those of whites, where by 1919, 49 percent of the nonwhite population over the age of ten was illiterate as compared to 37 percent of whites. In addition, only 429 Afro-Cubans in that year received professional or academic degrees compared with 10,123 Cuban white males.[35] Literacy requirements for voting meant that many Afro-Cuban males were often disenfranchised, and their representation in the public sector was far unequal to their proportion of the population. As 33 percent of the population, they constituted 8 percent of the teachers and 26 percent of the soldiers and police force. Land ownership by blacks actually decreased from 1899 to 1931 from 16 percent to only 8.5 percent in 1931, which was largely due to foreign investment in sugar production.[36]

Black organizations did usher in small victories with respect to racial discrimination. Presidents Carlos Prío Socarras and Fulgencio Batista created anti-discrimination legislation that would prohibit discriminatory hiring practices in employment. These successes were accomplished through pressure by the Afro-Cuban associations, but were limited to the labor market. Outside of employment, there were no laws that were created to curb the social segregation that existed in Cuba at the time. Beaches, recreational facilities, and other social spaces were segregated, albeit informally, and kept blacks out. Blacks were also subject to discrimination in their social and professional mobility through these informal practices put into place by white associations and individuals. The continued racial disparities motivated black organizations to speak out against them. In 1931, Club Atenas, an exclusive Afro-Cuban society, protested the immigration policy in Cuba and called on the government to stop immigration into the country, citing the damage that it had done to levels of unemployment among Cuban natives and particularly among people of color.[37] They argued that those that fought for

---

35. Pérez 2006.

36. De la Fuente 2001a.

37. More formal means of black exclusion emerged during the whitening campaign in Cuba, where an attempt to lighten the Cuban population was publicly promoted and funded through incentives for European immigration. The immigration in turn displaced many Afro-Cuban workers. This campaign, coupled with the overall lack of access to employment and health

the independence of the country were being ignored and forgotten.[38] Despite continued racism, the attention to the issue by the Cuban government demonstrated the importance of civil rights organizations to promote black advancement.

The rich history of black activism in Cuba during the period of the Republic does not suggest that racial consciousness and black solidarity were always congruent and consistent among all of those involved in racial organizations. Black consciousness was nuanced, and organizations varied in their commitment and articulation of black demands. As Melina Pappademos argues, while black elites did court the black vote, they operated more under a system of patronage for personal gain with white politicians rather than out of a duty to black communities.[39] Many of these groups envisioned black progress in different ways and black elites more often subscribed to ideas of racial uplift and assimilation into white culture and actively communicated Africanisms and blackness as backward. Pappademos makes a critical argument that racial consciousness did not occur consistently, particularly among black elites, and often promises made to black constituencies were left unmet. Moreover, discussions of racial disparities, black poverty, and opportunity were rarely articulated by black elites and politicians. During the first decades of the Republic, black elites remained silent or neutral on problems of structural racism in an effort to promote the raceless narrative of the government and adhered to individual notions of progress such as racial uplift. In addition, these elite organizations and their members often distanced themselves from the black popular class.

Although racial ideology had a clear effect in limiting the ways in which some groups chose to articulate issues of racism, voices did openly challenge ideas that promoted racial uplift and the backwardness of Africa and Africanisms. During the 1920s and 1930s several black activists, scholars, and writers were voicing messages of black affirmation and pointing to the socioeconomic gap between blacks and whites perpetuated by anti-black racism. The publication *Adelante* was one of the voices at the center of this emergence. The editors often wrote of the importance of social and political equality for blacks and the experience of discrimination that many suffered in

---

benefits for the majority of nonwhites in Cuba, highlighted the ways in which whites, regardless of nationality, occupied a privileged position in Cuba, at the expense of nonwhites.

38. Montejo 2004.

39. Pappademos 2011.

Cuba. Moreover, they often highlighted the importance of racial solidarity between blacks and *mulatos* in the struggle against racism in Cuba. On the subject of discrimination, in 1937 Zenobio Mustelier wrote,

> This requires an immediate and courageous solution. The discriminatory position in which people of color currently find themselves in Cuba requires blacks from Oriente to be completely united in order to confront this problem, without a spirit of aggression against anyone, but with the purpose of creating CUBANIDAD, or better, NACIONALIDAD. Having been born on this soil, black Cubans cannot emigrate to any foreign country; we can only require that things become the way they should be in our country.[40]

The messages within this newspaper expressed ideas that were contrary to the elites that sought to become incorporated into the white circles. Racial affirmation and solidarity were recognized by this group as being essential to the fight against subordination. One of Cuba's most noteworthy black intellectuals, Gustavo Urrutia, wrote in *Adelante* during the same period that in order to achieve equality, blacks had to first achieve self-determination.

> Blacks are differentiated in the economic and social realms and need, in a steadfast manner, to know deeply, from their own conscious, their position within the Cuban predicament in order to formulate a suitable critique to resolve the problem and discover the specific reasons for racial contempt. We must define the differences in order to eliminate them; this does not mean erasing biological differences, but making them innocuous ... In order to create the new black man, we must use our own values and mobilize them in favor of our community and initiate the process of self-determination, defining to ourselves what the black man signifies for the world and for Cuba.[41]

Indeed part of the ideology of racelessness meant obscuring the social position of blacks and *mulatos* relative to whites. Without this awareness, attention to the reach of racism was unlikely.

---

40. Mustelier 1937.

41. Urrutia 1937.

Much of the writing that came from the Afro-Cuban elite served as a challenge to the myth of equality, yet stayed within the limits of nationhood espoused by the dominant ideology. In 1939 journalist Alberto Arredondo, in his book *El Negro en Cuba*, wrote that "the fact that blacks are the *most exploited factor of our nationality* does not mean, and would never mean, that blacks constitute a nation within the Cuban nation. It only means that among the integral groups of the nation the black group is the most exploited."[42] A common theme among black Cuban thought throughout the Republic (which continues today) is the recognition that blacks have not been granted equal rights coupled with the simultaneous reinforcement of Cuban over black identity. Accusations of racism, inequity, and discrimination were often made by black associations and their leaders throughout the years following independence up until the revolution in 1959, but these complaints were always couched in the ideal of universal inclusion and the supremacy of nationhood.

It is crucial to point out these differences in black political thought throughout the period of the Republic because similar debates occur today. Calls for a black movement within the revolution, an integrationist movement, or the continued legitimacy of the racial harmony rhetoric that contends that the revolution erased most vestiges of structural racism are all present within black political thought in Cuba. These variations in thought circulate throughout black communities today not only among elite circles and well-educated blacks, but among black Cubans from all levels of education and occupations. During my research, regardless of the strategy or ideology that each person espoused, there was a consistency in blacks' investment in black progress and representation. Even the most ardent supporter of racial democracy in Cuba who insisted that race was no longer relevant when considering opportunity, felt personally connected to black progress. During the period of the Republic, while black solidarity did not exist equally across communities of black Cubans,[43] evidence of racial activism and consciousness was present despite the power of the ideology of racial harmony. Moreover, the existence of a "black vote" and the racially specific campaigning conducted to gain such a vote suggest that there were communities of blacks within the popular classes that expected black officials to work for their collective good and toward increased opportunity. Even though elites did not make good on

---

42. Arredondo 1939.

43. Pappademos 2011.

their promises and were operating via self-interest, their racial identity still mattered. In addition, although some elite organizations would not identify with poor blacks, the national myth of racial transcendence caused the clubmen to discuss the state of race relations in Cuba in the public sphere for fear of race being erased all together. This is coupled with the evidence of more radical thinking that pushed the boundaries of racial democracy, encouraging solidarity and even mobilization. Following this logic, there is little reason to believe that the desires for black progress or even black affirmation were erased after 1959.

Initially, the revolution was thought to address blacks' concerns in ways that leaders had not before this period, but the silencing of the black voice—a black voice that was well established just a few years prior—and the reality that the deeper roots of inequality and racism remained intact, created a dissonance. There were many voices at the start of the revolution that expressed support for a movement to truly eradicate racial discrimination at its root.[44] As the following chapters will discuss, this discontent among nonwhites, the desire among revolutionaries to tackle racism more comprehensively, continues today.

Conclusion

The racial ideology in Cuba succeeds in creating a lens that inhibits racial explanations of phenomena that are often connected to race and racism. It also creates an ethos that both supports integration and eschews those who wish to make claims of discrimination and racism, a combination that poses significant setbacks for black progress. Moreover, the characterization of Cuba as a mixed nation (neither black nor white) has been used since the period of abolition to maintain racial unity, while excluding black cultural forms and voices. Black elites during the period of the Republic were limited in their ability to draw attention to racism, and black consciousness was often undercut due to the power of racial ideology in Cuba. Nonetheless, those that were dedicated to increasing awareness about racism in Cuba created spaces for themselves and others to do so. Through press, writings, and organizations, there was a clear black voice in Cuba that was crucial in creating a black counterpublic that challenged the dominant voices of the public sphere.[45]

---

44. De la Fuente 2001a.

45. Dawson 2001.

Black political attitudes were not always in open opposition to racial democracy, but they were present and varied.

The ability of racial democracy to decrease the saliency of race is crucial for its longevity. In other words, the presence of racial consciousness among nonwhites will be one of the most important variables necessary to challenge the ideology of racial democracy and combat racism. We can expect that the impetus for any movement to dismantle racial inequalities will depend on blacks' collective consciousness. The significance of black consciousness and solidarity lies in its ability to provide the foundation for certain levels of progress to be made amidst a racist system. This point is made clearer via the historical tradition of black activism that worked to secure civil rights for nonwhites and raise the question of racism in Cuba. Throughout the Americas, the growth in the number of black professionals, university students, and government officials, black representation in the media, and the increase in equality of opportunity overall, has required collective racial solidarity. In the second part of the book, I discuss the collective consciousness of blacks in Cuba today and the development of ideologies from below that form the foundation of black solidarity and black political thought in Cuba. Although I argue that these informal and private collectives are crucial to understand the contemporary black voice, they would be far more powerful if granted even the limited space that black expression was granted during the period of the Republic.

4 INSTITUTIONALIZING IDEOLOGY

RACE AND THE CUBAN REVOLUTION

Fidel Castro and the Cuban government have married socialism and the ideal of racial harmony to create a formidable ideology that is an integral part of Cubans' sense of identity and their perceptions of racism in their country. By promoting an anti-discrimination ethos, desegregating spaces, diminishing class differences at the onset of the revolution, and declaring the end of racism, Castro was able to unite belief in the revolution to belief in the erasure of racism. The ideology is bolstered by rhetoric that simultaneously embraces diversity, but collapses it into one singular national identity, which discourages racial affirmation. The working of Marxist ideology with racial democracy is vital to the analysis of racial politics in Cuba because socialist ideology and belief in it strengthen the power of racial democracy in the country.

This chapter will explore racial ideology in Cuba as it merged with socialist ideology and follow its development until the Sixth Party Congress in 2011. It will also discuss the ways in which the government institutionalized racial democracy, further bolstering its staying power. The ideology of racial democracy has been historically predominant in Latin American and Caribbean countries and is not particular to Cuba. Rhetoric that negated the presence of racism and racial inequality was part of the nation building process throughout the region. At the same time, this rhetoric in Cuba alongside a Marxist revolution that also downplays the role of race is unique to the Americas. The initial advances that the revolution was able to make by increasing opportunity for blacks and increasing class equality provided strong support for racial democracy in Cuba and connected the possibility of racial equality to socialism. Supporters of the revolution became believers in the claim that racism had ended in Cuba through their defense of the new government and its policies. The final sections of this chapter will demonstrate this connection between political attitudes and belief in racial democracy for supporters of the revolution with interview data.

With such widespread initial support of the revolution, the policy prohibiting race-based organizations and discussion of racism on the island was legitimized for many. Although it could be argued that support for the revolution has waned since the early decades, the idea remains that an organization based on race is not relevant for Cuba. Furthermore, the silence that was mandated regarding racism in Cuba continues to operate as a norm. While other issues of social justice, such as women's rights, have been given official spaces to organize throughout the history of the revolution, racial justice remains a topic that is taboo. Silence was thus institutionalized not only through dialogue, but throughout the revolution's mass organizations.

Challenges to the silence and to the ideology of racial democracy were few until the emergence of the economic crisis caused by the fall of the Soviet Union in 1989. The Special Period in the Time of Peace marked the first serious challenge to racial ideology in Cuba as inequalities increased with significant racial dimensions. Racism and discrimination became much more visible, particularly by nonwhites. I will examine the change in rhetoric regarding race among the leadership in response to the crisis and how racial ideology was altered during this time. As highlighted previously, racial ideology, in order to remain relevant, must be flexible and adaptable to political change. The Cuban government allowed for racial dialogue to enter into the public sphere in a limited fashion and admitted to some prerevolutionary legacies of racism that were not yet eradicated, but never abandoned the negation of systemic racism. The power of race continued to be silenced and denied, despite the adaptations that the government made to adjust to the rise in discrimination during the Special Period.

Race and the Start of the Revolution

The end of the Batista regime and the start of the Cuban Revolution began a promise of inclusion for previously marginalized sectors of the Cuban populace. The initial phase of the revolution was ushered in with messages of equality, democracy and social justice. The government openly discussed racial issues and for the first time, acknowledged and rebuked racial discrimination. This impetus did not only come from Fidel Castro and his leadership. As early as January 6, the Communist Party newspaper, *Hoy*, highlighted racial discrimination as one of the "most immediate tasks" for which the government should create policy. In addition, Afro-Cuban intellectuals and political leaders also began to bring forth public discussion on the racial issue.[1]

The new government's initial task was to create a society that was free of prejudices and free of obstacles barring black access to employment and education. In a speech to a labor rally in March of 1959 Castro said,

> Of all the forms of racial discrimination, the worst is the that which limits black Cubans' access to jobs because it is true that in some sectors of our country the shameful practice of excluding blacks from jobs exists . . . In this way, we commit the crime of denying, precisely to the poorest group more than anyone, the possibility to work. While colonial society made blacks work as slaves, more than anybody else and without any compensation, we commit the crime in our current society, which some have called a democratic society, of doing just the opposite and trying to prevent him from working to earn a living.[2]

His inclusion of Afro-Cubans in the overall picture of social justice solidified his support among a group who had historically been left out of the political process. A 1962 survey found that 80 percent of Afro-Cuban workers were "wholly in favor of the revolution," whereas only 67 percent of white workers were.[3] Afro-Cubans were vital for the revolution's support and success. Consequently, the beginnings of the Cuban revolution were characterized by rhetoric that vilified a racist past and glorified a future of equality and an end to discrimination. Embedded in Castro's speeches were not only promises of an end to systemic racism, but calls for a new man, free of personal prejudices as well.

The professed duty of the revolution was to equalize access for blacks by abolishing segregation and class disparities to generate equality of opportunity. The consequences of creating this parity would be a similar ideology of racial harmony from the past, but with increased legitimacy due to revolutionary social and economic reform. Although Castro's rhetoric of racial democracy was strikingly similar to that of other Latin American nations, Castro was able to claim that he did a better job at eradicating racial discrimination than these nations through policies of desegregation. Castro's March

---

1. De la Fuente 2001a.

2. Castro 1959.

3. De la Fuente 2001a; Saney 2004.

1959 speech addressed not only free access to employment, but to all previously segregated social spaces.

> Let whites and blacks all agree and come together to end hateful racial discrimination in work centers. In this way, we will forge our new country step by step. In public school, blacks and whites will learn to live together as brothers and if they join each other in public school, they'll later join each other in recreation centers and everywhere else. But when we are educated separately, and the aristocrats educate their children apart from blacks, it is logical that later whites and blacks cannot be together in cultural or recreational centers either.[4]

Following this speech, the Cuban government began its gradual process of desegregation. The beaches were the first to be nationalized; many of them were private beaches owned by country clubs and hotels from which nonmembers were barred.[5] Although many white country clubs carried informal rules regarding membership, their practices of racial exclusion were clear. These clubs, along with exclusive professional organizations for which membership was dependent on family income, were nationalized one by one and several were converted into "workers' social circles." Low-income workers began to replace the elites as members of these workers' circles throughout Cuba.

Fidel Castro's initial speeches addressing the issue of race and discrimination received mixed reactions from whites that were traditionally on the receiving end of the benefits of racial segregation.[6] Desegregation did not come without resistance. Many clubs refused to integrate and alternative, integrated clubs with similar functions had to be created. As Devyn Spence Benson argues, many of the white, affluent Cubans who left Cuba in the early years of the revolution did so as a reaction to the threat of integration.[7] While the government did insist on integration, often resistance was not met with enforcement. Segregated clubs were allowed to continue to exist initially without experiencing any repercussions. The practice of redesigning and creating new institutions that would not discriminate often created a

---

4. Castro 1959.

5. De la Fuente 2001a.

6. Speeches that talked of integration in schools and workplaces received mixed reactions from Cubans. Many whites were in fact quite threatened by the changes that the government would begin to impose (Spence Benson 2012).

7. Spence Benson 2012.

façade of integration while many whites continued to remain separate from blacks. Exclusionary attitudes and structures continued to operate despite the revolution's attempt to create racial equality.[8] Nevertheless, the government's project of opening clubs and facilities to all Cubans changed the landscape of Cuban society markedly.

The project of desegregating facilities and social circles did not address structural inequities. Housing still remained largely segregated with whites remaining in more desirable, central neighborhoods and blacks living in historically poorer neighborhoods. Quality of housing also differed among these neighborhoods, giving whites a clear housing advantage. Furthermore, although after 1961 the government was put in charge of hiring state workers, few blacks were found in prestigious government positions.[9] Despite the incomplete nature of introducing racial equality to Cuba, the Cuban revolution provided opportunities and advancements for blacks that were unprecedented and accounted for much of their support of the revolution.

While the government did indeed institute these acts of desegregation to "rid" Cuba of racial discrimination, building national unity and maintaining white support of the revolution was a priority as well. Much like the period of consolidation that Cubans faced during the independence wars, Fidel Castro sought to consolidate the state and herald in a strong sense of nationalism among the populace to confront threats to national unity and to the revolution. Thus, the government's refusal to create legislation outlawing discrimination and its reticence to engage in race-based hiring was an avoidance of radical policies that may have alienated white Cubans. In the same speech quoted above at a labor rally in Havana in 1959, Castro stated,

> It shouldn't be necessary to pass a law to establish a right that is earned by the mere fact of being a human being and a member of society. It should not be necessary to pass a law against an absurd prejudice. What should be passed is anathema and public condemnation against those men, full of past vices and prejudices, and who are unscrupulous enough to come and discriminate against Cubans, to come and mistreat Cubans, over matters of lighter or darker skin.

---

8. De la Fuente 2001a.

9. Adams 2004.

Desegregation was done carefully, so as to not upend white backing of the revolutionary process and the government did not instate any laws pertaining to discrimination until the 1976 Constitution.[10] Whites were not pushed to change their lifestyles by mingling with Afro-Cubans in social and professional circles.[11] In this way, the revolutionary government sought equality, but not at the price of national unity. Later on, the silencing of the black voice when pertaining to racial issues by barring any public discussion of the topic would not only help to consolidate unity, but would maintain the notion that the revolution is free of racial problems.

Institutionalizing Silence

Following the desegregation process, the Cuban government announced that it had taken all of the required steps to ensure equality. On the second anniversary of the revolution, Castro proclaimed the end to discrimination and prejudice:

> The revolution was able to do away with prejudice, with unjust and cruel discrimination. The revolution was able to create hope; to awaken in sleeping people the noblest aims and ideals.[12]

With the race problem "solved," there would no longer be a need to address race or racism in Cuban society. Racist attitudes were characterized as a thing of the past in exchange for more noble, revolutionary ideals. Within the revolution, racism ceased to be an issue and any critical discussion was removed from both the government's script and from public debate. Castro would continue to present Cuba as a model for racial equality and tout his government's ability to eradicate discrimination, but any discussion beyond racism as part of history was eliminated. Speeches by Fidel Castro that followed focused on racism as a part of the past, or an international matter that other countries were still struggling with, but Cuba had overcome.[13] Consequently, in

---

10. Articles 41 of the constitution of 1976 states that discrimination motivated by race, color, sex or national origin is prohibited. Article 42 outlines various spaces that citizens, regardless of race, color, or national origin, have the right to access employment, the armed forces, education, medical assistance, housing, public services, and public spaces.

11. See Moore 1988, 212.

12. Castro 1961.

13. Castro and Taber 1981; Castro 2000.

Cuba the revolutionary government has, from the first months of the revolution's triumph, described a racial reality that in fact was not at all visible on the ground. As racism was proclaimed solved and subsequently banned from public discussion, racial ideology took on a clear strategy to mask racial divisions and disparities in exchange for national unity. Racial ideology was quite deliberate in Cuba.

Castro's discourse of historical legacies to explain any continued existence of racial prejudice in Cuba was—and continues to be—the foundation of state rhetoric on race. Defining racism as an evil inherited from Cuba pre-1959 relieved the new socialism system from any responsibility to further examine racial inequality beyond class. Consequently, the government banned all race-based publications, organizations, and societies.[14] Castro used José Martí's ideas regarding racial unity to negate the importance of racial difference. By prohibiting discussion of race and racial organization, Castro effectively legislated Martí's ideology and as a result, Cuban identity and racial thought.

In their article titled *Race and Inequality in Contemporary Cuba*, Cuban scholars Espina and Prieto offer three reasons for the subject of race "disappearing" from the public sphere at the start of the revolution.[15] The first, they argue, is the fact that racial inequality had not only become minimal, but remnants of racism depended only on individual and personal effort. As such, the problem of racism was declared solved. Second, the need for the government to secure national unity meant that any mention of racial issues became unwelcome and subsequently, the subject became taboo. The third reason that the authors give is a general disinterest from below regarding racial inequality during this time, largely due to the revolutionary fervor that most from below were experiencing. They argue that there was no social base for such a movement and that most were more interested in national unity during this time.

There is no doubt that there was overwhelming support for the revolution among black Cubans and that the measures that were taken to equalize opportunity and transform education, health care and housing were an integral part of that support.[16] I would argue these components were also an integral part of the support for the declaration that the race problem was in fact solved. Yet there were several prominent black figures that advocated for

---

14. De la Fuente 2001a.

15. Espina Prieto and Rodríguez Ruiz 2006.

16. Saney 2004.

a continued struggle against enduring racism and pointed to the need for the government to address the issue directly.[17] It is then the second reason that the authors offer that is most relevant in the "disappearance" of the discussion of racism and the attention that it received by the government and its citizens. This taboo, in turn, became a norm of silence.

It is important to note that silence in Cuba has significant structural and institutional implications. Race is not only absent from public discourse; its absence is institutionalized.[18] Organizing, writing, and discussing race in Cuba in a formal or public manner were prohibited. Consequently, the way that race was lived changed completely. It was no longer acceptable to affirm one's race, engage in Afro-Cuban cultural and religious practices, or perceive race to have any connection to relationships, opportunities, or lived experience. Race was also removed from the country's historical tradition through education and control of information whereby societies, publications, and organizations that existed to affirm blackness, bring attention to racism, or provide a voice to a marginalized community were all erased.

Organizations based on race were not only erased from historical memory, but were reinvented as racist projects. Carlos Moore argues that the nonracial outlook of the revolution involved stamping out black cultural expression.[19] Both Moore and De la Fuente cite assaults on Afro-Cuban religion, the abolition of the Afro-Cuban mutual aid *Sociedades de Color*, the persecution of the *Abakuá* secret societies, an unofficial offensive against Afro-Cuban language patterns, and attempts to discredit African religions as primitive as evidence that black culture was derided and stifled.[20] Moore also argues that though the government maintained tolerance toward the Catholic Church after a brief period of tension between the clergy and the government, this protection was not provided to the Yoruba religion.

Even among the revolution's supporters, discussions of racism during the early years of the revolution were met with suppression. Lillian Guerra discusses a particular example in 1969 when black intellectuals, through both

---

17. Fernandez Robaina 2009.

18. This practice is unique to Cuba except in the instance of Brazil during the period of authoritarianism. During this time, racial ideology was similarly enforced through the prohibition of racial activism and racial scholarship. As Reginald Daniel (2005) argues, "efforts to mobilize along racial lines were racist, subversive, a threat to national security and punishable by imprisonment" (92).

19. Moore 1988.

20. Ibid.; de la Fuente 2001a.

cultural production and an official meeting with the Ministry of Education, challenged the government's silence regarding racism.[21] The group sought to engage, from a revolutionary standpoint, the racist practices and culture that still existed nine years into the revolution and they were sanctioned and repressed as a result. The black voice was reframed as divisive and a threat to national unity, rather than as legitimate expression within the public sphere. We see this come to life in the survey data, which shows that 60 percent of the sample stated that a black organization would be just as racist as white organizations that excluded blacks.[22]

The level of access to information and alternative ideologies is an integral part of the wide support and the level of dominance that the myth of racial democracy achieves among the citizenry. As Van Dijk argues, elite ideologies may be widely adopted if there are no strong popular alternatives or these alternatives are unknown or marginalized.[23] Further, if elites are able to prevent or limit access to these counterideologies from the public domain, dominant ideologies are able to enjoy broader support. In the case of Cuban racial politics, dominant ideologies counter much of the reality on the ground, yet state control of media, expression, and information play a significant role in mitigating such contradictions. Challenges to the notion of racial harmony are controlled nearly completely by the state and as such, do not reach a large percentage of the population. The government's power over space determines who is able to meet, discuss, and express their views in public. Even within spaces of contestation that are permitted, limits are placed on what can be published, sung, performed, and discussed. Challenges to racial ideology in Cuba do exist, but their reach is quite limited, which not only lends more legitimacy to the dominant ideology but also puts constraints on awareness at the individual level should one want to actively participate in such a challenge. The lack of access to alternative information serves to keep marginalized groups in their subordinate position by silencing alternative ideologies and masking the effects of race on life chances, while permitting Cubans in general to ignore race.

Education, mass media, and even families are social teachers that have great influence on what issues are important to whom and what values one

---

21. Guerra 2012.

22. See chapter 9 for a discussion of this survey result and opinions on racial organizing in Cuba.

23. Van Dijk 1998.

holds. In Cuba, state control of all institutions and institutional space creates a centralized framework through which to support certain projects and ideas and discourage or silence others. The two particular institutions that have been most directly involved in the dissemination of ideas are education and the mass media. Both institutions have historically omitted the subject of race relations and have been narrow in their representation of black Cubans. History textbooks written for primary and secondary levels, for example, talk about the Afro-Cuban experience only through slavery and place little to no emphasis on the black contribution.[24] Television in Cuba does not only support silence regarding racism, but also has been notorious in its scarce representation of blacks.[25] Television shows that highlight racism in Cuba as personal prejudice keep information about structural racism away from the public. Finally, the continued media presence of racism outside of Cuba promotes a particular definition of racism that includes violence, riots, segregation, and resistance, rather than subtle institutional practices that maintain the country's racial hierarchy.

There are several institutional spaces created in the early years of the revolution for the debate and discussion of social concerns. Citizens are able to voice issues to their neighborhood and society as a whole through their small neighborhood associations that are connected to the local government. These Committees in the Defense of the Revolution (CDRs) support local issues, but racism in Cuba is not a subject welcome in CDR meetings.[26] It has always been counterrevolutionary to be racist, and even more counterrevolutionary to point to racism.

In addition to discussion on citizens' issues, the Cuban government created spaces at the start of the revolution for the advancement of women. The Federation of Cuban Women (Federación de Mujeres Cubanas or FMC) was founded in the first years of the revolution to address issues of opportunity, access, and prejudiced attitudes against women. The problem of sexism and women's rights was given deserved attention and the FMC served not only to include those who were left out of the national project prior to the

---

24. Torres-Cuevas and Loyola Vega 2001.

25. Morales Domínguez 2007.

26. Several of my interviewees shared that race or racism were not topics that were discussed in the CDR meetings and were understood as something that political candidates or those connected to the party will not bring up. A president of a CDR shared that there were some racial tensions in a solar in her neighborhood but this was brushed aside and not treated as a political concern because one cannot control others' attitudes.

revolution, but they were given the support to fight for and publicly demand gender equality.

The creation of the FMC without a similar organization to combat racial inequality reinforced the notion that the rights of women should be fought for on a consistent basis while the rights of blacks do not require such a struggle. The battle against sexism throughout the revolutionary regime has never been deemed divisive. Discussion of gender inequality is a topic that is open for discussion, unlike discussion of racial inequality, which people avoid because of political sensitivity or a belief that such discussion is against the revolution and national unity. The ideological framing that the state has given to sexism versus racism has significantly influenced how people view these two issues and whether they feel open to talk about them. The FMC created a national consciousness regarding the rights for women that continues today. Throughout the past decade, Cuba has launched many campaigns and a *batalla de ideas* to overcome the country's challenges and injustices without any reference to racism.[27] As an interviewer pointed out, the revolution is in a particularly advantageous position because they can guide policy and rhetoric regarding any particular issue. "Why not a racial discrimination campaign?" he asked.

During the first years of the revolution, the Federation of Cuban Women included many blacks and *mulatas* among their ranks and the inclusion of nonwhites served as evidence that blacks did not need their own organization. If blacks were subsumed into other organizations that addressed social ills other than race, they were not being excluded. While the same argument could be made about the inclusion of women into mass organizations, women were given their own organization and the freedom to address issues specific to their demographic. This policy supported black inclusion and simultaneous invisibility not only in terms of the government, but among the citizens as well. The institutional structure, and the organizations that existed within it, supported the erasure of the black voice and black rights as a whole.

---

27. The *batalla de ideas*, or battle of ideas, was a national campaign that was described as "the total comprehension of the ideals of the Cuban people, the wish of sovereignty independence, peace and development. It is a battle for justice that has been converted for us into a life attitude." The campaign focuses on economic recovery, education, culture, peace, and the freedom of the five Cubans imprisoned in the United States (Borjes 2007). The campaign was eliminated after the Sixth Party Congress in 2011, as it was found to be a very expensive endeavor for the Cuban state. Nonetheless, the government still is able to promote a public campaign to increase awareness and battle racism without the monetary commitment given to the *batalla* initiatives.

Ideology that promotes the idea that a race-based organization is divisive and prohibits its existence has a significant influence on society's perception of the racial activism and expression. Moreover, the illegality of creating such an organization without the approval of the state deters efforts among those that do recognize the need to organize based on race. Citizens believe that promoting black rights and black identity is indeed divisive and institutional frameworks discourage any action or organization despite possible opposition to the ideology. As Mary Jackman writes, "The surest strategy of social control is to confine the agenda within which a challenge might take place."[28] The state in Cuba is able to do this quite easily as it controls space on the island: space to live, space to meet, and space to convene, such that any official challenge to state ideology must be done within the state's parameters. The state must let you in before you can challenge it. Thus, the state controls the boundaries of the expression of counterideologies and consequently, to what extent that expression reaches others.

Ideologies similar to racial democracy throughout the world often propagate the idea that leaving race behind, in the past, is a progressive act that signals social and national advancement.[29] Governments and proponents of this racial ideology declare the end of race as the beginning of progress. It is thus seen as the solution to racism, one that requires much less work, sacrifice and unease than actually addressing racism. As David Theo Goldberg argues,

> The moral and legal insistence of racelessness has tended to rest upon a historical narrative promoting it as the only fitting contemporary response to pernicious racist pasts. On this account, any contemporary invocation of race for policy purposes, affirmative or not, comes to be equated with the horrors of racist histories.[30]

Why is colorblindness and silence regarding race seen as the way to fix racism? There are clear transnational patterns and calls to forget race and move past the ugly national histories are not only present in Cuba, but throughout the Americas, including the United States. It represents an approach to racism that seeks to forget about it, but keep it around. The notion invokes the lack of commitment toward racial equality, but also the belief that racism is indeed a mechanism of the past, easily identified by slavery, segregation, and

---

28. Jackman 1994, 67.

29. Goldberg 2002.

30. Ibid., 201.

racial violence. What this notion of progressive racelessness truly represents is racism below the surface: the desire to allow racism to live untouched alongside the unequal status quo.[31] Silence and the subsequent forgetting of racism provides a break between history and the present such that we do not connect the historical legacy of racism to what we might experience today—silence represents a new chapter that is free of the past.

Pushing race into the past does not mean that race has ceased to be ubiquitous within structures, practices and language.[32] As seen throughout this book, race remains a pervasive and significant component in the way that Cuban society is organized, making the forced silence on the topic particularly damaging. The presence of black consciousness refutes Cuba as a colorblind nation, but blacks cannot express this, act on it, or organize around this consciousness to demand more from their government, to open up dialogue and increase awareness of the issue. If we look at other states with levels of black consciousness, such as Brazil or the United States, we see examples of groups that are actively challenging this ideology and making strides (via activism and race conscious policies) to lessen its dominance and continued hold on racial inequality.

The presence of racism and racial movements outside of Cuba fit into the national rhetoric of racism as an external issue. Race was discussed in an international context throughout the first three decades of the revolution. In 1975, Castro made a significant racial appeal during the military campaign in Angola. Castro, explaining the decision to go to war, said,

> The leadership of the Cuban Communist Party did not have more than twenty-four hours to make the decision, which it did, without vacillation, on November 5, in a long and serene meeting. On another November 5, this one in 1843, a slave from a sugar mill in Matanzas, named Black Carlota, had risen up at the head of a slave rebellion, machete in hand, and was killed in the act. In homage, the actions of solidarity in Angola were named after her: Operation Carlota.[33]

The military involvement in Angola, and the fight against South African Apartheid that accompanied the struggle, were highlighted by the Cuban government as a representation of solidarity with Cuba's black heritage.

---

31. Ibid.

32. Winant 2000.

33. Castro and Taber 1981.

Castro declared that Cuba was an "African Latin" nation and the military effort reflected this Diasporic connection.[34] Half of the Cuban troops that were sent to Angola were black, which represented a much larger percentage than their share of the total population,[35] as well as their share in the military. Black soldiers were purposefully recruited from different regions of Cuba. The racialization of the military during this operation was meant to create a degree of racial parity among the Cuban and Angolan troops.[36] Although the battles across the Atlantic did summon recognition of Cuba's black population, the effort did not veer from the characterization of racial injustice as an external problem that did not affect Cuba.

A significant component of racism as an international (rather than domestic) problem is well displayed in a speech by Fidel Castro in April of 1981. Castro used the commemoration of the twentieth anniversary of the Bay of Pigs to emphasize the connection between socialism and racial equality in contrast to the United States. Here he proclaimed,

> When I mentioned the things that socialism made possible, I left out another one of our great successes: the end of the cruel discrimination that existed in our country, the discrimination on the grounds of race or sex. So we can also ask this question: Has the United States eradicated racial discrimination? Has the United States eradicated discrimination against women, the exploitation of women, or the prostitution of women? No! A thousand times no! These are truths. The facts speak for themselves; they are convincing facts, which explain and demonstrate what socialism has meant to our country.[37]

Castro is explicit with his association between racism and the United States. The United States is used as the primary example of a racist country both to tout Cuba's racial achievements and to solidify the use of the United States as a common enemy both to Cuba and its citizens. The United States is thus

---

34. Sawyer 2006.

35. Census records for 1970 do not include race in the published version and the 1981 census is the first record of racial make-up in Cuba since the start of the revolution. The 1981 census documents blacks as 12 percent of the population and mestizos as 21.9 percent. The 1953 census, the last record previous to 1981, marks the nonwhite population slightly lower (grouped into one category, other races) at 27.2 percent.

36. Domínguez 1978.

37. Castro and Taber 1981.

everything Cuba is not: capitalist, exploitative, imperialist, and discriminatory toward nonwhites. The United States also buffers the silence on race domestically: Castro discusses racism often in his speeches throughout the decades of the revolution, but he discusses it in an international context. The state-owned media also supports this rhetoric by reporting on racism and racial resistance around the world, without mention of the issue in Cuba.[38] Racism is always in the context of an external issue, further reinforcing the absence of racism in Cuba.

The United States is a crucial component to racial ideology in Cuba, and the government has used it to justify the recognition of national identity over racial identities. Against a colossus such as the United States, Fidel Castro is able to push for national unity so that challenges to this unity could serve as detrimental to national strength in the face of US opposition. Castro attaches national unity and identity to the survival of socialism, making serious discussions of racial hierarchies inimical not only to national cohesion, but to the endurance of the system. In this way, supporters of the revolution have a high stake in promoting the governing ideology of racial democracy. While the use of the United States both as a racist nation in comparison to Cuba and as a threat to the Cuban Revolution was more pronounced in the earlier decades of the revolution, it continues to be a part of governmental rhetoric today. Evidence of the continued American struggle with racism often appears in issues of the national newspaper, *Granma*.[39] The United States is also an integral part of the definition of racism in Cuba. The presence of segregation prior to the civil rights era coupled with contemporary racial incidents such as riots, killings, and brutality covered in the media help to paint a picture of racism as an overt phenomenon connected with violence and the separation of the races. Examples of racism within the United States and throughout the world link racism to capitalism as well, allowing for socialism to continue being the solution to racism.

---

38. Headlines such as "Uruguayans March Against Racism and Discrimination, FIFA Implements More Sanctions Against Racism and Discrimination, Greek Schools Are Against Racial Discrimination" and others appeared in 2013 in *Granma* to highlight international struggles against racism and violent racial acts around the world.

39. Most recently, coverage of the widely publicized trial of George Zimmerman for the killing of Trayvon Martin in Florida appeared in various issues of *Granma*, stating that "One hundred fifty years after the Emancipation Proclamation . . . the United States has not been able to close the bloody wounds of hate and prejudice because of the color of one's skin, despite having elected a black president for the first time" (*Granma*, July 2013). The many cases of police brutality that have been publicized in the United States are consistently covered in Cuban media as well.

The revolution's silence on domestic racial issues was broken for the first time since the early years of the revolution during the Third Party Congress in 1986. Perhaps due to the statistics reported in the 1981 census that included the race question, President Castro acknowledged the need to increase the representation of blacks, women, and youth among the ranks of government officials. He signaled that representation of previously marginalized groups could not be left to chance and put forth an affirmative action policy to encourage their participation.[40] As a result of this push to secure greater levels of equality through policy, members of the Central Committee that were elected during the Third Party Congress made the Committee 28 percent black, a considerable increase since the previous Committee. After this Congress, however, these numbers dropped again to the lower percentages seen previously, which was under 15 percent in 1980.[41] The reforms were never implemented in the long term and had little effect on representation. At the time of the increase of racial diversity in the Central Committee, the leadership did not initiate any further dialogue on race or representation and the lack of attention to this matter was further exacerbated by the fall of the Soviet Union in 1991. During the economic crisis that followed, blacks experienced considerable losses in equality with whites and racism became exacerbated by the reforms of the period. Chapter seven will outline the economic policies that were implemented during the Special Period and the resultant increase in racial inequalities and racism discrimination. The following section details the government's response to these changes and the modification in ideological rhetoric by its leaders.

The Special Period and Ideological Alterations

The increase in racial disparities during the Special Period has led to some increased recognition of the problem by the Cuban government, albeit infrequently, throughout the 2000s. This attention, while a slight departure from the revolutionary rhetoric of the previous three to four decades, did not lead to a fundamental change in the government's ideology of racial harmony. Instead, it was only slightly modified to acknowledge the revolution's inability to completely rid the country of racism after forty years. The role of race as irrelevant to one's life chances or opportunities did not change, and race

---

40. Saney 2004; de la Fuente 2001a.

41. Adams 2004.

continued to be a silenced topic among the leadership with a few isolated references from the government.

Although racial ideologies are historically embedded, they are also malleable and while states make race, they can also alter racial ideologies. As Eduardo Bonilla-Silva argues, the flexibility of ideologies bolsters their legitimacy as they can be changed to accommodate the needs of the state and new information or conditions.[42] Similarly, Charles C. Holt writes that race must "be reconstructed as social regimes change and histories unfold," but these new constructs are never entirely new and have elements from the past embedded within them.[43] In his book *Racial Politics in Post-Revolutionary Cuba*, Mark Sawyer develops the theoretical framework of race cycles to describe the changing rhetoric that has taken place in Cuba throughout history to suit the needs of the state. Sawyer argues that racial politics are driven by crises or critical events that create a new equilibrium where racial ideology and policies that support the ideology are altered.[44] These authors coincide in their recognition that while states may make ideological adjustments when economic or political transformations call for it, the foundational elements of the ideology remain the same. These foundational elements have survived throughout the nation's history and are often as old as the nation. While the Cuban regime did show a limited amount of flexibility in its rhetoric in response to the new set of conditions that emerged during the state crisis, it is important to clarify between a change in rhetoric and a fundamental change in the ideology. The Special Period, indeed a profound state crisis for Cuba, produced a new opening for racial dialogue as the state was forced to acknowledge that the revolution had been unable to completely eradicate racism and racial disparities. While the racial democracy ideal still holds in Cuba (according to state rhetoric), the Cuban government has begun to sporadically discuss race and inequalities, altering the rhetoric.[45] The state has been able to adapt its characterization of social conditions in Cuba but the core of the racial ideology remains true to its historical origins.

---

42. Bonilla-Silva 2001.

43. Holt 2000, 19.

44. Sawyer 2006, 3–5.

45. My use of "sporadically" is generous in that the presence of racial disparities or racial discrimination has been documented in speeches by the Cuban leadership only four to five times since the year 2000 when it was first mentioned (Adams 2004). There have also been a few television shows primarily for young people pointing to racial prejudice as ethically wrong.

This change in rhetoric is most clearly seen in Fidel Castro's speech in 2000 at the Riverside Church in Harlem, New York:

> I am not claiming that our country is a perfect model of equality and justice. At the beginning, we believed that when we had established full equality before the law, complete intolerance of sexual discrimination in the case of women and racial discrimination in the case of ethnic minorities, these phenomena would vanish from our society. It was some time before we discovered that marginalization and racial discrimination are not things that one gets rid of with a law or even with 10 laws, and we have not managed to eliminate them completely, even in 40 years . . . There has never been and there never will be a case where the law is applied according to ethnic criteria. We did discover, however, that the descendants of slaves who had lived in slave quarters were the poorest and continued to live, after the supposed abolition of slavery, in the poorest housing . . . We do not have the money to build housing for all the people who live in what we could call marginal conditions. But we have a lot of other ideas which do not need to wait and which our united and justice-loving people will implement to get rid of even the tiniest vestiges of marginality and discrimination.[46]

This speech, one of the only speeches on racial discrimination given by the Cuban government during this time, demonstrates the shift in rhetoric by Fidel Castro while remaining true to the fundamental components of racial democracy expressed since the triumph of the revolution. Castro acknowledges that there are racial disparities in housing, yet he makes sure to frame these disparities as remnants from the past that the revolution inherited. He does not reveal what the solution might be to these problems, but he expresses that through unity, they will be resolved. The fundamental component of the revolution's racial ideology remains intact: racism is a vestige of the past not supported or maintained by the revolution. It should also be noted that this speech was given in New York rather than Cuba, and would not reach the numbers that a speech made on the island would have. Nonetheless, the rhetoric does mark acknowledgment of racial disparities that were not eliminated by the revolution.

---

46. Castro 2000, 59–60.

The Special Period necessitated a modification of discourse on racism because it became more visible, but it also provided a way for socialism to remain a legitimate way to end racial inequality. The introduction of semi-capitalist reforms to rescue the Cuban economy allowed for new discriminatory practices against black advancement in the emergent sector to be attributed to the presence of capitalism in Cuba.[47] The rise in inequality, the lack of opportunity for blacks to acquire hard currency, and so forth are said to be consequences of capitalism, in turn allowing socialism to continue to be the best way to combat racial inequality.[48] Thus the period after the economic crisis is often described as a resurgence or re-emergence of racism,[49] rather than a period in which racism and discriminatory practices became exacerbated. Castro's speech on housing disparities does suggest that there are problems of the past that the revolution was not able to eradicate, but it does not point to any racist practices that may have occurred after the revolution equalized opportunity for all races in the first years of the regime. The revolution can acknowledge a few areas that need special attention such as representation of blacks and *mulatos* in the Central Committee, but overall, the blame for continued inequality is placed elsewhere and the Cuban government is only responsible for the solution (albeit partially), and not the problem itself.

The role of silence and the absence of institutions both served to maintain racial inequality in Cuba. The government never acknowledges this fact, even with successes of the Federation of Cuban Women. In 2005, Fidel Castro spoke at the International Conference of Pedagogy and stated,

> Women, terribly discriminated against before, and whose reach was only in the most humble jobs, are by themselves today a decisive and prestigious segment of our society ... the Revolution, beyond the rights and guarantees reached for all of our citizens regardless of ethnicity of origin, has not accomplished the same success in our struggle to eradicate the differences in the social and economic status of the country's black population; even when in numerous areas of great transcendence, among those education and health care, they play an important role.

---

47. Morales Domínguez 2007.

48. This sentiment was argued for the public in the daily television show *Mesa Redonda* in 2010 and has been repeated in other subsequent discussions of racism on the show.

49. De la Fuente 2001c; Morales Domínguez 2007.

Given the progress that women's rights have experienced since 1959, racial organization continues to be prohibited on a mass scale. Until now, there have not been any concrete policies that have openly addressed the problem of racial inequalities in housing, nor have there been policies enacted to increase black representation in leadership positions. These speeches do, however, give some space for dialogue among the citizenry so that racism, over time, may be given more attention and acknowledged to be something that Cuba has not yet closed the book on.

One of the greatest changes regarding race that has occurred in Cuba following the Special Period was the political opening that allowed for academic and artistic expression on the issue. Beginning in the early 1990s, writers and scholars introduced various publications regarding racial prejudice in Cuba, inequalities, and black identity. The Union of Cuban Writers and Artists (UNEAC) was particularly supportive of such a debate and one organization, Color Cubano, came out of the new dialogue to discuss issues of racism in Cuba. There have been several scholarly and literary publications throughout the past fifteen years that have dedicated issues to the subject and this has increased the awareness of racism, at least among those that seek out academic material. A documentary about racism on the island was created in 2008 in which the Vice Minister of Culture was interviewed on the subject and the state's daily television program, *Mesa Redonda* or Roundtable, hosted discussions on racism in Cuba in 2010, 2014, and 2015. Keeping with the dominant rhetoric, however, the *Mesa Redonda* panelists were quoted as saying that racism "exists among social relations at a very low intensity, more differential than exclusionary" and that racism still exists in "interpersonal relations" rather than structurally.[50] In sum, the Special Period marked both an increase in racial inequality and a significant change in the previous silence on racial issues, but the foundational elements of racial ideology in Cuba remain the same.

Signs of Change

During the Sixth Party Congress of the Communist Party of Cuba in 2011, Raúl Castro pointed to the need to increase the number of young people in the Central Committee and build new leaders to take over for party veterans. He also outlined that top positions should not only be given to those who

---

50. Mesa Redonda 2010.

have worked for them and display merit, but that there should be a stronger political will to assure that women, blacks, *mestizos*, and young people are represented.[51] Furthermore, in reference to the representativeness of the government and other top positions in the country, he stated,

> Issues such as these, that define the future, should never go back to being guided by spontaneity, but rather, via foresight and the firmest political intention to preserve and perfect socialism in Cuba.

Consequently, black and *mulato* representation increased considerably after the Congress.

The Cuban government consists of five bodies that include the Politburo, the Central Committee of the Communist Party of Cuba, the Council of Ministers, the National Assembly of Popular Power, and the Council of the State. The executive and main decision-making bodies are the Politburo, the Council of Ministers, and the Council of the State. The largest increase in nonwhite representation was achieved through the new appointments to the Central Committee, which rose to 31.3 percent from 13.3 percent in 1997. According to the 2002 Cuban census, blacks and *mulatos* together make up approximately 34 percent of the population, and thus the current Central Committee comes the closest in history to representing the population statistics.[52] There are one *mulato* and nine black members of the Council of the State (out of a total of thirty-one), which make up about 32.2 percent of the membership.

Within the Council of Ministers, there are three black members and three *mulatos* out of thirty-seven members, representing 8.1 percent for each group.[53] Two of these members were newly elected following the initial appointments in 2011. Among the presidents of the nineteen Provincial Assemblies there are two black presidents, of Matanzas and La Habana,

---

51. This call was part of the Central Report (Informe Central) for the Congress, given on April 17, 2011. The speech was reprinted in *Granma*.

52. There are estimates that place the percentage of nonwhites at a higher number, which would make the levels of underrepresentation higher (Moore 1988; Adams 2004).

53. The two ministers who were recently elected are in Information Systems and Hydraulic Resources; however, the nonwhite ministers prior to the new appointments were the Minister of Labor and the President of the Cuban Institute of Sports, Physical Education, and Recreation, two positions that can be considered stereotypical appointments for blacks.

representing 10.5 percent of the body.[54] The Politburo, historically the body least racially representative of the population,[55] currently has three nonwhite members out of fifteen, one of which was newly elected in 2011 during the Sixth Party Congress. Thus, there seems to have been an attempt following Raúl Castro's speech to add nonwhite members to the top governmental positions and nonwhite representation has increased significantly in the Central Committee, but it is unknown if this is an effort that will endure beyond the changes of 2011. Membership continues to be below the proportion of the nonwhite population particularly among the Council of Ministers and the Politburo, the two bodies with the highest decision-making powers.

As the historical narrative has shown, racial harmony in Cuba has been a foundation of racial ideology in Cuba since independence. The Cuban revolution did not give birth to this ideology, but it held a much stronger claim to it through socialist policies that increased both racial and economic equality and through its promotion of anti-racist, revolutionary attitudes. The government from 1959 until today has been able to promote an anti-racist program and assert that it has created racial equality so that those who believe in the revolution also should believe in the absence of racism in Cuba. Even after visible disparities and a change in rhetoric, the ideology remains the dominant narrative and supports an argument that the revolution has the ability to solve whatever remnants of racism it thought to have solved by 1961.

Racial ideology and socialist ideology can reinforce each other and create a formidable ideology that both strengthens national unity, but ignores racial inequalities at the same time. For this reason, I connect the power of the two ideologies to enduring racism in Cuba. The government has not addressed racism outside of the ideological framework, and without policy changes the modifications do not represent a tactical change or a weakening of racial ideology in Cuba. The following section will explore the ways in which Cubans attach the absence of racism to socialism and the Cuban Revolution.

Racial Ideology and Socialism

A socialist revolution that ushered in a more equitable society than the previous regime provides for a distinct case in which to study the power of racial

---

54. Information regarding percentages were calculated by using the website of the Cuban government, which lists the members of the main organs of the government. In addition, *Granma* also provided information about those officials who were newly elected during the Sixth Congress.

55. Adams 2004.

ideology based on egalitarianism. Exploited classes can often threaten ideological projects because of the contradiction between rhetoric and reality.[56] In the case of Cuba, the ideological frameworks constructed by the revolutionary government promote a racial ideology that seems to be in favor of the exploited classes. Consequently, racial democracy in Cuba acts at best as an improved reality from previous regimes, and at worst as an ideal to strive for against which there is little resistance. Much of Louis Althusser's work, and others in the Marxist tradition, discuss ideology as exploitative in a capitalist context, arguing from a leftist vantage point.[57] These scholars often do not examine the power of leftist ideologies to use rhetoric that seems to support previously marginalized groups, but in fact seeks to silence these groups. Racial democracy coupled with socialist ideology seeks to incorporate previously marginalized or exploited groups and has the potential of generating high levels of support among nonwhites. By incorporating nonwhites and silencing racial resistance (both indirectly through incorporation and directly through prohibition), racial ideology in Cuba becomes exploitative even as it appears to lessen racial inequalities. Thus, we see today that blacks are indeed threatening the racial project that the leadership has promoted since 1959 as they become more vocal about its contradictions.

The revolution, when compared to previous regimes in Cuba, has heightened legitimacy with regard to racial equality. Marxist thought relies on a class centered approach to racial inequality and today Cuba continues to rely on this approach which 1) attributes any evidence of racism as vestiges of the capitalist system pre-1959; 2) names the Cuban Revolution as the solution to racism and releases it from responsibility for current inequalities; and 3) creates a strong link between support of the revolution and belief in its racial ideology. The rhetoric still serves to exonerate the government from further obligation to Afro-Cubans: with racial harmony achieved, the government rejects the need to address race or racism and the link between race and access is barely acknowledged. Fidel Castro, by openly including nonwhites in the national image of social justice and creating higher economic equality, politicized race in a way that Latin American leaders had not.[58] He connected socialism to the eradication of racism and the end of black exploitation.

---

56. Althusser 1994.

57. Mannheim 1991; Althusser 1994.

58. This is not to say that other countries in Latin America with similar rhetoric have a weaker level of support for racial democracy, only to point out that Cuba has connected this belief to political support of the revolution.

The Cuban leadership did not only claim to eradicate legal racial discrimination; they argued that through socialism, racial equality and human rights were achieved. Political rhetoric conveyed no doubt in the erasure of racial discrimination and thus, political supporters of the revolution should have no doubt in their minds either. For Cubans, particularly supporters of the revolution, there is significant difficulty in making the connection between a government that came into power to solve problems of inequality and social injustice with one that is also complicit in reinforcing racist practices. The message that a socialist or revolutionary government could not support structural racism is a powerful one and is strengthened by the rhetoric that connects the government to social justice. It is here where revolutionary ideology has been able to make believers out of the citizenry in favor of racial democracy despite examples of racism and racial inequality throughout the island.[59]

Racial Ideology and Political Ideology: Interview Data

The explicit connection that is made between socialism and racial equality does not fall on deaf ears in Cuba. Data revealed that strong supporters of the revolution are often believers of the racial narrative communicated by the government as well. Many of those who spoke highly of the revolution highlighted the fact that the revolution eradicated racism. A white male actor shared,

> Racism is according to how you see it. With the triumph of the revolution, equality was established. There is always latent racism that is maintained in magazines, in sayings, and it's present on television as well. But we are not as racist as the North-American.

Racism is described as latent, despite the fact that the interviewee recognizes its presence throughout society. As long as equality under the law is established, which the revolution did, racism no longer exists in any significant way, particularly in comparison to the United States. The United States was continually communicated during interviews to be the example of a racist

---

59. My characterization of revolutionary and racial ideology together creating a false consciousness does not suggest that Cubans are living in a fantasy world. Rather, it is to emphasize the power of ideology in creating alternative explanations for social injustices (Van Dijk 1998; Eagleton 1991).

society, a rhetoric, as argued above, that is integral to the marriage of social-ism and racial democracy in Cuba.

Those that were alive before 1959 were strong supporters of the changes that the Revolution brought in regarding racism. A sixty-five-year-old black psychologist, who expressed staunch support for the revolution, shared the following opinion:

> In my personal opinion, let me tell you since the triumph of the rev-olution until now, things have changed 100 percent. Moreover, the problem was so bad before the revolution that we had black societ-ies, white societies, *mulato* societies. Today, I think that if you go to the university you see a mass of black people; there are a lot of black doctors, black officials. Today, I have no problems. Maybe others have problems, but I have no problems. I don't feel discriminated against; I can enter Habana Libre.[60] Maybe I can't enjoy certain things because I don't have CUC,[61] but no one can tell me that I can't come in. Maybe what is missing is that blacks should try to progress more; because in order to study, there are no differences. If someone wants to be an engi-neer, they just have to study. We have the same opportunities.

Here the problem of access into certain spaces is attributed to economic issues, and not race. This position is particularly interesting considering blacks are summarily kept out of tourist spaces by hotel workers and security, regardless of their spending capabilities. Moreover, the existence of universal education coupled with high levels of access for all races, a major component of the Cuban Revolution, leads people to believe that those who seem to be absent at the university (nonwhites) suffer from motivational shortcomings. The successes that the government was able to bring to blacks at the start of the revolution remain as testimonies to the absence of racism.

The lack of overt policies that would exclude blacks leads to an under-standing that racism no longer exists. Other respondents explained that the lack of racism is specific to Cuba because of the revolution and the society

---

60. Habana Libre is one of the more famous hotels in Havana, and with its central location and shopping complex, it is visited by many Cubans and tourists alike. My interviews highlighted quite a few instances where blacks were either barred from entrance or given a hard time at the door in order to get in. This particular interviewee, because of his age and professional dress, has probably not had many problems entering hotels in Cuba. Those that are targeted are often younger black males or those dressed in a nonprofessional way.

61. Cuban Convertibles (CUC) is the hard currency in Cuba, replacing US dollars in 2004.

that it created. As a black male accountant expressed, the revolution has created solidarity that transcends racism in ways that other countries have not
been able to accomplish—a sentiment that the government has espoused
throughout the life of the revolution.

> I think that above all, the Cuban has a trait of solidarity, union. It's a
> matter of Cubanness. Since always. That feeling has to do with the rev-
> olution. The revolution triumphed and people started to understand
> that racism is an injustice. That is very real. I think we have less racism
> than other countries because of that. That's how I see it. We are a bit
> better with this issue.

This particular interviewee did not display strong support of the revolution throughout the interview, but nonetheless felt that the revolution
and socialism were responsible for diminishing racism in Cuba. He also
argued that the revolution did so within people's minds through a feeling
of solidarity, not just within institutions. Despite the common characterizations that downplayed racism by revolutionary supporters, there were
some I interviewed that connected the revolution's racial ideology to the
problem. Those that work on the subject of racism in particular, have much
different ways of seeing and interpreting the problem. A young black male
who actively works to increase black consciousness talked about the contradiction between revolutionary ideals of unity and solidarity and awareness
of racism.

> The racial issue in Cuba has *never* caused a problem because the peo-
> ple have not complained. They are ignorant of it. The black person has
> an invisible bill [*billete* invisible] and they don't know that they are
> enslaved! They don't know who the master is either. Am I imprisoned
> or aren't I? Am I a slave or aren't I? The slave knew he was a slave. He
> knew who was keeping him a slave. When the revolution came into
> power and said we are all equal, could black people see who was rac-
> ist or and who was not? They couldn't see it. In the United States you
> *knew* who the enemy was—the white man. But here, no. You get stuck
> in the strategy of unity. The responsibility does not only lie with the
> government, there is a great responsibility among those that suffer. You
> can't let someone step on you; you have to fight against it. And the
> black Cuban is waiting for the other guy to do it, or they don't even
> realize what's happening.

The emphasis on unity in fact maintains racism because it keeps people locked in a false consciousness. While the interviewee doesn't say that racial ideology in Cuba is a racist one, he does point to the ways in which it can perpetuate the problem of inequality by keeping people in the dark about the issue.

The treatment of race by the government was clear in many of the interviews with individuals that were connected to the government. They espoused elements of the dominant ideology giving similar views of race in Cuba, declaring that race is irrelevant in Cuba because people do not notice racial difference. In an interview with a white member of the Cuban government, I asked how she views racial issues in Cuba. She talked about race as irrelevant in Cuba and dismissed any cultural connections that blacks may have with Africa due to racial mixing.

> Afro-Cuban does not exist here because we don't have anything from Africa. There is no connection with Africa; not in the music, or the culture, or anything. That is not part of our history. We have all mixed. That's why Color Cubano does not interest us,[62] because we do not see skin color. Skin color here does not matter. They got Afro-Cuban from the African Americans. There is a tendency to view the Cuban reality with a North American eye. But we don't have the same problems. A black male athlete is just as good-looking as a blond woman with blue eyes. Just go out into the street and you see a white man with a black woman or a black man with a white woman everywhere. We don't have any kind of differences between us. There is a saying here that says, "*el que no tiene de Congo tiene de Carabalí.*"[63] We have a mix and there is really no pure black person. That doesn't exist here. What we have are cultural differences, cultural discriminations but not social or racial discriminations. For example in black relationships, it's custom for the man to pat the woman on the butt. White people don't do that; they don't understand it. Those are cultural differences.

---

62. The interviewee referred to the organization Color Cubano, which arose out of the Union of Cuban Writers and Artists, without me making reference to it. She was saying that we, the government and the Communist Party, are not interested in the organization's goals—to address racism and black invisibility in Cuban society.

63. The saying refers to the mixing of the races in that everyone has a bit of blackness. It can be translated as "he or she who doesn't have roots from the Congo has roots from the Carabalí," which are two ethnic groups or regions in West Africa.

Her discussion of race relations in Cuba draws heavily from the ideology of *mestizaje*, which suggests that racial mixing erases the saliency of race. If everyone is mixed to some degree, race becomes insignificant because there is no way to tell who is black and who is white. Alongside the critique of Cubans not seeing color, however, she makes reference to black and white physical difference when talking about interracial relationships and then even suggests that there are cultural differences between blacks and whites. Her example shows that rather than cultural differences, she is pointing to behavior among blacks that whites would never engage in. She makes references to black stereotypes by discussing black male athletes and what she perceives as a black cultural tendency to make inappropriate gestures with their mate, a practice that she insists white people do not understand. What her central point is, despite her clear recognition of racial difference, is that the government does not want to give race any societal significance, much less an organization like Color Cubano, which advocates open dialogue regarding racism and black opportunity. Although Color Cubano was founded within a state organization (UNEAC), some of the members that I interviewed, particularly the woman quoted above, did not support its existence.

In sum, all of the interviewees that expressed support for the revolution also expressed a belief in its racial ideology as well as many who were not staunch supporters or members of the Communist party. The only exceptions were those who have become activists on the subject. In all of my interviews, it was clear that even those that point to racism, make a connection between socialism and racial equality. In addition, many make the same comparison between Cuba and the United States that the government has made for decades. The Cuban government has succeeded in creating the belief among many that the revolution had noble ideals in bringing out racial equality and through its socialist policies has made racism much less severe than pre-1959 and the United States.

Conclusion

This chapter has examined the ways in which racial ideology has been used throughout the history of the revolution to foment national unity and consolidate political strength at key historical points. The rhetoric suggests that the racial hierarchy is to be ignored since race has no place in a nation of mixed-race people. Moreover, the role of racism in barring blacks from equal opportunity and access has been negated with the triumph of the revolution.

In essence, a mask has been placed over the role of race and the government's maintenance of inequality through institutionalization of silence, such that supporters of the revolution, despite the reality on the ground, largely believe in equal opportunity for all Cubans. Those that continue to deny the relevance of race often do so through their identity as revolutionaries, which is still powerful in Cuba. While this chapter argues for the salience of race and the role of racial ideology as a mask over existent racism, it also argues that this ideal continues to have a hold on notions of identity in Cuba. I contend that this is especially true in contemporary Cuba due to the union of revolutionary and racial ideologies.

The Cuban government has slightly adjusted its rhetoric and the limitations placed on its citizens regarding racial dialogue in order to adapt to the new environment of increased racial inequality brought on by the Special Period, but the lack of institutions to ensure equal rights for blacks suggests that officially, racism is not yet a national concern. Moreover, racial representativeness in mass organizations continues to be low. Although the FMC does claim membership that is racially proportional to the population, currently the National Secretariat, or the governing body of the FMC, does not have any nonwhite members and the rest of the leadership (classified as "other members") has 25 percent nonwhite membership, with blacks constituting 14.7 percent and *mulatas* at 10.2 percent of the eighty-eight members. Women of color are not represented within the top positions, and are underrepresented in the lower positions of the leadership as well. While the two essential pillars of the FMC are to defend the revolution and the struggle for equality, there is no mention of race within this struggle. The organization is quite vocal about the process of inclusion for women, the responsibility of the revolution to promote women's rights, the need to enact policy to support equality, and the inclusion of women in the national historical memory and educational system.[64] They also receive a high level of support from the Cuban government.

The elimination of black institutions and racial dialogue cannot be understated when examining the work of racial ideology and the trajectory of black gains during the revolution. Indeed, not enough attention has been placed on the silence that Castro ushered in when he banned black institutions and organizations. Castro removed any relationship that the state would have

---

64. Federación de Mujeres Cubanas 2009.

with black Cubans and in this way controlled any gains or losses that blacks would experience. The importance of racial inequality was at the discretion of the government without any input from those that were left at the bottom of the hierarchy. A population was silenced, but also made to believe that the gains that they did achieve were enough to consent to the silence.

5 "THERE IS NO RACISM HERE"

ANTI-RACIALISM AND WHITE RACIAL ATTITUDES

During my time in Cuba, when I would approach people about the presence of racism, I often received a similar answer. Irrespective of the person's actual opinion regarding racism, the first, almost knee-jerk response was *aquí no hay racismo*, or there is no racism here. This narrative, while not always believed by its preachers, operates in society as a quick explanation for racial issues. After some thought, much of the time, the person would abandon this initial characterization for one that was closer to the reality in Cuba and to their own conceptions. Yet whether people would admit that racism does or does not exist in Cuba, the individuals always insisted that they never harbored any racist sentiment, which inspired the title of this chapter. This way of answering a question about racism, often without even thinking, is just as important as what people really believed when probed a bit further. The words that people chose, "there is no racism here," is emblematic of the way that people first wish to describe their country, which corresponds with the way that the government describes the country, but it is also representative of a lack of reflection on racism in Cuba.

The absence of racism refers not only to laws and institutions in Cuba, but to Cubans' own attitudes and imaginaries as well. I describe this as an ethos of anti-racism or anti-racialism where race is of little consequence to societal realities and people, particularly as products of the revolution, do not harbor any racist sentiments. This chapter presents survey data that show the tendency for Cubans to tout the lack of racism, both in Cuba and in reference to their individual attitudes, through the idea of harmonious social relations. At the same time, the data also demonstrate anti-black sentiment among whites, which complicates the notion of anti-racialism. Anti-racialism is a norm that is communicated by many Cubans, but is superficial and only serves to hide the strong presence of racism and anti-black sentiment that exist. The consequence is a lack of reflection on what is racist and how racism operates on the island, much like the norm of silence discussed in the previous chapter. A second and equally important consequence is the survival of racist attitudes and anti-black stereotypes that are accepted and often expressed in Cuba openly, yet are never deemed racist or harmful. The national tolerance of anti-black expression and stereotypes is predicated on both the norm of anti-racialism as well as a general acceptance of white superiority, which is demonstrated in the language, phrases, and jokes that are drawn out in this chapter.

There is a double mechanism where racial ideology relegates the subject of racism only to private spheres and everyday conversations, but also creates a norm in which racism remains pervasive and unchallenged in these private spheres and whites and some *mulatos* feel comfortable participating in racist expressions and actions. Racism is thus shunned and protected by the state at the same time. Its location among private conversations and attitudes removes it from the purview of state control, but racism lives within a rhetoric of denial, which allows it to continue.

Anti-Racialism in Cuba

The Cuban revolution came into power with a program to not only change societal and economic structures, but to create a set of attitudes that would complement the goals of the revolution. This new consciousness was based on support for the nation, for the people, and for social justice.[1] It also included a commitment to ending prejudice and racial discrimination. Thus, the silence regarding the presence of racism in Cuba promoted shortly after the start of the revolution was accompanied by discourse that championed an abandonment of racist attitudes among the populace. Fidel Castro made several speeches that vilified racial prejudice and talked about the new revolutionary Cuban with nobler ideas than those of the past. The social norm of anti-racialism developed through this rhetoric, which declared Cuban revolutionaries free of racial prejudice and Cuba free of racism because of the accomplishments of the revolution.

---

1. Perez-Stable 2012.

Today, television and print media occasionally address the topic of prejudice, but it remains a topic with little national reflection. In a 2005 article in the state newspaper *Juventud Rebelde*, the writers cite a study that finds that 68 percent of young people attribute more interracial relationships to the revolutionary process that has overcome racial prejudices and taboos. The article acknowledges the presence of racial prejudices (particularly among the elderly) but highlights in the byline that "The future is mestizo. It can be seen in the streets and research confirms that today's young people do not worry about that future."[2] The emphasis in the article (and the rhetoric overall) is on progress rather than what might allow these racist attitudes to continue, how we define them and how we can challenge them.

The framework of Cuba's racial ideology supports the notion of racism as something incompatible with the revolution. Consequently, the presence of racism is devoid of analysis or significant attention. Citizens are not made to think about their own attitudes regarding race, and as a result it remains a topic that is untouched, yet pervasive. The reforms targeting racial segregation in particular were policies that signaled to the country that the tangible and visible patterns of racism had disappeared. These moves by the government, along with speeches that championed a strong anti-racist stance, were enough for many to show that racism would be a thing of the past and that talk of racial difference would be detrimental to national unity. While government rhetoric boasts the anti-racist nature of the state, the revolutionary qualities of its people are also based on anti-racialism. In this way, if someone cannot be a racist, then their derogatory language and the language of others cannot be racist either.

The notion of being nonracist, coupled with the notion of white supremacy, produced a particular attitude among some where racism was blamed on black Cubans. In my conversations with nonblack Cubans, I found that racist attitudes were said to be a problem in the black communities, so that nonblacks did not have to be accountable. I would often ask about racism in Cuba and be met with one of two responses: 1) blacks are racist against themselves, it's not us; or 2) blacks are racist against white people. The first response would attribute the perception of black inferiority to blacks instead of whites, suggesting that blacks hate themselves and thus are the ones who perpetuate anti-black racism. It was thus an admission of white superiority with an omission of white guilt. The second response would often be an attempt to

2. Perera Robbio et al. 2005.

redirect the blame away from whites to suggest that black people's negative feelings for whites should be the focus of inquiries into racism.

I use the term "nonblacks" here, because although racism was often communicated throughout my interactions in Cuba as a black/white paradigm, *mulatos* were part of this equation, albeit in different ways. I found that mulatos displayed anti-black racism and were the targets of such racism as well. *Mulatos* occupy a complex middle ground, where they can emphasize their position above blacks in Cuba's racial hierarchy. Nonetheless, I often found that white racism was not reserved only for blacks, but nonwhites. The ways in which *mulatos* navigated this contradiction varied significantly. In one interview, when asked about racism in Cuba, a thirty-year-old *mulato* pointed to a black man sitting near us and said, "*Those* people are the ones that are racist!" When I asked how he came to this conclusion, he conceded and said, "We *mulato*s are often more racist than white people." We thus see how anti-racialism can be used to hide racist attitudes, even among nonwhites.

Racial Attitudes

Scholars have made arguments both supporting and negating the importance of racist language, actions and attitudes as they relate to structural forces and racial ideology. The study of racial language and everyday expression is of particular importance to work on racial ideology, as it serves as an example of the kind of culture that a particular ideology produces. As Imani Perry writes regarding the study of individual actions with regard to race, "It allows us to recognize that we have a cultural practice that is diffuse."[3] While I recognize that structural, historical, and ideological patterns facilitate a racist culture, my definition of racism is a comprehensive one that includes these patterns, as well as the attitudes that they create.[4]

Racist language, although not necessary for the maintenance of white privilege,[5] is quite pervasive in Cuba. Both whites and blacks participate in the perpetuation of anti-black stereotypes (black people have bad hair, are lazy, do not want to succeed, are prone to criminal activity). When that kind of rhetoric is established as a norm or "cultural practice," it supports white

---

3. Perry 2011, 35.

4. Winant (1994) offers such an approach to the study of racism in that its analysis should not be based on either attitudes or structural elements but should take into account that ideology influences structure and social structures give rise to beliefs (74).

5. Bonilla-Silva 2014.

privilege and whites' systemic location in the hierarchy. Thus racist expression is important to me not necessarily to interpret people's individual psychological positions, but because they form part of racial norms. They represent a standard of white superiority and a lack of attention to the operationalization of racism on the ground. Indeed, racial ideologies that deny racism carry an acceptance of racial hierarchy as a constant and have survived on this fact.[6] Racial democracy not only professes that racism does not exist, but must also, in order to secure consent, regard racial hierarchy and black subordination as acceptable. In other words, it is fine to say that black people have bad hair, do not wish to work hard, are unacceptable partners for one's child, or that a black man with a white woman "looks ugly." If such commentary and perceptions of black people are tolerated and accepted, this is not only indicative of the social position of blacks, but it reinforces this position. Anti-racialism works to support racist attitudes as well as racial hierarchies.

Scholarship that examines social norms, social desirability, and racial attitudes has focused primarily on the United States. Moreover, social norms are most often explored within a context of intolerance for racist commentary, rather than the opposite. In their book *Racial Attitudes in America*, Schuman et al. point to norms or social desirability as a constraint, preventing people from exhibiting racist attitudes both on surveys and in their behavior.[7] They highlight the transformation of social norms pertaining to race from the pre–civil rights era to the present, where the acceptability of overt racist expression and actions has slowly diminished. These normative changes have led to the overall finding that racism is considered to be a socially undesirable trait in the United States. This can be seen in Maria Krysan's work in that some white respondents feel pressure in an interview situation to appear more racially liberal than they would indicate under conditions of greater privacy, and that this tendency is probably accentuated for more educated respondents.[8]

Racism in Cuba is also considered to be a socially undesirable trait, yet openly racist commentary is part of everyday conversation and often not attributed to racism. The boundaries for what permissible language and opinions are among "nonracists" are quite wide. Although citizens do not claim racist attitudes, there is little reflection on what constitutes such attitudes. In the interview setting, for example, when the interviewee would claim that he

---

6. Perry 2011.

7. Schuman et al. 1997.

8. Krysan 1998.

or she was not racist, as the interview went on, racist comments would surface with a high degree of comfort. The response in the chapter's title, "there is no racism here" or "I am not racist," was not just reserved for me as an interviewer, but is a response that would be given to anyone in Cuba. It was not my position as a scholar of another race and nationality that elicited this response; rather, this is the normative response when asked about race or racism. I would observe this response both among Cubans and in conversations with Cubans that I developed personal relationships with.

Within the norm of anti-racialism, it is important to analyze what people consider to be racist. My ethnographic research suggests that people perceive racial preferences (or anti-black sentiment) as nonracist. Thus, issues of social desirability as a constraint in obtaining a true assessment of individuals' racial attitudes was not a significant issue for me as a researcher in Cuba. Although it is critical to know whether or not interviewees are displaying their real attitudes, it is equally important to understand social norms and how they guide race language. While norms calling for equal treatment based on race are now dominant in most countries, including Cuba, the language often does not match the norm. There are competing norms that both support nonracist attitudes, but tolerate openly racist language. The former supports the latter in that because citizens consider themselves to be nonracist, their racist language can be dismissed.

A major element of the denial of the existence of racist attitudes among the citizenry is the use of racism and humor. Racist expression is often declared as humorous or benign without containing any real malice. While there are many jokes that are tied to anti-black racism, there are also ways in which incidents involving racism are laughed at in an attempt to delegitimize their derogatory content. In a conversation with someone involved with foreign student groups, a story was told about a study abroad group that he described as all white ("Aryan white" was the term he used), except for one black student. He immediately started to laugh at the mention of this student saying that wherever they went, the police would ask for the black student's ID card. He started to laugh even more, assuring me that when this happens it is a just a joke (*una broma*) and that it is nothing bad, which is how the students should take it. He went on to say that he has been accused of being racist because he often does not want the students engaging with Cuban black men that hang out around the hotel. He insisted that this was not related to race, he just didn't want the students being around hustlers. Each time he mentioned a black student or a black Cuban, he would point to his forearm and say "de color" or "of color." He was able to laugh at his own racist attitudes and had never been forced to confront them as such. Anti-black phrases or sayings were often laughed at or dismissed by many nonblack interviewees as language that should not offend.

In a column in the newspaper *Juventud Rebelde* titled "Humiliating Laughs," a writer discusses the tendency to treat racist jokes as normal. He describes racist jokes as being in fashion and even seen as one of the "noble attributes of Cubans."[9] He goes on to write that many consider themselves to be anti-racist champions without taking into account racist sensibilities that are historically and culturally embedded in the country's norms. The presence of the article in the newspaper is noteworthy, as it stands as one of the few that highlight the issue of racist language in Cuba. It does not, however, go very far to explain these historically entrenched racist sensibilities, or how they can be combated. In their study of Mexico and Peru, Tanya Golash-Boza and Christina Sue argue that the interpretation of racial humor in everyday discourse as nonracist reproduces racialized systems of power.[10] Similarly, Kia Caldwell has done work on verbal forms of racial discrimination in Brazil that perpetuate the "subordination of Afro-Brazilians in culturally and linguistically specific ways. Racial epithets serve to erase the personhood of Afro-Brazilians and replace it with a racialized sense of difference that, by virtue of being marked particular and nonuniversal, is inherently inferior to whiteness."[11] Caldwell goes on to write that responses to these negative comments and jokes are often dismissed as exaggerated because the comments are inconsequential, and thus "the popular acceptance of symbolic violence against black women delegitimizes efforts to denounce it."[12] Caldwell talks about how black women have to deal with norms of anti-black aesthetic in their daily lives and how these norms are embedded within social practices in Brazil. The perception that responses against racist language are exaggerated is part of the idea that racism is not something that anyone should waste their time with. The characteristic of being a nonracist society enables racist language to remain within the lexicon with little backlash.

I witnessed various uses of racist humor in Cuba in which those telling the jokes never expected any rejection of their choice of language. In 2008, I entered a taxicab near Santa Maria beach in Havana and the engine shut

---

9. Ronquilo Bello 2008.

10. Golash-Boza and Sue. 2013.

11. Caldwell 2007, 84.

12. Ibid., 85.

off—a common occurrence for a 1950s Chevrolet.[13] The driver, who was white, called his friend over, who was *mulato*, to take a look at the car so that he would not lose the fare. As he was fixing the car, the driver turned around to me, smiled wide, and said, "You see? The white people drive the cars and the *mulatos* fix them." The driver was very surprised by my reaction of offense to the comment and insisted that it was only a joke. The joke was no doubt connected to actuality. There are few *mulatos* and blacks in Cuba that have access to a car and taxi drivers are overwhelmingly white. The humor allows people to laugh at unequal conditions, without having to think about the reality of those conditions.

Social Relations: Survey Data

One of the primary ways in which anti-racism is communicated in Cuba is through the notion of harmonious social relations and interracial friend-ships. Interviewees of all races embraced the notion that relationships are free of racial considerations. While blacks' awareness of the racism that non-blacks harbor against them is present, this awareness does not seem strong enough to dismantle the perception that race does not affect social relation-ships. Edward Telles uses the concept of vertical and horizontal relations to show that racial discrimination and economic exclusion (vertical relations) can exist simultaneously with racial mixture and harmonious social rela-tions (horizontal relations).[14] He argues that in the case of Brazil, while rac-ist practices exist to produce racial inequality and lack of opportunity for blacks, social relations among Brazilians are relatively pleasant without a high emphasis on race. Mark Sawyer found that Cubans generally felt that race relations were better in Cuba than in Latin America and the United States.[15] Though the survey questions regarding social relations presented below do not challenge previous findings on the subject, interview data that demon-strate white racial attitudes and black experiences with discrimination, as well as survey data that document the perception of anti-black racism, do indeed call the idea of racial harmony into question. The ethos of anti-racism is there, but my data suggest that while members of all three racial groups deny

---

13. This beach is particularly for tourists in Cuba. Being at the beach and taking a taxi both were signals that it was likely I lived outside of the country.

14. Telles 2004.

15. Sawyer 2006.

the existence of racism, blacks have a more complex view of race relations due to their own experiences with racism. Furthermore, interview data show that whites exhibit attitudes that reveal both a perception that social relations are harmonious, coupled with anti-black attitudes that *prevent* harmonious social relations, particularly romantic relations.

Survey respondents were asked whether 1) their social relations had a lot to do with race; and 2) whether blacks and whites have more commonalities than differences. In accordance with dominant ideological rhetoric, I would expect to find that blacks will perceive race to be unimportant in their social relations. Since the start of the revolution integrated neighborhoods, high levels of economic equality, and the lack of social segregation should provide for interactions where race is not a consideration. It should be noted that while I expect Cubans' perceptions to reflect harmonious social relations, this does not mean that race is not a salient category in people's lives. I use the term "perceptions" because anti-black sentiment among whites is a reality in Cuba and can affect people's relationships.[16]

For the first question, whether social relations have a lot to do with race, a majority of the sample, 63.8 percent, answered that their social relations are not based on race (see Figure 5.1), while 21.3 percent thought that their social relations did have a lot to do with being black. We can glean from this result that friendships can often be of mixed race as well as other types of social relationships. Race does not seem to factor into many people's opinions of how they relate to people or build friendships. Nonetheless, as I will discuss in a later chapter, among those that had experienced discrimination, many of the respondents (41.7 percent) cited being discriminated against by individuals or in a relationship. While there are many that may have interracial friendships and even relationships, the role of race still plays a part in how people relate to one another.[17]

If we examine the data more closely, there is a significant relationship between having an experience with discrimination and responding positively to the question of social relations being race-based (see Table 5.1). Experiences with racism can trump the perception of colorblind relations, but we should

---

16. See Nadine Fernandez (2010) for a detailed account of interracial relationships in Cuba, anti-black sentiment, and the ways in which racial attitudes influence social relations. Fernandez finds that despite the high level of racial mixing in Cuba coupled with the ideal of racial harmony, interracial relations are transgressive and their presence "rubs against the grain of society in some fundamental way" (3).

17. Fernandez 2010.

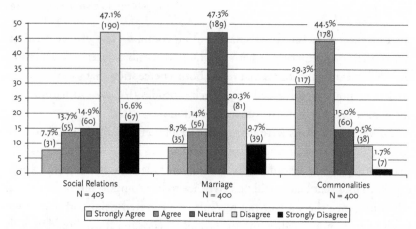

FIGURE 5.1 Social Relations

Note: The questions read as follows. Social Relations: "My social relations have a lot do to with the fact that I am black." Marriage: "It would be beneficial for blacks to marry whites." Commonalities: "Blacks and whites have more commonalities than differences."

Table 5.1 Relationships Between Social Relations

Social Relations Colorblind	Agree/Disagree	Neutral/Disagree
Discrimination	1.74***	1.05***
Less than High School	0.81	0.17
High School	0.60	−0.12
Some College	−0.31	−0.44
Gender	0.67**	0.40
Cohort fifties	−0.68	−0.79
Cohort sixties	1.59***	−0.08
Cohort seventies	0.59	0.73
Cohort eighties	0.56	−0.06

Note: Entries are odds ratios from a multinomial logistic regression on a categorical variable with responses of agree, neutral, and disagree; disagree is the base category (strongly agree and strongly disagree were collapsed into the agree and disagree categories). The measure of social relations reads, "My social relations have a lot to do with the fact that I am black." A value of 1 indicates there is no predicted difference based on the independent variable. The first significant coefficient under the agree/disagree column, for example, may be interpreted to mean that those with an experience with discrimination are 1.74 times more likely to respond Agree to the question than those that did not have an experience with discrimination. The dummy variables for age are separate by cohort according to the decade in which they were born.

Model χ^2 (20) = 75.61***

N = 361

*** p < 0.01, ** p<0.05, * p<0.10

also take into consideration that among those who reported an experience with discrimination, a majority said that social relations were not race-based compared with those that responded affirmatively. Discrimination certainly is an element that challenges the discourse of racial democracy, but the rhetoric is still a powerful one. Males and those born in the 1960s were also more likely to report that their social relationships had a lot to do with their race. Chapter 7 will show that these two variables, age and gender, were also significant when reporting an experience with discrimination. Males and those in their forties were more likely to report an experience with discrimination, and that experience also seems to be driving their perceptions regarding social relations.

The saying *todos somos cubanos* does not only refer to national unity, it also represents the idea that regardless of race, all Cubans share the same culture. Thus, racial ideology suggests that differences of skin color are only matters of phenotype. Similar to the question on social relations, Cubans should not believe that there are major differences between blacks and whites. To suggest affirmatively would be to suggest that there are significant cultural differences and that race would be significant among social relationships and interactions. A small minority expressed that blacks may have clear differences from whites, which parallels the results for the first question regarding social relations. In response to the question asking whether blacks and whites have more in common than differences, 73.8 percent either strongly agreed or agreed, while only 11.2 percent thought that blacks and whites have more differences than commonalities. One of the respondents expressed that she feels fine socializing with people of any color and that she does not take into account any differences between blacks and whites. Although respondents expressed differing opinions regarding interracial marriage and intimate relationships, the majority found that among their friendships race is not taken into consideration. This is reflected in the survey results for both questions in this section.

The data suggest that the argument by Edward Telles regarding horizontal relations also applies to Cuba. Indeed, when asked on a survey if race factors into social relationships the majority of blacks replied that it does not, similar to Mark Sawyer's data as well. Interview data, however, indicate that antiracialism is at work, and many respondents answered the question regarding social relations with the same knee-jerk response that whites give when they say "I am not racist." Although Cuban perceptions of race relations differ widely among different racial groups, the majority of the interviewees initially stated that their social relations had little or nothing to do with race. Everyday observations of interracial marriage and friendships were talked about frequently among interviewees, particularly by those who wanted to point to their own tolerance and nonracist attitudes. As the interview progressed, many pointed to contradictions and frictions that suggested racial harmony was in fact not as prevalent as the survey, or they, would suggest. In each of my interviews with whites, racist sentiments were expressed throughout the interview. The claim of harmonious social relations, then, was the normative response that did not reflect actual attitudes. More importantly, this response is not one that is perceived as a lie by the interviewees. During the interview it was clear that they did not consider themselves to be racist, even when challenged after admitting to having a preference for white people or an aversion toward black people. Black interviewees who thought that social relations were colorblind, but added conditions to that characterization (usually when talking about romantic relationships), did not veer much from their original position. If we go back to Edward Telles's findings regarding horizontal relations, we see that it is crucial to have data that give us an idea of race relations beyond the normative answers and perceptions.

In an interview with a seventy-year-old white woman retired from a factory job, she initially discussed racial relations as harmonious even within her own experiences, but later expressed a rejection of blacks as a potential partner for her children.

INTERVIEWEE: I'm going to be honest with you. I have very good friends of color and I believe that there are blacks and whites that are good people and there are those that are bad people. I get along with whomever. My best friends are *mulatos* and when I worked I had a lot of friends; good, good friends of color.

INTERVIEWER: Well what about marriage, would you be bothered if your children married black people?

INTERVIEWEE: I'm going to be honest. I really wouldn't like, and I'm not talking about in the old days I'm talking about now, I wouldn't like for my daughter to marry a black man. Maybe a *mulato* (*Quizás un mulatico*). But when it comes to that (places her hand on her chest) I . . . um . . . well, I always tell my daughter that females are the most precious.

Her initial reaction, despite anti-black attitudes that she has, was to describe herself as anti-racist because her friends have been of all colors. Yet at the same time, she clearly views blacks as inferior to whites and unworthy of marriage with her daughter. She feels that she must protect her daughter from a man who is nonwhite, as indicated by her comment that daughters are the most precious. Finally, it can be gleaned from this interview that she has expressed these attitudes to her daughter as a teaching mechanism.

Many black interviewees expressed being on the other side of this experience, where romantic relationships were not welcomed by whites. A nineteen-year-old black waiter told me that he has always had trouble with families when he has dated a white or a mixed-race woman.

> I had a white girlfriend when I was in HS and her father was in the military and they did not accept me at all. And the military is supposed to be this accepting, progressive institution that follows the ideal that we are all equal and they are never supposed to be racist because they represent the government. But forget it, her father would not allow her to be with a black guy.

Experiences such as these reinforce for blacks the contradictions that exist between the state's racial ideology and what is practiced on the ground. For this reason, experiences of discrimination are often the impetus for blacks' rejection of the dominant ideology.

In an interview with a nineteen-year-old white woman, she explained to me her view of racism in Cuba coupled with her first (and only) experience in a relationship with a black man:

INTERVIEWEE: With friendship there's no problem. At least in my case. I can have best friends that are black but with respect to relations, that mix doesn't work for me. Especially after my experience. I dated a black man just to test it, to see if it was in me and I realized that it didn't fit. I was with a man of color. You know, he smelled good, he was very friendly, he didn't have any black characteristics and he treated me like a princess. But well, what I felt was disgust.

INTERVIEWER: And had your parents ever taught you anything about race? Did they say that they preferred you to be with a white person?

INTERVIEWEE: My father always had that thing where white women look ugly with a black man.

While most nonwhites in my sample did not talk much about race in their homes, white interviewees expressed that their parents passed their prejudices against blacks onto them. In a conversation with a friend in Cuba, he said that he had never dated a nonwhite woman because his mother taught him "whites with whites and blacks with blacks." She told him that he should never bring home a girlfriend who is not white and he adhered to (and agreed with) that rule. Much like the above interviewee, he did not interpret this as anti-black prejudice because he socialized frequently with black people and had many black friends. The above interviewee did not consider herself to be racist even after such an admission because she too has friends that are black and *mulato*, and only discriminates in intimate relationships. Her characterization of black people as smelling a certain way or acting a certain way would not, to her, be considered anti-black. A *mulata* woman expressed to me a similar sentiment:

> A leader of the [Communist] party once told me that they would never have relations with a black man. I've heard sayings like, "I've never drank petroleum." One day another person from the party told me in a theater that you don't have to be scared of black people, what you have to do is learn to dance with them. These are phrases. Is that not racism?

One of my interviewees, after explaining that she was not racist and had many friends who are nonwhite talked about the city of Guantánamo where she is from, which historically has been a majority black area.

> When I traveled to Miami I didn't see that many people of color. But in Guantánamo, it has changed. Guantánamo has gotten worse and before it wasn't like that. I came to Havana nine years ago and back then there were white people [in Guantánamo], but honey, now it's *mulato*, black, *mulato*, black and there are few whites. In Guantánamo and Santiago.

All of those that I interviewed said that they did not pay attention to race in their friendships, whites and blacks alike. When asked more questions, however, whites displayed anti-black attitudes especially when considering intimate relationships and blacks discussed experiences that suggested race played a significant role in their social lives. The interview above even expresses dismay that nonwhites are taking over the population on the eastern part of the island. All of my white and some of my *mulato* interviewees either would not date a black person, or had family members that did not want them to do so. Social relations then, are not harmonious with regard to race and are only interracial to a limit. There is a false sense of harmony that many adhere to as part of the notion that racism does not exist in Cuba coupled with the norm of anti-racialism.

Racial mixing or mestizaje has been presented as proof of racial harmony for centuries not only in Cuba, but throughout Latin America. The presence of interracial relationships and a large mixed-race population is viewed by many as a way to gauge whether or not racism is present in society and whether there has been progress over time. A black male says,

> Since the colonial era the Spanish were mixing with the blacks, for whatever reason, but they were mixing. Many people here don't care about having relations, sexual or a friendship, whatever it may be, with blacks. After the triumph of the revolution that has gotten better, or it is getting better. What I do not want to say is that there are no manifestations of racism, because you can't change someone's mentality. But to speak publically in a debate or a meeting in a racist way or to attack a black person can bring a person a lot of problems here. Many people are racist, maybe not at the magnitude that a North American can be, but you can't change people's mentality. The revolution changed many things, but that is not going to change here.

This quote represents much of the ideological rhetoric of the government, being expressed by a citizen. This particular interviewee points out 1) the ability of the revolution to improve race relations among individuals through socialist policy and rhetoric; 2) the characterization of race as a matter of mentality among individuals only; and 3) the notion that a US citizen is more likely to display racism, a stronger brand of racism than any Cuban could. Without these interviews with questions that probe further into people's opinions regarding race relations, we would not be able to discern the true nature of social relations in Cuba, which are clearly guided by racial difference.

Racial Perception

The contradiction between the survey data that suggests harmonious race relations and the presence of racism in people's individual experiences is further elucidated through the following set of questions regarding racial perception among blacks. These questions examine anti-black stereotypes and blacks' perception of how significant they are in Cuban society. If blacks are comfortable in their social relations with whites and race does not affect these interactions and relationships, then it would follow that blacks do not think that most whites hold anti-black stereotypes. Revolutionary rhetoric promotes the idea that racism may lie with a few individuals, but contends that these racist or prejudiced attitudes are only present among a few and anti-racialism is far more prevalent. To be racist is to be unpatriotic, and thus my expectations are that while some do recognize anti-black attitudes among whites, most will believe in congenial race relations and a lack of these attitudes among whites.

The questions in this section are as follows: 1) blacks are respected by others; 2) many do not consider blacks to be as efficient as whites; and 3) many white people distrust or are suspicious in their relationships with blacks. For the first question, because race was not specified here, the answers are not specific to whites, but to all groups. The answers were distributed across all categories in that 45.8 percent claimed that blacks are respected, 24.2 percent said that they are not and 30.0 percent were neutral (see Figure 5.2). This is similar to the expectations: while the highest percentage thought that blacks were respected, a minority recognized anti-black sentiment among the population.

While the results of the first question suggest that anti-black stereotypes or negative perceptions of blacks are not very significant, perceptions of black competency, especially among whites, lean more negatively. In the second question regarding black efficiency when compared to whites, the majority of

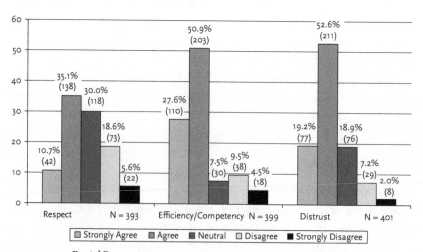

FIGURE 5.2 Racial Perception

Note: The questions read as follows. Respect: "Blacks are respected by others." Efficiency/ Competency: "Many do not consider blacks to be as efficient as whites." Distrust: "Many white people distrust or are suspicious in their relationships with blacks."

the sample, 78.4 percent, confirm that many think that blacks are not as efficient as whites, and only 14.0 percent disagree with the statement. This result is quite surprising, and shows that there is a substantial perception among blacks that whites hold negative attitudes regarding their competency. A similar number, 71.8 percent, think that many white people distrust or are suspicious in their relationships with blacks. This last result in particular suggests that although blacks may have friendships with whites and *mulatos* and do not think about race when building these friendships, the role of race does play a part in how they believe they are perceived. Personal relationships may be interracial, but not colorblind.

Experiences with Discrimination

Experiences with discrimination are often connected to how blacks view racism in Cuba and black interviewees often used examples to show how pervasive racist attitudes are. Indeed, experiences with discrimination can create the idea that blacks are seen as less efficient or that they should distrust whites, and produce the kinds of survey results presented above. The quality of being one of the few blacks at the university, for instance, has produced experiences of discrimination for black students in the classroom, and some of my interviewees discussed scenarios where they were openly spoken to in an offensive way by their professors and the comments were passed off as jokes. A university student described to me a situation in which he was singled out by a white professor as the incompetent black student in his classroom.

> I'm sitting in the classroom and the professor comes in with this crazy presentation and then asks if there are any questions or doubts. I say that I don't really understand and I wasn't the only one, but I was the only one who spoke up. So the professor says, "Oh come on, it's the black student who doesn't understand," rubbing his arm.[18] I got mad and turned around and asked the class, "Is there anyone here who understands this?" Everyone said no. Then I turned and looked at the professor and said, "Do you see that no one understands this and it's *not* because I'm *black*??? Do you realize this??" I know that he did it unconsciously because in Cuban society that's a really normal thing, it's become common. It's always like this; society is like that and we

---

18. In Cuba, the gesture to describe someone of color is to rub your finger along your fore arm, as if pointing to the different skin color.

have to live with these things because there is no consciousness, no
education, no culture.

Following the class, the professor apologized to the student saying that he
didn't want to upset him, it was a joke and that he did not mean for the comment to be racist. He also made mention of black friends that he has. For this
kind of dialogue to be used in front of a classroom, expectations of a reaction such as the one the student gave are low. In other words, a lack of consciousness about what should be rejected as discriminatory allows for these
racist comments to continue without being checked. During a conversation
with a *mulato* physics professor at the University of Havana, he explained to
me that there is equal opportunity in Cuba, but admitted to a lack of black
university students. He said that this phenomenon occurred not because of
racial inequalities, but because blacks are lazy and do not want to study. The
role of silence on the issue of race and more specifically regarding opportunity for blacks and the presence of racism cannot be understated. Without
any admission from the government or public dialogue about this problem,
anti-black stereotypes will continue to prosper among both the educated and
uneducated.[19] Racist attitudes in Cuba are not exclusive to class or level of
education, which makes them even more pervasive.

In an interview with a *mulato* manager of a company, he talked about his
experience when he married a black woman. He said that his parents were
shocked and disappointed when he brought her home even though he had black
people in his family. His college roommate asked him why he would date a black
woman if there were plenty of white and *mulata* women to choose from. After
many years, he encountered the roommate again on the street and was told,
"You're still with that black woman? What is your problem?" He noted that this
reaction was not uncommon and that many of his friends and family members
did not approve of his relationship.

Black Image and Black Inferiority

Anti-black discourse is part of a societal culture and amidst the mantra of "we
are all Cuban" or *todos somos cubanos*, there is a constant practice of pointing to

---

19. I do not argue that racist attitudes such as the one held by the university professor are not
present in societies that have a more open dialogue on race and operate under a different racial
ideology. I do argue that under Cuban racial ideology these kinds of attitudes enjoy an open
position among everyday conversations, are so pervasive that they have become a part of the
culture, and are communicated in the presence of whites and nonwhites alike.

difference and, more specifically, black inferiority. Although the previous sections in this chapter pointed to white racial attitudes, blackness can be viewed as subordinate among all races. In a conversation with a black woman, I asked her if she sees any differences between racial groups in Cuba. She said, "No, we are all equal; Castro did away with racism in 1959." She then touched her hair and said, "although we lost here." Similarly, in a conversation with a black musician he described an attractive black woman by saying, "She is so pretty she looks white." These common phrases, as well as the most well-known *"tenía que ser negro"* or "he had to be black," which is used when a black person has engaged in negative social behavior, are indicative of a culture of inequality. Moreover, the presence of anti-black discourse most likely motivated the answers to the survey questions on racial perception that caused blacks to distrust whites or acknowledge that they are seen as inferior or less competent.

Comments that may seem to be markers of description can also bear a derogatory meaning by pointing out racial difference and racial inferiority. The interviewee below describes a situation in which he is subject to pejorative comments that are often passed off as jokes.

> People will always say, man, *"esto es un tipo de negro"* or *"el negro de clase y el clase de negro,"*[20] which are different things. *El clase de negro* is almost always used negatively. They can call me a black man with class, but what does that mean? It's derogatory and I still need to work harder than whites because if not, forget it; at the end of the day, you are black. Those sayings have a lot of interpretations. I have had a lot of problems with that. I don't like the saying. I don't like the way they call me black. I have stopped people who call me *negro* and say, "How do you mean to say that?" Because in English, for example, they have the word nigger and that is an extremely negative word . . . here we don't have that. Here they say *negro* normally but on the inside it has a lot of meanings and it is the same thing.

What the interviewee does not directly say is that calling someone a black person with class suggests that they are in the minority; most blacks do not have class. Sayings that are popular in Cuba, such as "you have to do things the way white people do them" or the term "blond black woman" to refer to

---

20. *Esto es un tipo de negro* means "this is quite a black man." "Clase" in Spanish can mean class or type/kind, and thus the difference between *un negro de clase* (a black man with class) and *un clase de negro* (quite a black guy) have different meanings, where the second refers to the type of black person.

a black woman who is classy, professional, or educated, perpetuate the idea of black inferiority. Moreover, because they have become part of the normal lexicon they are not recognized as such. Although ignored, these comments perpetuate a damaging view of blackness that is widely consumed and often accepted.

The declaration and subsequent belief by the population that true equality of opportunity exists, leads any examples of inequality to be attributed to individual shortcomings among blacks. Although the pairing of egalitarian and racist ideology can be found throughout the Americas interacting with various political and economic systems, in Cuba it is particularly strong in that socialism, in theory, increases equality of opportunity and government rhetoric supports this claim. Individual weaknesses are used to justify any remaining social inequalities as part of the ideological framework of socialism and racial democracy. In other words, the belief that all Cubans are equal due to socialist policies and the leadership's efforts to end racism assigns the blame for inequalities to deficiencies in black character or motivation. This point is not explicitly stated by the government, but is a consequence of the rhetoric of racial equality in a country where racial equality does not exist. Moreover, the presence of blacks in high numbers in the health care and education sectors provide examples of black success and a lack of systemic discrimination. If we return to Edward Telles's terms, vertical relations in these two sectors remain relatively flattened, which give more fodder to the argument that race is of little consequence in Cuban society. Several authors discuss this in studies of racial politics in the United States. In the post–civil rights era, where formal obstacles to black advancement have been eradicated and significant advances have been made to secure equality of opportunity, the lack of black achievement and socioeconomic parity with whites is attributed to their lack of work ethic or desire to succeed.[21] In several of my interviews, as evidenced in my conversation with the physics professor, this conclusion was made: if education is universal and anyone can go to the university, blacks are underrepresented because they do not wish to study.

The rationale that there is equal access to the university, for example, derives from the fact that 1) there is no charge to attend the university, and 2) primary and secondary education is equal and universalized regardless of neighborhood. The small number of blacks and *mulatos* that have indeed succeeded also reinforces the notion that opportunity is there, but blacks do not

---

21. Bobo 2004; Forman 2004.

take advantage of it. In this way, white privilege is maintained with little to no accountability or recognition of such privilege. Teun A. Van Dijk writes that egalitarian norms are not inconsistent with the maintenance of privilege and exclusive access because "the acts controlled by the ideology are not perceived as discriminating in the first place: if they qualify, then minorities may well occasionally be admitted."[22] However, there continue to be many sectors in Cuba where blacks are unable to advance, complicating the rhetoric of equal opportunity.

The claim by the Cuban leadership to have created equality of opportunity, particularly through education, attempts to erase history from the black experience and as Paul Gilroy would argue, contains blacks in the present.[23] In sum, it is not only overtly racist ideologies, but also those ideologies that do not promote a racist message and deny its existence, that can be seen as a strategy for "containing blacks." Embedded in racial democracy under socialism are the same racist ideologies that we find in discourses of the past. Black affirmation is prohibited, discussion of racial inequalities is silenced, and blackness continues to be tied to inferiority if black advancement remains stagnant. While it is important to make distinctions across different ideologies, in the end, an ideology that supports and maintains racism by denying its existence is also an ideology that perpetuates black inferiority by trivializing the central role of race.

Conclusion

One would not imagine that embracing the quality of being anti-racist or nonracist could support racist ideas and language. Yet encouraging citizens to be nonracist while living in a country where racism has been declared history, but remains embedded in society, can deny a nation the exercise of examining just what is racist. Moreover, the dismantling of any civil rights organizations and black press also has an effect on black resistance, which is often crucial in bringing a discussion on racism and anti-back stereotypes to the table. I argue in this chapter that the ethos of anti-racialism actually supports racism. Racist jokes and expression are often trivialized at best, or at worst, taken as normal and in fact humorous.

---

22. Van Dijk 1996, 26.

23. Gilroy 1987.

Amidst the idea that racism does not exist among Cubans is the notion that social relations are harmonious, race does not factor into people's friendships, and those who point out the role of race are misguided or even racist. We find that social relations are harmonious only to a point, and in fact there is a clear sense among blacks that whites are distrustful of them in their relationships and often hold negative stereotypes about blacks being inefficient, lazy, or inferior. Indeed the idea by many whites interviewed that blacks were not good enough to marry either them or their children must have an effect on friendships as well. Despite the pervasiveness of the language, the norm of anti-racialism remains valid, even among nonwhites. It lives among a culture of white superiority where many (within all racial groups) consider blackness to be inferior. This is damaging not only to black image and self-worth, but it serves as an impediment to the development of black consciousness and pride.

6 THE POWER OF A FRAME

THE CHARACTERIZATION OF RACISM AS PREJUDICE

The Cuban Revolution has produced many political slogans. The slogans are more than just catchphrases—they represent the goals, mission, and accomplishments of the revolution throughout its five decades in power. They are the ideological mantras that the government has infused into everyday notions of politics and society. Sayings such as *Todos somos iguales, Universidad para todos*, and *Revolucion es: igualdad y libertad plenas* are visible on billboards, presented in various media outlets, and often appear within popular culture, conversations, and educational curriculums; they are indeed ubiquitous.[1] The notion that we are all equal, that the university is available for everyone, and that revolution is equality and freedom are ideas that reinforce egalitarianism in Cuba. The level of equality that the revolution has achieved is celebrated by many on the island and continues to guide not only support for the revolution, but perceptions about identity, access, life chances, and outcomes, regardless of people's political leanings.

Ideas about equality also shape public opinion about racism in Cuba and strengthen racial democracy. Racism is framed within the context of egalitarianism, and consequently the concept is defined as individual prejudice by both elites and the populace. One of the most significant successes of racial ideology in Cuba and throughout Latin America was to define anti-black racism in

---

1. These are translated as "We are all Cuban," "University for Everyone," and "Revolution is: Full Equality and Freedom."

this individual based framework rather than as a structural phenomenon. As Fidel Castro stated in 1960:

> Democracy is this, in which you, black Cubans, have the right to work without anyone being able to deprive you of that right because of stupid prejudice. Democracy is this, in which you, women, obtain full equality with all other citizens ... This can only be done by a government that is truly democratic, where the majority governs![2]

By trivializing racism as "absurd" or "stupid" attitudes that are morally wrong, Castro suggested that it was the citizens' responsibility to combat racism. If racism is defined only as acts of individual prejudice, it takes the onus away from the government, as it makes the problem a moral issue that is beyond its realm of control or influence. Employment discrimination in this speech was deemed an outcome of prejudice, rather than an institutional practice. Early on as the revolution's leader, Castro denied the government's responsibility to enforce or even create anti-discrimination laws, because such an act should not have been necessary. He justified the lack of legislation within the context of Cuba as a fully democratic and equal society. Through rhetoric of social justice coupled with the social transformation that Cuba experienced during the time, definitions of racism as absurd prejudice rang true to citizens.

The racial frames that the government created also guided its decisions regarding institutions. The government did not examine discrimination of a structural nature and did not establish institutions or policies to report or address discriminatory treatment since racism became miniscule following the measures taken by the revolution in the first two years. In this way incidents were largely undocumented, and discrimination could be ignored if citizens had no institutional mechanism through which to report such an experience. The denial of structural racism also benefited from public opinion, which at the start of the revolution leaned toward the belief that full equality of opportunity was reached.

The way in which the Cuban leadership discusses racism today follows a similar framework. The Special Period in Cuba marked a decided change from the early revolutionary claim that racism and discrimination had been completely eradicated. Fidel Castro's speech in 2000 in New York

---

2. Castro 1960.

gave evidence that the government acknowledged more work needed to be done. In December of 2009 Raul Castro discussed the problem of racial representation in government, pointing to the lack of women and blacks in top leadership positions:

> Personally I consider the insufficient advance on this subject in fifty years of Revolution to be an embarrassment. Despite the fact that 65 percent of the work force is composed of women and that the citizenry forms a beautiful racial rainbow without any formal privileges, they subsist in practice. Still in societies such as Cuba, derived from a radical social revolution, where the people reached full and total legal equality and a revolutionary educational level that threw out the subjective component of discrimination, it still exists in another form. Fidel labeled it as objective discrimination, a phenomenon associated with poverty and a historical monopoly on knowledge. I will do my part to exert all of my influence so that these harmful prejudices continue to give way until they are finally suppressed and that women and blacks are promoted to leadership positions at all levels for their merits and professional qualifications. It is necessary to select and prepare our pool of cadres with this perspective, to take into account the ethnic and gender composition of our population.[3]

The speech marks a much different rhetoric from the early decades of the revolution, but continues to point to prejudice, rather than racism as the cause for any inequalities that may exist. Racism continues to be framed in the same way as it was in the early years of the revolution and although the rhetoric is altered, the racial norm that negates structural racism continues to be strengthened. Raul Castro's words note that equality of opportunity indeed exists in Cuba, whereby after the revolution "people reached full and total legal equality and a revolutionary educational level that threw out the subjective component of discrimination." Blacks and women are not promoted to higher positions because of "harmful prejudices," and the solution to this is to prepare citizens of the revolution with a perspective that promotes equality. Racial inequality is defined in terms of the past, when the elimination of segregation and inequality under the law were the obvious signs of structural racism. Indeed,

---

3. Castro 2009.

in 2013 an article in the Cuban national newspaper highlighted a new book about race in Cuba, stating, "The revolution eliminated prohibitions to access to public places for blacks . . . and universalized health care and education. Nonetheless, the author laments that the country needs a more defined legal framework against attitudes or mistreatment based on the color of one's skin."[4] The more subtle, hidden forms of racism that exist institutionally that prevent blacks from ascending to higher positions of leadership and employment continue to be attributed to individual, unenlightened attitudes. Although Raul Castro vows to fight these attitudes in his speech, it is clear that a true change of perspective is quite difficult to combat through policy.

The use of the terms "prejudice" or "racial discrimination" is quite purposeful. Within the body of the speeches that address the racial issue throughout the past fifteen years, the word "racism" is often, if not always, replaced with the term "prejudice" or "racial discrimination" (unless the speech refers to racism outside of the island). In the 2009 Cuban documentary *Raza*, the Vice Minister of Culture, Fernando Rojas, says, "I think that racism exists. It is not on a scale minimally comparable to that of any other country in the world, or, of course, to prerevolutionary Cuba . . . although the more common expression is racism, I prefer to say that racial discrimination exists. I would like to emphasize that it exists to a much lesser degree than other realities and to a much, much lesser degree than what we had before 1959." Thus there is a deliberate frame that the leadership created in the early years of the revolution, which persists until today and serves to shape Cubans' ideas about racism both domestically and internationally. The frame 1) defines racism in Cuba as prejudice and discriminatory acts by individuals that is outside of systematic practices; 2) defines racism in general as de facto racism that supports inequality legally and in policy; 3) highlights the revolution's role in creating an egalitarian society that offers equal opportunity and access to all levels of society; and 4) locates systematic racism outside of Cuba.

Why has racial democracy been so successful in winning over public opinion regarding racism throughout Latin America and the Caribbean? The way in which racism is framed throughout the region is an understudied topic in the literature on racial democracy. While there is extensive scholarship on racial democracy and its effects, there is little that has been done to

---

4. Delis 2013.

examine the reasons for its staying power, even in nations with persistent racism and racial inequality. Perceptions of what racism is, how it operates, what effect it has on people's lives, and how it can be diminished has much to do not only with what people believe about equality in their country, but whether racism even receives public and private attention. The framing of racism as individual attitudes is one of the most important components of racial democracy and accounts for much of the apathy and denial surrounding the issue.

In this chapter I highlight the third mechanism of racial democracy, the framing of racism as prejudice, demonstrating its consequences: it confines the debate on racism, maintains the status quo of racial inequality, exonerates the government from policy commitments, and portrays solutions based on education, the passage of time, or the will of the people rather than policy-oriented solutions. People in all racial groups in Cuba see the government as a supporter of racial equality. The way in which people conceive of societal racism has great implications for both its staying power and the level of opposition it receives. Many citizens think about racism as something that resides solely in the realms of lawmaking or individual enlightenment. Eradicating racism from each individual's mindset becomes a project that has no real chance at working and its existence is accepted. If information about how racial inequality persists is either low or incorrect, then it maintains apathy around the issue and affects levels of racial consciousness among nonwhites who suffer from racism.

Racism is, in fact, embedded in the country's institutions. Through survey data where respondents report an experience with discrimination, I find that many of these experiences stem from structural mechanisms such as access to employment and racial profiling by the police and within tourist spaces. Despite these reported experiences that give evidence of systemic racism, the majority of the respondents still view them as problems of prejudice. While perception is attitudinal, evidence suggests that structural racism does indeed exist in Cuba. Racial frameworks that portray racism as psychological and not economic or political create a barrier toward activism, organization, and reflection on the issue in relation to the revolution.

Frames

The literature on framing often draws from Goffman's work titled *Frame Analysis* to define the concept as the framework that "allows its user to locate, perceive, identify and label a seemingly infinite number of concrete occurrences defined in its terms."[5] David A. Snow defines frames as "articulation mechanisms" that allow one set of meanings rather than another to be conveyed.[6] Their significance, Snow argues, is such that actions and experiences cannot be meaningfully understood apart from the way that they are framed. In his study of the rise of black insurgency during the years of the civil rights movement, Doug McAdam highlights the differences between objective and subjective grievances, arguing that how people view an injustice is much more important than what the injustice looks like objectively.[7] Framing can often serve to guide perceptions that view a certain social ill as unchangeable rather than an injustice, which in turn discourages mobilization or other actions. Within an ideology of racial democracy, it can also keep the subject off of the table. In the case of Cuba, the revolution's claim of eradicating structural racism is believed by many, even if its attempt to eradicate individual racism is not. While people's personal beliefs and actions are hard to control or change, the presence of structural racism could not only be changeable through policy, but accountability would point to the government. The racial frame that the government of Cuba has to promote is one that recognizes the presence of racial prejudice, but still adheres to the notion of equal opportunity and equality that is not only promoted, but was created by the state.

Racist practices by individuals are perceived as unfortunate, but state-sponsored racism is an injustice. We can take this idea beyond the example of Cuba and look to the frames that shape grievances regarding racial inequality in the Americas. In the United States, for example, the practice of Jim Crow and anti-black violence was seen as an injustice and inspired mobilization, particularly when it was publicized via national media. When we think about the more subtle forms of institutional racism that we see today, many do not interpret this as an injustice, particularly in comparison to the state-sponsored racism in the pre-civil rights era. Moreover, the racism of today is often viewed in terms of individual attitudes and practices, rather than a systemic pattern, which is bolstered by colorblind ideology and the success of the civil rights movement.[8] The waning popularity of affirmative action in the United States is based on frames that rely on equal opportunity: racism is

---

5. Goffman 1986, 21.

6. Snow 2004, 384.

7. McAdam 1982.

8. Brown et al. 2003.

something that individuals practice, but not institutions.[9] Throughout Latin America, this vision of state-sponsored racism as the only kind of racism often features the United States as the regional culprit. In Brazil, those that argue for racial democracy and against affirmative action policies use this example of racism in the United States as something foreign to Brazil. Racism is instead described as something that is an aberration and any discussion of the problem leads to national divisions. We could imagine that it would require a transformation of how racism is framed to move people to act against structural racism or to support some kind of policy that would undercut racial inequality.

Framing is not the only tactic that is utilized by government elites; it is coupled with state control as well. In a socialist and authoritarian regime where organization, space, and expression are managed and supervised by the state almost completely, discouraging discontent can occur in ways much different from a democratic system. Often social movement activity or even public expressions of grievances are directed toward appropriate authorities to challenge unequal conditions.[10] Who are these appropriate authorities when we are interpreting everyday racism? Organizing on the basis of race on a mass level remains prohibited in Cuba. A state organization has never been created to address any grievance related to racism or discriminatory treatment, nor are there local institutional mechanisms for a grievance. This institutional environment has existed since the start of the revolution and consequently the prospect of seeking justice for discrimination is not part of societal norms. One can address a grievance of any kind through the Communist Party; however, this is not an institution that is specialized to address racial discrimination. The absence of appropriate authorities, coupled with the interpretation that the government cannot control individual attitudes, show that racial frames and the institutions that support them are crucial in the interpretation of black grievances and a lack of organization.

Cuba and its political system are also able to discourage grievances in ways contrary to a capitalist authoritarian government. The frame that defines racism as prejudice is successful at managing discontent not through force or repression (although that may occur), but via more noble claims to social justice. In other words, the Cuban revolution can prohibit racial organization and activism not just through control of its citizens, but as a logical policy attached

---

9. Bonilla-Silva 2014.

10. Snow 2004.

to the idea that the revolution's commitment to social justice has meant that racial inequality is nearly defeated. Indeed, in a survey conducted by de la Fuente and Glasco in 1994, a majority of whites and blacks thought that discrimination had ended, but racial prejudices still exist.[11] Thus there would be little need to organize under the banner of racial solidarity, because the government has brought about national solidarity thanks to measures taken to diminish racism. What is the result? Many blacks, aware of the presence of racism among Cuba's individuals, would argue that to organize as blacks would be against what the revolution stands for, and because the regime does not support racism, would be misdirected and unnecessary.[12] The importance of race as a social cleavage diminishes as blacks and *mulatos* are present in other organizations whose identities *are* recognized as essential in the struggle for equality and representation: women, unions, and youth groups.

Individual versus Structural Approaches

The study of racism has produced various definitions of the concept ranging from structural, ideological, and/or attitudinal components as the driving forces of racial inequality. Public opinion about racism and its origins is very much influenced by the state's racial politics. Eduardo Bonilla-Silva argues that scholars have often offered a "clinical approach to race" in that they focus on the racial attitudes of individuals rather than identifying ideological and systemic forces that maintain nonwhite subordination.[13] An approach to the study of racism that only focuses on attitudes is not only incomplete, but misdirected as well. There are ideological forces at work that shape racial beliefs and in turn are reproduced by individuals. Ideological frameworks seek to steer the conversation away from societal structures and toward individual racial pathologies.

Scholarship in Cuba on race often mirrors state rhetoric on race, analyzing individual attitudes almost exclusively. Scholars that reside in Cuba are also limited in the ways that they can write about racism in published works, which contributes to these academic boundaries as well. Thus the focus by authors on individual prejudice and stereotypes in Cuba not only leaves out a structural and ideological explanation of racism, but is a product of

---

11. De la Fuente and Glasco 1997.

12. See chapter 8 for survey results that demonstrate this perception.

13. Bonilla-Silva 2001.

ideological forces that define racism in that very way.[14] Cuban scholar Estéban Morales, who has talked publicly at length on the presence of racism and is a member of the Communist Party, serves as an example when he writes that "where stereotypes and racial prejudice exist, racism is present. It does not exist or manifest itself in an institutional way but rather, in the consciousness of individuals or certain groups."[15] We do not know if political constraints, political loyalties, or belief in the frames are what drive the mode of inquiry for each racial scholar. During an interview with an academic in 2008, he was only able to show me his research on racism in private and he kept his results hidden from other colleagues. Regardless of the motivations, racial scholarship in Cuba reinforces racial democracy by utilizing the frames of individual prejudice.

While there are certainly instances of blacks who have been discriminated against by individuals in their personal relationships (as noted in the previous chapter), scholars have highlighted instances of blacks being denied jobs, promotions, and educational opportunities because of their race.[16] Through interviews and observations, some works do point to the continued exclusion of blacks in certain employment sectors, high positions, and within the government as well.[17] Alejandro De la Fuente points to the absence of blacks in the "state sponsored media" as well as the government enterprises that reproduce racist practices, particularly in the tourism sector.[18] The following section outlines interview data that show both of these tendencies at work: reports of structural racism, but expressed as individual prejudice, or a phenomenon that exists outside of the system. I thereby expand scholarship on racial politics in Cuba by examining how frames support the existence of and trivialize the anti-black stereotypes and racist attitudes that previous scholars have highlighted.

Individual Conceptions of Race: The Interviews

Among those interviewed, 70 percent characterized racism in Cuba to exist primarily among individuals; three cited racism to be structural or systemic,

---

14. Alvarado Ramos 1996; Espina Prieto and Rodríguez Ruiz 2006; de la Fuente 2008.

15. Morales Domínguez 2007, 51.

16. Duharte Jiménez and Santos García 1997; Sawyer 2006; Morales 2007.

17. Adams 2004.

18. De la Fuente 2001a.

and ten thought that it was a combination of both. The three interviewees who clearly viewed racism as systemic were also the three interviewees who described themselves as being opponents of the revolutionary government. Although those who were strong supporters of the revolution described racism as a product of individual prejudice, there were those who defined it in the same way, without having strong ideological ties to the revolution. In other words, although attitudes in favor of the revolution shaped the way that the interviewees viewed racism, belief in equality of opportunity and the absence of systemic racism existed also among those that were not members of the party or declared supporters of the revolution. Those who cited both structural racism and individual prejudice were mixed in their views of the government, but were all black Cubans. All of the white interviewees expressed racism as a consequence of individual prejudice, and the *mulato* respondents were mixed in their views. Some *mulatos* referenced their own experiences of discrimination while others argued that racism did not affect them, but most agreed on attitudinal definitions. Although different groups define and perceive racism according to their location in the hierarchy (i.e., whites tend to defend the racial status quo), I find that due to the policies that the revolution implemented and its strong claims of racial and economic equality, people in all racial groups hold an individual conception of racism that has real implications for racial consciousness and the racial status quo, or racial inequality. Nonetheless, whites tend to support the revolutionary rhetoric on race, regardless of their views of the revolution, and nonwhites have a more critical and nuanced view of race and racism in Cuba.

What is most notable about the tendency for interviewees to define racism as a matter of individual prejudice is that their descriptions of racism were largely structural. Interviewees recognized the presence of racism, even structurally, but still characterized it as something that can only be seen among individuals. Lack of opportunity for blacks, employment discrimination and little black representation in high positions, including the government, often did not translate as structural discrimination for respondents. I asked respondents how they defined racism and if they viewed it as a phenomenon only among individual attitudes or as something systemic. A thirty-year-old black hair stylist said,

> I see racism among people, not within the system. I never had an experience with racism but it's there. There are jobs that are for whites and jobs that are for blacks. For example, it is rare to find a black person working in stores or as cashiers. In the hotels, in all the places of higher

rank and money, there are only whites working. Some white teachers also show preference to white students. With respect to jobs, whites have more opportunities than blacks, at least here. Also, within the better jobs, whites tend to always help another white person, but blacks have a hard time helping another black person to get a position.[19]

Employment discrimination in the emergent sector and the lack of access blacks experience to jobs connected to hard currency are systemic problems occurring after the Special Period. This interviewee, however, does not see these institutional barriers. There are very few blacks in these industries, which also may be why the few who have ascended to these positions seem reticent to show racial solidarity to others.

Observations of what would be considered examples of structural racism did not lead to reproach of the government or a call for policy changes within the revolution. An accountant shared an opinion quite similar to the dominant racial ideology, although he claimed that the government was not completely open in their characterization of attitudinal racism.

The system doesn't advocate racism. Really. Now, I will say there are things from the past, things that are not seen in public but everyone knows that they exist. We are still struggling against that. The revolution has preached that racism doesn't exist, that it can't exist, that it has ended. That is what they say to people. *It exists.* There are feelings from the past, very subtle and hidden, that still prevail. It's very simple: I have never heard of a group of whites getting into trouble and someone has said, "They had to be white." (Laughs.) No! It's always, "Damn, they had to be black."[20]

The conversation continued in this way:

INTERVIEWEE: There is a lot more to be done. Here there are opportunities for everyone, but not really for everyone. In some cases yes, in some cases no. It's true that to get high up professionally, there are few blacks;

---

19. Employment that provides Cubans with access to hard currency, such as working in dollar stores as a cashier, is considered to be a job with privilege.

20. *Tenía que ser negro*, or "he or she had to be black," is a common expression denoting blacks propensity for getting in trouble or doing something wrong.

however, when it comes to sports, we are favored. We are appreciated. In boxing for example, we are the good ones."

INTERVIEWER: Why do blacks excel and ascend in sports and not other areas?

INTERVIEWEE: Sports are not on the same level as professional positions.

INTERVIEWER: So then it's a question of power?

INTERVIEWEE: It's a question of power. A university graduate in physical education is not the same as an economist or an engineer.

After thinking about my questions, he begins to think about stereotypical positions that blacks are able to advance in as opposed to those that come with a measure of prestige and influence. Despite this realization, he does not attribute the lack of opportunity to anything institutional and uses the past as the only place where racism was created and supported.

A major component of racial ideology in Cuba uses the example of the United States and their policies of Jim Crow from the past both to define racism and to locate it outside of Cuba's borders. Indeed, half of those I interviewed made some reference to the United States as the model of both structural and individual racism, whereas Cuba, with a more mixed population, did not suffer from that kind of racism. One young *mulato* musician told me, "We have racism here in Cuba, but it's a mild racism; not a violent racism like in the United States." Similarly another interviewee compared Cuba to a segregated United States and South Africa.

> Everyone has different racial views. In my opinion, I don't believe the concept of racism exists here. Here's an example: I can go to any place that I want to. In South Africa, there is a zone for blacks and a zone for whites. In the United States, there are areas where blacks don't go and areas where whites don't go. That doesn't exist here. That's why I say people have different points of view or prejudices, which is different than the concept of racism. Racism is segregation, racial separation. Racial prejudice exists. There can be an instance where someone does not want to marry a black person. There are a lot of people that think like that, but they are not the majority.

Portrayals by the Cuban media of racial events in the United States, such as race riots and more recently, police brutality help to paint the overall characterization of the United States as racist. Moreover, many interviewees had a current view of the United States that was based on formal segregation and racial violence from the past. This leads to a contrasting view of racism in Cuba as something that occurs only among individuals and is not promoted by the state. If opportunity is legislated to be equal and there are no overtly racist laws, then logic follows that the system is not racist.

A female scholar not only characterized discrimination as a phenomenon that had to be legislated by the state in an interview, but she discounted the role of individual prejudice as something that could cause any unrest in Cuba. She stated,

> There is no official discrimination, that's a fact. But there are famil-ial patterns that get transmitted from generation to generation. When I was the president of my CDR,[21] there was a woman who would not let her daughter play with another girl in the *solar* [housing tenement in Havana] that they lived in because she was black. Despite these examples, it's not a social pattern. It's not anything that could produce a movement or struggle. Prejudices exist and we should work on that, but it is not a social problem. My children don't see color; Afro-Cuban doesn't mean anything to them. They meet a person and they don't remember what color they are.

It is unclear whether, as a member of the Communist party and a former president of a CDR, this interviewee expressed these sentiments because she believed them or she wanted to portray a raceless Cuba to someone from the United States. While she did acknowledge individual prejudice among some, she claimed that others have no perception of race. Her answers seem to be a justification to downplay racial prejudice. Another interviewee who was a recent university graduate expressed a similar sentiment regarding the absence of overt racist policy, but did look to the government to provide some sort of dialogue about the issue:

> Racism escapes a systemic conception because the system is established so that everyone has the same opportunities. At the same time, when you put a white manager in a particular hotel and he hires his white friends, which almost always is how managers acquire their personnel and control everything, racism is linked to that. They are part of the system but at the end what is produced is only part of a link, so the

21. CDR stands for Committee for the Defense of the Revolution, which are local governmen-tal organizations or committees which were created to encourage mass political participation. Each neighborhood has their own CDR.

actual system is not producing any racism. Within the system we all have the same rights. Yes, it's true that the system is a part of the reason that we do not discuss the issue because we solved the problem a long time ago. That is one of the achievements of the revolution. In that sense, the revolution has contributed to the fact that there is little discussion about racism. The system is implicit in that because they don't make any concrete actions in order to make the debate more open.

Those that defended the revolution throughout their interviews often pointed to the revolution's accomplishments in 1959 and did not attribute any remaining evidence of racism to the governments' actions or lack of action on the subject. The older generation, in particular, who saw the vast improvements that were made toward black advancement and equality of opportunity, often pointed to those changes when describing the presence of racism today. One sixty-five-year-old black doctor said,

> When this revolution started, defending blacks, and when Fidel started, the houses that the rich left behind were made into schools. Racism exists in Cuba now, but much, much, much less! Here we have black doctors, black nurses, black professors; we have a lot of blacks in health care. The vice president, Lazo, is black—so black he's almost blue! He's *black*. There are two or three black members of government in Santiago de Cuba. There are black people inside the Central Committee of the Communist Party and I feel proud of that. There are blacks, there are wonderful doctors . . . you can see there are whites and blacks in these professions.

The gains that the revolution made in opening up opportunities for blacks in health care and education are often used as examples of equal opportunity and the end of formal racism. This particular area of progress allowed for a higher level of racial equality in Cuba, but also facilitates arguments that the racism in other sectors is a function of some other phenomenon.

Despite the majority of the sample that defined racism within the limits of people's attitudes, there were some that did attribute inequalities to society's structure. A black sixty-six-year-old self-employed worker said,

> Of course the system is racist. The country is racist if all of the bosses are white and all of the higher positions are for whites. There are very few blacks in high positions; they are the minority. There is racism.

Even Raúl said that we have to put more blacks in these positions. It's there. If there were more blacks in government then that would change something. If they occupied those high posts it would change.

This particular interviewee was very adamant about his desire to leave Cuba and his disagreement with the government and its policies. He rejected most of the rhetoric that has been espoused by the government, which may have been part of the reason that he was comfortable to speak frankly about the role of the government in maintaining racism in Cuba. Nonetheless, he did make a direct connection between lack of opportunity for blacks and systemic racism that others did not.

Racism, Discrimination, and Experience: Survey Data

The passages quoted above are some of the many examples of how racial democracy holds a strong influence on attitudes toward race and racism. Although the dominant racial ideology in Cuba influences everyone differently, even the most racially conscious have elements of this ideology infused into their own mental framework when locating racism. Racial democracy both in and outside of Cuba is expressed as an acceptance of racism among individuals rather than on a systemic basis, which would deny any ongoing anti-black discrimination by the government or its institutions.[22] Survey data suggests that although there is a conception of racism as a psychological phenomenon, reported experiences of discrimination point to another reality. Structural forms of discrimination were reported by a significant number of respondents, suggesting that racism is indeed an institutional problem.

Within the survey, respondents were asked whether they had an experience with discrimination, with a choice of yes or no. If they answered yes, they were asked to explain the experience in more detail. This section of the survey allowed me to capture a more nuanced idea of their experience and gather more qualitative information among a large sample. Surveys often do not allow for more in-depth answers, and in this way I was able to extract what form of discrimination people were experiencing and their opinions on the subject.

The detailed positive responses on the discrimination question were separated into two categories—structural discrimination and attitudinal

---

22. Hanchard 1994.

discrimination. Responses that pointed to discrimination on a systemic basis such as governmental or employment discrimination, racial profiling, or racism due to lack of access or opportunity for blacks were categorized as *structural discrimination*. Those that pointed to discrimination on an individual basis pertaining to relationships, incidents on the street, or disparaging remarks by friends or family were placed into the *attitudinal discrimination* category. This type of categorization was employed to test whether the rhetoric associated with racial democracy in Cuba that defines racism as everyday attitudes actually represents the reality for blacks. The responses show that while we do indeed find instances of discrimination that are attributable to attitudes, there are many instances of structural discrimination that fall beyond the boundaries of what the government has defined as vestiges of racism left from the Republic. Although there are those that do attribute discrimination to individual attitudes or isolated incidents, a higher percentage of those that experienced discrimination were of a structural nature (See Figure 6.1). Those who cited being discriminated against due to individual attitudes, 38 percent of those who reported an experience with discrimination, most often described the parent of a white partner that did not accept them because of their skin color. Others discussed looks that they received from whites, racist comments that have become part of the culture, and preferential treatment of whites in everyday interactions. One respondent, for example, wrote that

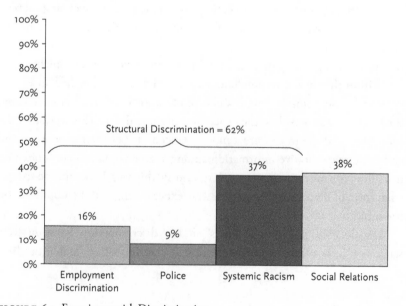

FIGURE 6.1 Experience with Discrimination

since middle school people have told her that she is *una negra blanca o una negra rubia* (a white or a blond black person) because of her politeness, her intelligence, and her level of education. She found this to be the worst experience of discrimination that she endured because good qualities, character, and intelligence are normalized as white.

A total of 62 percent of respondents that explained their experience with discrimination cited some form of structural discrimination. These respondents pointed to inequalities produced by the government, absence of representation in government and in media, lack of access to managerial positions, and a devaluation of blacks by the government and society as a whole. Respondents also expressed that Cuba is a racist country or that the political and economic systems in Cuba are racist. A twenty-six-year-old male writes, "Cuban society continues to be a racist society and this manifests in all spheres of life in Cuba." A female university student wrote, "Despite all that can be done to eliminate discrimination here, you confront it daily when applying for a job, when you put on the television, in every relationship, in popular phrases, etc." A young man working as a welder expressed that Cuba is racist "from the television to the hierarchy," while another wrote that blacks in Cuba "are not valued." A thirty-six-year-old woman expressed the sentiment that the government is to blame for racial disparities. She writes, "Because of Cuban society and the policies of the heads of the country, the best positions are for whites only."

Within the category of structural discrimination, 16.7 percent of those that had an experience with discrimination cited specific incidents of job discrimination. A forty-year-old male professor, for example, wrote, "Promotion always has a limit for blacks here in Cuba," while a forty-nine-year-old female wrote, "Job offers and exchanges are subtly managed by whites. Whether you have money or not, they only accept other whites."[23] Another respondent expressed that whites always have better opportunities in Cuba. The responses also included references to tourism and other jobs that provide access to hard currency, but are unavailable for blacks. Networks factored into people's responses as well and because whites occupy most of the managerial and administrative positions, they are likely to hire their friends and family, barring access to black job seekers. Several of the responses pointed to this practice, which aside from the issue of job discrimination, also points to some form of racially defined social relations. One respondent wrote, "Because job

---

23. Her response refers to the practice (albeit illegal) of purchasing employment opportunities in the most lucrative sectors such as tourism.

opportunity is done via friendship, whites only hire each other." Another expressed that even blacks in positions of authority will not hire other blacks. She wrote, "In institutional and work spaces blacks experience discrimination doubly, both by whites and blacks."

The absence of institutional channels to report discrimination is a consequence of the government's negation of institutional racism. Several respondents referred to their inability to hold employers and others accountable. A thirty-eight-year-old female author explained, "Cuba has always been a racist country. Discrimination here is invisible therefore those that are discriminated against feel impotent. In governmental terms discrimination does not exist and one has nowhere to go or a place to complain when you are mistreated." Another wrote that "sometimes being black or *mulato* has put brakes on advancement in certain fields and although it is never said directly, you are made to feel inferior or blocked out of opportunity."

The most common response among young males referenced poor and unequal treatment by the police. A male university student wrote, "Most of the time, the police force is racist and detain young black males in the streets without having committed any crime." Many respondents referred to the practice of asking for identification, which the police seem to reserve almost exclusively for nonwhites. One young artist described racial profiling as being "defined by the police" when walking through the streets, while another expressed an inability to walk in public with white friends without being stopped by the police. Both tourist and white spaces are firmly protected by the police, primarily from black bodies which hold an association with criminality. While Cubans are generally discouraged from interacting with tourists, nonwhite Cubans, both male and female, are surveilled at much higher rates.[24] Black and *mulata* women are often read as hustlers or *jineteras* when seen with tourists, and black males are stereotyped in similar ways as hustlers or criminals.

Discrimination within the schools was also a concern for respondents. One male artist wrote that in high school he was blocked out of the career that he wanted when the opportunity was given to a white student, despite the fact that his grades and performance were ranked better than hers. At a very early age, he wrote, that affected him deeply. It is difficult to decipher whether career tracking in Cuban schools are affected by race, but

---

24. I was stopped by the police and asked for my identification multiple times while traveling with American students. Often as the only nonwhite person in the group, I was the only one who was asked to furnish my ID because I was often mistaken for a Cuban.

respondents did report racist attitudes from teachers in the classroom. Although universal education continues to stand as one of the major triumphs of the revolution, the systemic racism that may exist within this institution deserves more study. This is particularly important as career opportunity and access for nonwhites are intimately connected to issues of racial inequality. If nonwhites students are less supported less in the schools or encouraged to pursue less lucrative or socially estimable careers, they are less likely to be represented at the university and in the more sought-after fields.

Conclusion

The way in which racism is framed in Cuba and throughout Latin America and the Caribbean accounts for much of the credibility of racial democracy. The perception that the phenomenon can be explained through the attitudes of a few supports the idea that full equality exists and systemic racism is not a reality. The Cuban revolution's policies at the start of the revolution, coupled with the ideological frames and mantras that juxtapose socialism with social justice and create erroneous definitions of racism, further strengthen racial democracy. As a result the ideology remains intact, even when citizens identify instances of racial discrimination supported by institutions.

Legacies from the prerevolutionary era and individual attitudes among some white Cubans continue to be the only concession that the government is willing to make regarding the presence of racism in contemporary Cuba. The survey data show that there are indeed instances of employment discrimination, racial profiling, and barriers toward access for blacks in general. The following chapter will show that experiences with discrimination are not only often of a structural nature, but they are quite common among the sample. Despite this reality, interview data show that Cubans consistently view racism as a form of individual prejudice and downplay its importance or effect on Cuban society. Although some blacks do point to systemic racism, many also continue to view racism as attitudinal even when discussing experiences and observations of systemic racial discrimination. Thus we find that structural discrimination exists, but is often viewed as manifestations of individual prejudice, largely by whites, but by blacks as well.

The mantra of equal opportunity has been quite effective in its influence on public opinion in Cuba—so much, in fact, that it can sometimes trump experience for blacks. The view on this issue takes attention away from any governmental role to combat the presence of racism and its ability to create a solution. Individual prejudice is seen as something that is difficult or even impossible to tackle and not an issue that would inspire protest, dissent, or organization. Consequently, the racial status quo of inequality and lack of opportunity for blacks remains unchallenged.

7 *TODOS SOMOS CUBANOS, PERO NO TODOS SOMOS IGUALES*

HOW RACISM WORKS IN CUBA

When I began my field research in Cuba in 2008, I aimed to gather data that can give the best analysis we have of what racism looks like today in Cuba and how it affects blacks in their everyday lives. This task holds such importance because as compared to other countries in the region, Cuba represents one of the only countries where this data is not available. If we can identify how racism operates in Cuba, we can begin to understand how particular structures and practices produce disparate experiences for whites and nonwhites. As I argued at the start of the book, the presence and awareness of anti-black racism creates a formidable challenge to the power of racial democracy in Cuba. This chapter puts together original interview, survey, and ethnographic data to show that racism in Cuba is embedded in social practices and institutions and cannot be relegated to racial prejudice.

The racialized social structure in Cuba was, of course, created with the institution of slavery and codified during the period of the Republic, following abolition.[1] Although the Cuban Revolution was able to open access to *mulatos* and blacks and create a more equitable society, structures and institutions in Cuba remained racialized throughout the revolution and became exacerbated during the Special Period. An analysis of racism today must include not only the successes of the Cuban revolution, but the intimate connection that the Special Period and its recovery measures had with the increased visibility of racism and its social and political implications in Cuba. It can be argued that the increase in racialized

---

1. See Bonilla-Silva 1997.

outcomes and the decrease in black access was an unintended consequence of the recovery measures, but these were also outcomes of the silence on racial issues that preceded the crisis. The racial implications of the economic recovery hardly exist in a post–Soviet bubble; they are the aftereffects of a history of racial exclusion, a culture that maintains black inferiority and a national denial of the embeddedness of race and racism in the societal structure, both despite the revolution's efforts and due to the revolution's lack of attention to these problems.

This chapter serves to do several things: 1) demonstrate how racism and discrimination operate today to exclude and surveil blacks; 2) reveal that discrimination is a common experience among black Cubans, and more likely to occur for those who grew up during the Special Period; and 3) argue that the Special Period and its recovery measures created new spaces for racism and marginalization of black Cubans in various ways. Although this chapter argues that the economic crisis and the recovery measures indeed worsened racism in Cuba, I want to separate this argument from the strand of scholarship that contends that racism arose during the Special Period. Thus, while demonstrating that racist practices increased after 1990, I also will argue that racism was present well before the Special Period in Cuba, despite the revolution's efforts to dismiss it. Data and interviews point to experiences that demonstrate a racist culture and lack of representation in the media, government, and high levels of employment that were present before the economic crisis. The nature of the racist practices that are aligned with the development of tourism and the dollarization of the economy made racism more *visible* as it created a new racial environment that did not exist during the first three decades of the revolution.

The Cuban censuses of 2005 and 2012 both counted race; however, much of the data are not made publicly available. As a result, there is no empirical method possible to reveal the current correlations between race and issues such as socioeconomic status, housing conditions, and health indicators. Discussion of racial discrimination is largely anecdotal, and based on observation. For this reason, I aim to provide a more concrete conceptualization of racism in Cuba.

Economic Crisis

Following the fall of the Soviet Union, Cuba suffered an enormous loss from the collapse in foreign trade, credit, and Soviet aid, termed the Special Period in the Time of Peace. The profound societal changes brought about during the economic crisis produced inequalities not seen in the earlier decades of the revolution.[2] The financial watershed not only exposed the racial inequalities that the revolution failed to eradicate, but disparities (including class differences) were exacerbated and became far more visible due to both the crisis and the recovery measures implemented to restructure and save the economy.[3]

In the latter part of the 1980s, Cuba's dependency on the Soviet Union amounted to 85 percent of Cuba's exports and a comparable portion of its imports.[4] Cuba experienced a 75 percent fall in imports from $8 billion in 1989 to $1.7 billion in 1994.[5] The gross national product shrank by an estimated 40 percent from 1989 to 1993, and 60 percent of industry was halted.[6] Such a dramatic plunge was largely due to an end to the barter agreements between Cuba and the Soviet Union exchanging sugar for oil and industrial machinery. Cuba's primary export, sugar, left the country with little ability to lessen the shocks of its loss of economic protection. Food rations, public transportation services, and school and medical supplies declined severely. The shortage in petroleum severely reduced vehicle usage as gas prices increased exceptionally. Public transportation was not able to cushion this shock, and in fact, the shortage led to significantly fewer public buses. The government was able to maintain the social safety net that had always been the core of the revolution, however, at much lower levels.[7] Consumption experienced such a decline that even as late as 1998, Cubans had to purchase 60 percent of their protein needs, 50 percent of edible oils, and 30 percent of their caloric intake in dollarized markets.[8] While the government still provided a set amount of food and necessities, it was unable to cover the full quantity needed by the population.

Cuba's recovery from the economic shock largely depended on the development of tourism and the legalization of dollars. In August of 1993, the government legalized the possession of hard currency (primarily US dollars), a reform that became tightly intertwined with tourism and had major effects for the Cuban population. To gain further profit from the circulation

---

2. Fernandez Robaina 2009.

3. De la Fuente 2001c; Saney 2004.

4. Perez-Stable 2012.

5. LeoGrande 2000.

6. Dilla 2002.

7. Eckstein 2003.

8. Dilla 2002.

of dollars, the government created a domestic market economy, or "dollar stores." Cubans who held hard currency were able to shop at these stores, enabling them to purchase items not available among the state-provided provisions. Many of the stores were supermarkets with increased food options (including imports) and others sold goods such as appliances, electronics, home merchandise, and clothing. These stores were particularly important during a time when the government was no longer able to provide citizens with the previous standard of living. By 1997, dollar sales in these high-priced stores represented 17 percent of Cuba's total dollar income and by 1999, sales had reached one billion dollars.[9] What has resulted is a highly visible difference among those who have dollars (and necessities) and those who do not. This dichotomy did not end with the Special Period and remains the current reality on the island.

Uneven access to hard currency between blacks and whites has resulted in an increase in inequalities.[10] Hard currency is obtained either via remittances or employment in the emergent sector where salaries and bonuses are paid by foreign business owners or through tips from tourists. While there is no record of the race of families that send money to Cuba, it can be gleaned from the self-reported racial make-up of Cuban Americans in the 2010 US census where 85 percent of respondents identified as white and 4.6 percent of respondents identified as black, that the majority that receive remittances in Cuba are white. When asked if there was a disparity among blacks and whites that have access to the convertible peso (CUC), a sixty-six-year-old black, self-employed worker who made ends meet by painting and selling things on the side said,

> There are more whites that receive remittances and have CUC. Everyone knows that. Blacks left with the *balseros* and from Mariel,[11] but the white people that had money had already left. Look at where we are now. Almost all of those that are in prison are black. There are whites there, but very few because we have had less opportunity. And everything comes out of that. The government is aware of that.

---

9. Hostetter 2001.

10. De la Fuente 2001c; Espina Prieto and Rodríguez Ruiz 2006.

11. Two waves of emigration from Cuba to the United States occurred in the 1980s, called Mariel, because those who left were brought to the Mariel boatlift in Havana and in 1994 when Castro allowed those who wanted to construct their own rafts, or *balsas*, to leave for the United States. Both were associated with a higher nonwhite racial make-up compared to the first wave of those that emigrated during the beginning years of the revolution.

In a survey done in Havana in 2000, Sarah Blue found that whites have more access to hard currency than nonwhites via remittances, bonuses in state employment, and jobs in the tourism sector.[12] Remittances bring in an estimated two billion dollars annually to Cuba and constitute an integral component of economic sustainability.

Although close to the entire population relies on extra income in addition to state salaries, blacks are often scapegoated as the only group that engages in illegal activities to earn hard currency.[13] Some of the scapegoating is due in part to the fact that if blacks do not have access to jobs with hard currency, they are forced to engage in more visible activities to gain access. Whites are more likely to have jobs that handle CUC, and thus are able to create scams through their places of employment—activities that remain undetectable to the general public. I observed during my time in Cuba that most people who were able to pilfer money, goods, or food from their place of employment, did so. This was well known as a secret—but common—practice. Working a job in which Cuban pesos are the only form of payment leads many to engage in outside activities, with varying legality. It is clear that blacks do indeed have limited opportunities and limited access to hard currency: Rodriguez and Espina found that blacks are almost three times as likely as whites to rely on activities outside of their regular employment to earn dollars and make ends meet.[14] As argued in previous chapters, any disparity in opportunity is often not recognized, leading to conclusions regarding lack of black work ethic and a racial predilection toward criminal activity. The legalization of self-employment, for example, has been used by Cubans to open up room rentals and restaurants for tourists in their homes. Both of these opportunities have remained virtually closed to blacks and to a lesser degree, *mulatos*. Housing patterns, still racially segregated in many areas of Havana, do not allow for Afro-Cubans to benefit from the option to rent rooms to tourists or open up private restaurants, as do many white Cubans living in more attractive, less marginalized, and central neighborhoods. Various sectors that have been open to nonwhites in Cuba are those that pay in Cuban pesos and regardless of social importance, they are jobs that do not cover monetary needs. In the tourism industry, managers and owners of hotels, albeit not explicitly, make jobs only available to lighter

---

12. Blue 2007.

13. Duharte Jiménez and Santos García 1997.

14. Espina Prieto and Rodríguez Ruiz 1996.

Cubans, with the justification that these are the faces thought to be preferred by European tourists.[15]

Since the legalization of dollars, various economic reforms have taken place, particularly since Raúl Castro took over the presidency. Following the Sixth Party Congress in 2011, several changes were to the Cuban economy and structure to address Cuba's economic challenges and increase productivity. Among those related to access to hard currency, the government legalized the private sale of homes and cars, Cuba's state banks could now provide loans to those that were self-employed, and the options for self-employment would cover far more occupations and opportunities.[16] Smaller changes such as the ownership of cell phones, for example, were also made in the late 2000s. The Party Congress also announced the eventual elimination of the ration card, which provides staples such as detergent, rice, beans, sugar, coffee, bread, and milk for pregnant women and children. Although the products available at the *bodega* (stores selling rationed products) are not of the highest quality, many depend on them for their monthly consumption and cannot afford to purchase all of their food from *agromercados* (farmers' markets) or supermarkets. Those that are only receiving a salary in Cuban pesos are particularly vulnerable if rations are taken away completely. Thus, people with access to CUC are poised to benefit considerably from the new reforms and will not be affected by the loss of the ration card, or *libreta*. Someone with enough money to purchase a car or home, for example, can use that asset to earn money in various ways in Cuba. Those that do not have access to hard currency remain unable to take advantage of the reforms and find themselves still dependent on government rations. If access to currency continues to be correlated to race, racial inequality will increase.

Exclusionary practices in various sectors, coupled with the daily microaggressions against blacks that came with the advent of tourism, made racism more visible during the Special Period. Blacks are often profiled as criminals and summarily thrown out of hotel lobbies, being stereotyped by doormen and hotel employees as hustlers or pimps in pursuit of foreigners' cash. The increased attention from police that blacks received by being stopped in the streets for verification of their identification was also a reminder of a second-class status. These conditions increased the everyday significance of being black in Cuba and continue to create visible examples of racial inequality

15. De la Fuente 2001a; Duharte Jimenez and Santos García 1997.

16. Dominguez 2012.

that often cannot be ignored. Finally, it should be noted that access to hard currency is the primary preoccupation of most citizens on the island. If it is observable that blacks have limited access to CUC, whether due to remittances or employment obstacles, this can become a noteworthy issue. More than daily stops by police, if it is the case that blacks have less ability to take care of their families and purchase necessities when compared to whites, this is a disparity that bears great significance when considering how Cubans perceive structural racism and racial inequalities.

Experiences with Discrimination: Survey Data

Data on experiences with discrimination show that the economic recovery measures produced particular racialized experiences and exposed discriminatory practices. The data also show that discrimination in Cuba is common among blacks. The survey found that 176 (or 45 percent) of respondents experienced discrimination in some form. Although this percentage is significant on its own, it only marks those who had a direct experience in their lives. I suspect that there are other respondents that knew of instances of discrimination with friends or family, or observed others being discriminated against. Thus, I would expect that the number of those that observed some form of discrimination would be higher than 45 percent. Similar studies in the United States have shown that approximately 60 percent of African American adults experienced discrimination in their lives.[17]

In order to identify patterns of discrimination among different groups, the relationship between an experience with discrimination and gender, age, educational attainment, and occupation were explored. Previous studies do not identify a particular relationship with these variables and an experience with discrimination. In Cuba, it is common to hear the argument that black males are overwhelmingly targeted more than any other group by the police and thus may be more likely to have experiences with discrimination. The criminalization of black males is only part of the various mechanisms of racism in Cuba; however, it is an experience that is easily recognized as such. The institutional mechanisms that reproduce racial hierarchies are often subtle and not easily recognized by those that are affected by them. Lack of access and opportunity is not always something that people are cognizant about and would not necessarily point to systemic arrangements as racism. Racial

---

17. Kessler, Mickelson, and Williams 1999; Sanders-Thompson 1996 (also quoted in Sellers et al. 2003).

profiling by police is a systemic practice that is in your face (quite literally) and an experience that one might have multiple times.

The age of respondents and its relationship to discrimination may also relate to surveillance. Young black men, and to a lesser degree women, are often more likely to be stereotyped in tourist areas than those of older generations when entering hotels or being in the company of tourists.[18] When considering employment discrimination, it is unclear how certain demographics are affected. Although the tourism industry is most visibly exclusionary, there is evidence in the data of employment discrimination in various other sectors that affect the black population in general. Finally, while no official numbers are available, many have observed that the percentage of blacks both in higher education and in professional and managerial positions is well below their share of the population.[19] Those that have ascended to a university education may encounter more obstacles in these whiter spaces than those with lower levels of education. Studies outside of Cuba have also pointed to the increased experiences of discrimination that middle and upper class blacks experience as they move up the social and economic ladder to find that these spaces are dominated by whites.[20] Thus I would expect for significant relationships to show that experiences with discrimination are more likely for males and younger Cubans as a result of police and hotel surveillance, as well as those in higher educational levels. The following hypothesis reflects these expected differences:

H1: Experiences of discrimination are more likely to occur among a) young b) male Cubans and those in c) higher educational levels.

As shown in Table 7.1, there is in fact a significant relationship between experiences of discrimination and gender, where males are two and one half times more likely to report an experience. Within the total sample, 58 percent of males experienced discrimination while only 33 percent of females reported such an experience. In the descriptions of these experiences, males pointed to racial profiling by the police, the criminalization of black males, employment discrimination, and overall systemic racism, as well as racism from other individuals. They were far more likely to point to racial profiling by the police and

---

18. Sawyer 2006.

19. Adams 2004; Morales 2007.

20. Hochschild 1995; Krysan and Lewis 2006; Caldwell 2007.

Table 7.1 Logistic Coefficients and Odds Ratios for Regression of Experience with Discrimination on Gender, Education, and Age Cohort

Ind. Variables	Discrimination					
	Odds		Odds		Odds	
	(1a)	OR	(2b)	OR	(3b)	OR
Sex (Female Omitted)						
Males	.977***	2.65	.962***	2.62	.841***	2.32
	(.211)		(.214)		(.229)	
Education (4yr Degree Omitted)						
Less HS	—		−.483	.62	−.196	
			(.407)		(.428)	
H.S. Grad	—		−.184	.83	.001	
			(.300)		(.323)	
Some College	—		.108	1.11	.393	
			(.300)		(.324)	
Age Cohort (1950s Omitted)						
1960s	—	—			1.453*	4.28
					(.581)	
1970s	—	—			1.757***	5.80
					(.534)	
1980s	—	—			1.510**	4.52
					(.496)	
1990s	—	—			.559	
					(.532)	
Constant	−0.701***		−.622* -		1.965***	
	(.154)		(.254)		(.524)	
Chi-Square	22.47***		x***		51.13***	
df	1		x		9	

Note: Numbers in parentheses are standard errors. Number of observations is 385.

* $p < .05$ ** $p < .01$ *** $p < .001$ (two-tailed tests)

issues of criminalization. Many also pointed to tourism as the primary reason that blacks are confronted with their race on a regular basis. Racial profiling by the police primarily in tourist spaces is not reserved for males, as evidenced by my personal experiences and other observations in the field. Males, however, are more likely to be criminalized and targeted by the police, which is brought out in the survey data: only one female respondent reported being stopped by the police as compared to 20 percent of the male respondents that reported an experience with discrimination.[21] Black women are subject to many other racist practices and female respondents pointed to employment discrimination and racism experienced in a social setting or in the streets as the primary ways in which they experienced discrimination. Racial profiling is not the only variable driving the higher likelihood of men reporting an experience with discrimination, but I would argue that it is a significant experience for black males, particularly in cities like Havana that attract a significant number of tourists.

While black men in particular pointed to many instances of discrimination by the police, white and *mulato* interviewees also noted that the police stop black Cubans much more than those of other racial groups. One interviewee, a forty-three-year-old male, shared that racial profiling by the police was the only instance of discrimination that he could point to in his life.

> I haven't had too many problems with discrimination except for the police. They always stop you, "Hey! Good afternoon, good morning. Your ID card." One time, after the officer went over me and my friends' ID cards, I asked, "What did we do for you to stop us, was there a problem?" He said, "The problem is we are here to control." It happens all the time. Another time I asked one of them, "There are other people passing by of another race, another color and you didn't stop them. Are we doing something bad?" If something happened in that area or you happen to look like someone, forget it! And if you observe, the majority of people that they stop are black. Let's look at the prisons. I don't know exactly what the percentage is of blacks in the prisons, but I am absolutely sure that there are more blacks than whites; you can be sure

---

21. It should be noted that this number does not indicate that only 20 percent of the respondents were stopped by police, but that only 20 percent used an incident with police to describe discrimination they have experienced. Respondents who used other ways to explain discrimination in Cuba had been stopped by police as well, and shared this during interviews and conversations following completion of the survey.

about that. Anyone who tells you no is lying. My vision is at 100 percent and that is how I see it.

A construction worker had a similar sentiment noting that white people do not receive the same treatment by police.

Here they see the black man as a bandit. The police will ask a white person for his identification if he is going on a trip perhaps, but blacks are always asked for their identification. White people pass by a police officer and the police don't tell him anything; but to black people they always say, "Hey, what's this one doing?" They always stop him.

Black men have a unique experience with police. These experiences are frequently shared in conversations among them and serve to build sensibilities about race and the meaning of being black and male in Cuban society, particularly in Havana. Throughout my trip in Cuba, comments were made often about the practice of racial profiling in Cuba in and outside of the survey and interviews that were conducted.

Males in particular can often count on being stopped by police in areas of high tourist traffic even without being in direct contact with tourists. A twenty-three-year-old student stated that most black males can be expected to be stopped in the street at some point.

That is a big problem here. The police are always watching black men. They stop you from entering so many places. If you want to go into a hotel they are always watching you or questioning why you are there. Black people are seen as delinquents.

This experience is not unique to Cuba. Police activity against the black community is often an impetus for black political activism throughout the African Diaspora.[22] Wiezter and Tuch show that in the United States, blacks have differing views of the police when compared to whites because of disparate experiences with the police.[23] Blacks and Latinos in the United States are more likely to be stopped by the police and thus are more likely to recognize the

---

22. Davenport et al. 2011; Ogbar 2004; Cashmore 2001.

23. Wiezter and Tuch 2005.

prevalence of racial profiling. There are also various accounts of racial profiling by the police in Brazil's "racial democracy" where blacks receive disparate treatment from whites.[24] In Cuba, the treatment of blacks by the police has unearthed racism's presence in the form of everyday incidents, making them impossible to ignore. The common experience of young black males to be stopped and harassed by the police has contributed to a more conscious black population especially among the younger generation. Moreover, although these experiences are more likely in tourist areas, they can also happen in areas away from tourists. A twenty-eight-year-old male described an experience at the university:

> It has happened to me on the university stairs. I'll be walking up the stairs and there is a white person in front or next to me and the guard says to me, "Your identification please." And I'll say, "Did you ask for identification from that white guy?" He'll say no, and so I tell him that I'm not showing him mine either and I keep walking.

Differential treatment of blacks by police and barred entry from certain spaces are among the changes during the Special Period that lifted the veil that kept racism hidden or at the very least, sufficiently subtle to be ignored or glossed over by many blacks. This is akin to Patricia Hill Collins's concept of surveillance and containment where the police essentially contain blacks away from tourist areas and other *spaces of privilege* such as the university.[25] Blacks are kept under surveillance through identification requests and reminded of the spaces in which they are not welcome or expected to legitimately occupy.

In addition to reports of being targeted by police, males were also more likely 1) to report being the focus of pejorative comments in the street, such as "tenia que ser negro"; 2) to comment on blacks being undervalued in general; and 3) to point to systemic racism. There was little gender difference between those who reported employment discrimination or being confronted with racism in their social relations. Thus black males in the sample seem to be more likely to experience racism in public spaces in their everyday lives, whereas women are likely to experience racism in private spaces such as the workplace or a home setting. This could also contribute to the higher

---

24. Vargas 2004; Vargas and Alves 2010; Alves 2016.

25. Collins 1998.

likelihood of male reporting, but on its own is a noteworthy difference in the ways that men and women experience racism.

The results for age do not quite operate in a linear fashion from youngest to oldest, but the data show when ages of the respondents were grouped into cohorts by decade of birth, there was in fact a significant relationship with some of these cohorts and an experience with discrimination. The age variable was divided into five cohorts by decade: those born in the 1990s, 1980s, 1970s, and 1960s, and the last cohort represents those born during the 1950s and any previous decade. The results show that those born in the 1970s are most likely to report an experience with discrimination, followed by those in the 1980s and then the 1960s (other cohorts did now show any significance). Those born in the 1970s and 1980s were in their teens or twenties when the changes ushered in by the economic crisis began to take hold. These respondents were old enough to experience a rise in racial profiling as well as the emergence of a new employment sector that was virtually closed to them as they began to look for work, and thus may be more likely to both recognize and experience discrimination. They are the cohorts that had to rely on the dollarized economy to support families, whereas those born in the 1960s and before built families and careers in the more stable peso economy of the 1980s. Those born in the 1970s and 1980s have had more varied experiences in their social and work lives (those born in the 1990s could not be more than eighteen years old in 2008) as well. The responses that correspond with the group born during the 1970s are based more on structural discrimination whereas those that were born in the 1990s or early 1980s mainly discussed experiences in their personal relationships or with individuals in their everyday interactions. Those born in the 1970s and 1980s are more likely to be confronted with a racialized system in their workplace, in access to certain sectors, and in practices by the state police. It would follow that the more structural experiences reported by those in the middle cohorts have a more significant influence on conceptions of racial discrimination, and observations that are connected to structural inequities are more likely to be made by people in their thirties and forties. As I will discuss in the following chapter, those that were born in the 1970s display higher levels of racial consciousness than those of any other cohort as well.

There was no relationship found between discrimination and level of education. The survey results showed that experiences were almost equally distributed among all levels of these two variables. Despite the insignificant relationship between these two variables, survey respondents shared sentiments such as "people do not like when a black person reaches a professional level" or "people are uncomfortable with someone who is black and intelligent." For the age variable, although I expected younger Cubans to be more likely to report an experience with discrimination, the data show that the youngest cohort is not the most likely to report an experience. Although this finding does not match my expectation, it does match the argument that the Special Period did have a strong influence on the commonality of discrimination.

Employment Opportunities and Black Advancement

Black opportunity, particularly in employment, is one of the most important issues regarding racial inequality and one of the least addressed issues in Cuba. The government has made little reference to the presence of employment discrimination,[26] yet many of my black interviewees and survey respondents cite the problem as significant. The lack of data makes it difficult to know the extent to which employment discrimination blocks black opportunity. In the tourist sector in particular, the disparity is so stark that awareness of discrimination is noted by most, even if only by observation. Other areas of employment, however, are not as racially exclusive, and while many mention the lack of black managers and directors in all sectors, the evidence is only anecdotal. The results according to my data are mixed: 17 percent of those that had an experience with discrimination pointed to employment discrimination specifically, and , as noted, 62 percent of those that had an experience with discrimination pointed to structural discrimination in general. In the interviews, there were a good number of interviewees who felt that employment discrimination existed, but there are also many who did not believe that blacks can be denied certain jobs because of their race. Those that did believe that job discrimination existed were all nonwhites. What is clear in the interviews I carried out is that beliefs in both the revolution's establishment of equal educational opportunity, as well as absence of employment discrimination, drove the opinions of those that did not think blacks were left out of employment opportunities because of race.

If government rhetoric promotes the idea that employment discrimination can be defined as a law that bars blacks from being hired in certain positions or sectors, it is hard to identify more subtle practices as racism. One

26. Raúl Castro's speech cited in chapter 5 is the only recorded instance since the start of the revolution.

interviewee insisted that he could place himself in whichever position he would like to be.

> I believe that black people have to better themselves, come out on top and prepare because that's the only way to have a weapon to be able to fight. I always say, if you don't put me there, I'll put myself there. They can't limit me from anything. Race can't be limiting. What can be limiting is knowledge, because the person who doesn't know anything, white, black, Chinese, is marked; but blacks are definitely marked. I'm telling you, being black and having all the necessary qualities, they still eliminate you. Imagine if you have none. If you have none of them you're even worse off because then you're *un negro imbécil, un negro bruto* [a stupid or ignorant black person] and those words are qualifying.

As this quote indicates, there is a simultaneous belief in equality of opportunity and the presence of employment discrimination, which contradict each other. Jafari Allen discusses this contradiction,where he suggests that although the playing field for blacks is not level, the strategy of believing, as the interviewee does, that if you work hard you can put yourself where you want to be, can be a strategy to "facilitate successful navigation of treacherous systems."[27] It is clear that the interviewee is aware of the barriers, and so he convinces himself that with hard work you can overcome them.

The interviewee occupies the position of director of an institution and perhaps because of his position, he is able to believe that anyone can attain his level of success, but as he recognizes later in the quote, blacks are summarily eliminated from opportunities such as his. A black engineer shared a different initial view, saying that education may be framed as a guaranteed vehicle toward success, but in fact there are barriers set to keep black access low. Moreover, without equal opportunity, blacks must work doubly hard to succeed. A *mulato* who works in gastronomy said,

> If you are black and you want to be in a high position, you have to be so good that there is no choice but to hire you. If you are black you have to work twice as hard to get a position. Tourism is even worse because they hire according to how you look. There is a certain look that

---

27. Allen 2011, 88.

managers and owners look for and often credentials are less important. That is the reason that you'll hardly see black people in that sector. What is considered a pretty face here in Cuba is not associated with black skin. When I was looking for a job decades ago, it was skills that got you in. Now it's the way you look.

The association of beauty with lighter skin was mentioned in several interviews as just one of the ways in which blacks are seen as less desirable for certain jobs. Even in jobs outside of the tourist industry, the notion that black workers have to work twice as hard and be twice as talented evidences not only barriers to acquire employment, but to retain it as well.

Social networks are also important when considering issues of job opportunity and hiring practices. A *mulato* male interviewee commented on access to CUC, pointing to the practice of gaining good jobs through personal connections.

No one really gets paid in CUC. Only those that work with foreigners. There are blacks and white in those jobs, except for tourism. If a black person is smarter than a white person then he can get in there. But what happens is that a white person will pull someone in on the side and then the black person who could have gotten in and has all the credentials, does not and is told that there are no openings. Also, there are those that pay for job openings and get in that way.

There is a conflict between what people perceive as the rules of access that support equal opportunity and what actually happens when blacks seek jobs in high positions or lucrative industries. Social connections and systematic exclusion of blacks in tourism both have an effect on black access to CUC and to employment in the emergent sector in general. Outside of this sector, it is very difficult to determine the role that employment discrimination plays in Cuba. Through survey and interview data coupled with the field data included in this section, we can at least note that it does exist. This is evidenced by representation in the most lucrative positions and the awareness blacks hold that their race is an impediment to advancement.

Barriers to black access often occur subtly where blacks may not gain employment opportunities, but it is not explicitly stated that race is the reason. It is difficult to identify such instances because they are not overtly expressed as discrimination. One interviewee shared with me a case where it

was stated quite clearly why his sister, who is black, was kept out of an opportunity because of race.

> My sister wanted to enter into synchronized swimming; she was one of
> the best swimmers. They told her that she couldn't swim with the team
> because the problem was, that sport required a special pigmentation.
> Her pigmentation did not fit with that sport. My parents did not fight
> for it and because she was young, she didn't say anything either. My
> mother is a strong revolutionary and denies that racism exists in Cuba,
> even with that experience. Since then, I have looked and I have never
> seen an interracial synchronized swimming team. Because of that
> I think that black people have a lot more to show in this society that
> we live in, but we are not given a chance. Blacks in the US for example
> have succeeded in getting their own television channel—BET. They
> have their own way of dressing, their character; Obama is black. It
> seems to me that in the struggle against racism you are far ahead.

The above interview shows that there are clear practices to exclude blacks.
Although his family did not fight against what happened to his sister, there
are no institutions that exist where they could issue a formal complaint. The
lack of an official process through which to report an experience with discrimination not only leaves blacks disempowered when confronted with such
a situation, but produces a lack of awareness about such a right. Finally, for
this family and others, belief that racism could never exist under the revolution not only inhibits people's desire to report discrimination, but can lead to
the creation of alternative explanations for racist practices.

Although the above experience may point to a particular choice by an
individual to exclude another, these kinds of practices are part of a systemic
pattern that occur particularly in the higher valued professions. A university student identified these practices by referred to a glass ceiling regarding
opportunity.

> The system can say to blacks, "If everyone can study, then there is no
> racism." Everyone has the opportunity to study and human capacity is
> not limited. Those who can do, will do. But there is something called
> a glass ceiling for us. The system determines what they want us to be.
> First, we need to be able to have high administrative jobs. But what
> are they doing about that? Nothing. The head of the ministries are all

white. And how many blacks are there to be heads of ministries and institutes? Many! But we are not there.

The statement by the interviewee discloses a crucial consequence of the juxtaposition of silence and the continuation of racial discrimination: institutions embedded with racist practices determine black progress. The glass ceiling that he refers to cannot be challenged, and thus, as he notes, those that are qualified to ascend are faced with consistent and often unmovable barriers.

Jobs in tourism, dollar stores, and banking are some of the most coveted jobs in Cuba. In a single day in Havana in 2010, it was observed that among twelve banks and 156 employees, there were fifteen black employees (9.6 percent) and fourteen *mulatos* (9 percent), totaling 18.6 percent overall. Among seven major hotels in Havana, there were two *mulatos* and one black employee in visible positions (not including the cleaning crews). In an interview with a hotel worker, he told me that there were some black people, primarily male, that are starting to appear in the service positions in hotels such as bartenders and waiters, but that there are no black managers. Even so, in a more prestigious hotel like the one where we held the interview, Hotel Sevilla, he said that it would be hard to find a black person in any position except for cleaning. Indeed, there were no black workers in the hotel except for the cleaning staff. He shared that black women and *mulatas* are primarily in cleaning positions due to the maintenance of stereotypical roles of black women as maids and because these women are not educated thus they are relegated to cleaning and dishwashing positions. Black people, he thought, are mostly living in marginal neighborhoods and do not have the same resources and social surroundings as white people. Many fall into delinquent behavior or lose interest in their studies because of their environment. Black women, he opined, are often not given opportunities to educate themselves, although education here is free, and they end up in these positions. Perhaps the most important point that he made was that while he was in school studying tourism, his black professor warned him that he was going to suffer in the tourism business as a black man and that he had to be prepared to work twice as hard to prove himself. He felt that after his internship he would be able to keep his job as a waiter because there were some black workers already in the restaurant that would support him being hired. Thus while there is a keen consciousness of the lack of black representation in the tourism sector, there is also a measure of solidarity among blacks that are there in order to help one other succeed under difficult conditions.

Interviews: Tourism

Beginning in the early 1990s, tourism became the centerpiece of not only foreign investment but of the economic revival, growing significantly each year (as much as 20 percent). The expansion of tourism was spearheaded with joint ventures and hotel construction all over the island, but primarily in Havana and Varadero. In 1990, 340,000 tourists visited Cuba and in 2014 a total of 3,001,958 visitors were received through the country's airports, bringing Cuba from twenty-third in the Caribbean to second in the region in visitors and revenues.[28] The opening of the tourism sector led to the development of new employment that currently accounts for some of the most well-paid jobs in Cuba. Work in the hotels brings tips and salaries that are considerably higher than the average Cuban salary, with some Cubans making forty dollars per day or more in tips, a two-month salary for state workers.

Much of the blame for the lack of black presence in the tourism industry is placed on the foreign owners, who, it is said, keep blacks out because they prefer whiter employees. In several interviews with Cubans that work in the tourism industry, the European hotel owners are blamed for the lack of representation. However, there are reasons to believe this is excessively simplistic. The process of hiring in the hotels is largely left up to Cuban managers;[29] while European owners can express a desire to keep out black employees, Cubans in fact are responsible for hiring decisions. In order to be considered for a job in a hotel or restaurant, Cubans are put on a list through the state employment agency (*bolsa de trabajo*) and from there are selected on a first-come, first-served basis. All of the employees that I talked with who have a job in the industry said that they work there because a friend got them the job and they did not go through the formal process. This was the case not only for hotel and restaurant workers but for taxi drivers as well, another coveted position within the industry. Moreover, when positions are open for certain specialties within a hotel, preference is given to those who already work in the hotel. The hiring process is not colorblind, as those who enter the employment list are seldom chosen for the positions. The Cuban managers of the hotels, who are overwhelmingly white, have control over the process in each hotel. The waiter interviewed earlier in the chapter who worked in one of the top restaurants in Havana was able to get his job through his best friend's father. He emphasized that had he been given that opportunity, he would not have been able to get

---

28. Caribbean Tourism Organization 2015.

29. Eckstein 2003.

a spot at a restaurant. He explained that while black people may be given the chance to study tourism and enter into an internship, they will often not be hired and are kept out of the industry.

In an important interview with two hotel managers, it was clear that foreign tastes are not the only reasons for the lack of black faces in the tourism sector.

> There isn't much of a racial issue with the workers here; there are black workers. Now to have black bosses, that's a different story. For a black manager, he'd have to come from somewhere else, Jamaica or something, or perhaps if he is really good. There was one guy here, really black, that had to go—he did not get along with the manager of the hotel. I'll tell you the truth, in a hotel like this, if the manager says that he doesn't want blacks, there won't be any. And it is not the hotel owners that hire workers—Cubans hire the workers. We did have one Brazilian manager and he was used to black people, coming from Brazil. He got here and when he saw the boss was black, he said he didn't want a black guy to be a boss and he told him to resign. And he had to resign, saying he didn't want to be the boss anymore. That's always going to happen. Whether it be Cuba, the United States, wherever it is, blacks are black and they are always seen that way. I don't look at blacks that way, but foreigners are different and don't see blacks the way that we do. I can say, "Hey *negro*, what's up," but I see him as a person.

While the managers admit that Cubans are in charge of the majority of the hiring, they maintain that Cubans are not as racist as foreigners and place the blame on these outsiders in keeping blacks out of the industry and higher positions in particular. They maintain this argument despite their admittance that there are Cuban managers that will not hire black workers, particularly for higher positions. They point to blacks having to be either exceptional or foreign to be considered for a managerial position in the industry, indirectly suggesting that this is not the case for whites. Moreover, they were quite nonchalant about the exclusion of blacks from higher positions.[30] The black workers that they referred to were in positions that were not visible to hotel

---

30. At the end of the interview one of the managers told me, "Even though you are black, we can date or go out together if you'd like." The sheer arrogance coupled with overt racism that the managers displayed were indicative of the acceptance of such behavior in general.

patrons and therefore did not have access to tips. Their final reasoning for the lack of representation of blacks in the industry offers a justification for black subordination in every country in the African Diaspora as the normal state of affairs, although they of course exhibit the ethos of anti-racialism when discussing their own attitudes.

In a restaurant in the Vedado neighborhood of Havana, a waiter described the process of keeping blacks out of the industry.

> There is a lot of racism in the field and if they don't want you there, they will find a way to keep you out. A friend of mine was doing her internship at my restaurant and little by little they started to push her out because she was black. They told her that they were pushing her out because she wasn't working well but they told me that it was because she was black and not pretty enough. They said she didn't fit the image that they wanted. "Maybe if she were *mulata*, prettier," they said. She never got hired. I know that I have to work hard and not fit into the stereotypes that they have for blacks. I am on my best behavior.

The notion that blacks are less attractive leads to the perception that they are unfit to greet or wait on tourists. This is particularly true for women, who are subject to a standard of beauty in Cuba that favors whiteness. The waiter's interview expressed the same notion that others interviewed both in and outside of the tourism industry did: blacks need to work harder than whites in order to keep their jobs and escape the impression that they do not fit into most people's stereotypical conceptions of blacks. The interviewee had to, in other words, deracialize himself to appear as far away from black, which in his mind, meant being on his best behavior. In Andrea Queeley's study of Anglo-Caribbeans in Santiago de Cuba, she argues that respectability politics as a strategy "simultaneously challeges and reinscribes the racial heierarchy and Black marginality."[31] The waiter here is using what he views as an image of respectability to keep his job and break existing racial barriers, but he also (implicitly) acknowledges that it is a performance of whiteness. Performances of blackness, on the other hand, would convey traditional black stereotypes that pigeon-hole black males into certain jobs within the sector. In an interview with a taxi driver, he noted that blacks are often not present in jobs related to tourism, but that there are many doormen and taxi drivers

---

31. Queeley 2015, 5.

that are black. He said that "taxi drivers cannot be cowards; they need to be strong," and thus many blacks can serve in that position.[32] The image of blacks as physically strong, but less respectable or attractive than whites, allows them access to jobs as doormen and bars them from positions at the front desk, or as a bartender, waiter, or hotel manager.

It is difficult to identify or document overt discrimination in the tourism sector as there are no set policies that exist to keep blacks out, either of employment opportunities or as consumers. A black employee of a hotel in Havana stated that when you begin work at a hotel you are told that the hotel does not take into account characteristics such as your color, religious beliefs, or your political beliefs. Nonetheless, employers create a predominantly white environment where those at the top rarely hire black workers. He shared,

> There are very few blacks that work in my hotel, black people like me, not *mulato*. We always have to work harder, which is promoted subtly. Although it is not said directly, it is still obvious that people see the difference between whites and others. Even though we live here, even though we live with socialism in all that we do, the racial issue always remains. To get a job in tourism you have to enter through the lotto [state employment agency or the *bolsa de trabajo*] and many tourism graduates wait to be called after their internship. Who knows how many black people are waiting in the lotto but if you look in all of the tourist jobs there are very few blacks working or getting hired. In my personal case, I've had to go beyond everyone else; I speak two languages and I'm trying to learn a third. People are always watching me and so I need those tools. People in the hotel are always evaluating the black employees and we have to be extra good. Because they don't fire you outright, but they look for the chance to indirectly make a small problem a much larger one. In general, if I recall, there are only two or three hotels that have black managers. The rest are white. That's at least in tourism.

This interviewee, much like the last, points to constant surveillance by his superiors because of his race. The surveillance is not, as he perceives it, the same kind of scrutiny that white employees receive. Blacks in the industry carry a firm awareness that they must go above what is required of their white

---

32. Despite his stereotypical characterization of the ideal jobs for black people, there are few taxi drivers in Cuba who are black.

and *mulato* coworkers to keep their privileged position in tourism. This is particularly true because jobs are not often obtained through formal procedures and if blacks are lucky enough to win a position, they must work to keep it. His description of those workers that complete their internships and then wait to be hired provides evidence that the process is not based on colorblind practices; employees know who workers are because they have completed their internships and much like the woman who was pushed out of the restaurant, blacks are unlikely to be awarded a job following the internship period.

In addition to the process of gaining employment in the industry, exclusion from tourist spaces are one of the primary ways that blacks are discriminated against. Security guards and doormen (of any racial group) often keep blacks out of hotels or subject them to questioning before entering, and police will invariably stop black Cubans who are seen with tourists or within tourist areas. Stereotyping of blacks as delinquents, criminals, or hustlers leads to increased discriminatory treatment. Tourism has in fact, heightened blacks' sensibilities about racism due to these practices. A black security guard who used to work in a store in a hotel in Havana shared his experience where the hotel had a special code that they communicated to each other when black people entered the hotel.

When I was in tourism I was in a company that was called SEPSA.[33] I started working in a hotel and they told me that there was a code for the security team that we were to use to communicate. For men we would say H [hombre] and for women, M [mujer]. One day a black guy walks in, dressed in a typical way; not bad, but what they would stereotype to be the dress of a delinquent or a *jinetero*. He was dressed more or less like me with baggy shorts and a baggy T-shirt. So the security person says on the radio, "An H just walked in with the complexion that you are familiar with." And I said, "What does that mean, that I am familiar with?" She answered, "Yes, yes, the complexion that you are familiar with." In my gut I knew what she meant. I had a conversation with the person about it and they stopped using that code while I was there. I was there for a year and so many people would come in there trying to rob merchandise, but let me tell you, they were never black.

---

33. SEPSA is the state security agency and stands for Servicios Especializados de Protección, S. A. or Specialized Protection Services.

Another black man working in a hotel shared his experiences when standing at the door with the doormen.

> When I'm at the front door with the security guards at the front, I see it happen all the time. You'll be with a group of guards and a black man will be coming and they'll go, "Who is this here?" It's the comments that they make: "We're not letting this savage in here." If a black person comes in the hotel the guards will say, "I'm gonna get him." And sometimes, black guards fall into that same game. When I complain, they give me a laugh and say, "It's not like thaaaat."

The day before this interview a friend of mine came to visit, having just been barred from entering the hotel where the above interviewee worked. He visited me visibly upset because he was unable to purchase a phone card in the hotel. The security guards told him that he was not dressed properly to enter. His wife, a *mulata*, was allowed to walk in with the same style of dress. He felt that the security guards kept him out because he was black and that his dress had nothing to do with it. The interviewee, recalling the situation, confirmed that my friend was denied entry because of his race. To avoid accusations of racism blacks are given alternative explanations by hotel workers, but it remains clear to most blacks that the racial segregation of tourist spaces is real and does not carry an explanation other than the negative associations that accompany their blackness. Those that stand at the door, police and others who surveil and control entry, have the power to segregate and subordinate without any repercussions. Blacks are systemically kept out of spaces of privilege and questioned when they attempt to challenge this racial system.

The tourist sector represents one of the most visible sectors where there is a lack of equal access to employment or equal representation. The overwhelming number of whites that work in the industry coupled with the experiences of keeping blacks out of these spaces has been difficult to ignore. In a speech in 2000 Raul Castro declared that black people should not be denied access to enter into hotels or any other location related to tourism,[34] giving credence to the existence of the practice. Nonetheless, there are those in government that will continue to deny that there is a lack of opportunities for blacks, even in this particular sector. The former head of a CDR that I interviewed shared her view on why blacks are not present in the tourism industry:

---

34. Adams 2004.

It is true there are hardly any blacks in tourism but that has its reasons and causes. There were never black workers in tourism, even before the revolution—throughout history there hasn't been a tradition of blacks in tourism. Blacks have always been interested in working in public health, education and sectors such as these—it's traditional. This is why you'll notice that there are plenty of black professors in academia—because there are no racial limits in education.

The above interviewee ignored the reality that a job in tourism is the most coveted job in Cuba, by all races. While some justifications of the disparity will be present among Cubans discussing the tourist sector, most Cubans will agree that racism is present in the industry. Indeed, all of those I interviewed, except for two, agreed that blacks were kept out of tourism, received negative treatment when entering these spaces, and that race was significant in this sector more than any other even if they differed regarding the causes or consequences. Those that denied such a practice spoke of the revolution as having solved such a problem nearly fifty years prior. It was clear for these interviewees that their attitudes regarding the revolution would not let them confront the racial realities that were clear to others.

Issues of Representation

The emergent sector, jobs that were created under the economic reforms in Cuba in the early 1990s, only constitutes one of the visible areas where black access is systematically blocked. The issue of the relative absence of black representation in socioeconomic, cultural, and political circles, however, was present well before the start of the Special Period. Racism and inequality were indeed exacerbated starting with the economic crisis, but black visibility in other areas such as the media, historical texts, managerial positions, and government positions have suffered throughout the decades of the revolution.[35] Few studies have examined Cuban perceptions of racial representation in the media, yet when asked about representation or racism in general, several of the interviewees discussed the absence of positive black images on television. Furthermore, organizations on the island that are focused on racial equality have pointed to black images in the media as a significant problem.[36] The

---

35. Ibid.

36. Organizations based on racial equality and black rights, both past and present, have outlined the increase of black representation in the mass media among their goals.

following section details interview responses regarding three areas of representation: mass media, employment, and government.

Black access to desirable employment seems to have worsened since the economic crisis as the most desired jobs are those that are connected to hard currency. These are also the jobs that are least available to blacks, and *mulatos* to a lesser degree. Racial representation within the government, however, is cited by many nonwhites in the sample as a problem that has existed well before the Special Period. As one twenty-nine-year-old male stated:

> In Cuba there is no racist system that is sustained through laws, that doesn't exist; but let's look at the system itself. Although it is changing, it used to be difficult to see a black person on television . . . it still is difficult. There are so few blacks in government. The other day they held an event on the Anti-imperialist stage. It was a political event about terrorism and a black person gave the speech. That is one of the first times I have seen that.

This passage suggests that as a black person, he is cognizant of black representation both on television and by the government. When there is a slight improvement it is noticeable by many blacks, such as the example given here. Other respondents also pointed to the introduction of a black character or a black government official that appears in the media as something that indicated a small change in black images on television. Although the issue did not appear as frequently in my survey data, problems of black representation in various sectors were communicated in almost all of my interviews with black Cubans.

Black Representation in the Media

The issue of the black presence on television was one of the issues most frequently raised during the interviews I carried out. Blacks continually pointed to the lack of black characters on television that were not slaves, criminals, or had more than a marginal role. There have been some changes made on state television to reflect a higher representation of blacks and there have also been a few programs that aired sporadically regarding the importance of anti-racist attitudes in the past few years. These programs discuss prejudice only on an individual level, but it is an improvement from the complete silence that was practiced previously. In the newscast that is shown three times daily, a black anchor was added in 2008 to the evening lineup, one of the most visible changes to the racial make-up of state television. There are also nonwhite teachers and professors that appear in the *Universidad Para Todos* (University for Everyone) programming segment that teaches college level material through television. Blacks still remain largely absent from the most popular programming on Cuban television: soap operas, primetime series, and movies. Racial scholars and activists perceive the recent change in other programming as part of the sporadic attention that race is receiving by the government to respond to the growing concern by citizens.

The recent documentary that was filmed in Cuba about racism, *Raza*, featured an artist who talked about his son not having any figures on television that look like him. In the documentary he says that he suffers trying to find people in the media or dolls that are black so that his son is not traumatized by his blackness and his features. During a discussion about this documentary, one of my interviewees, a black graduate student, said:

> Sometimes I stop and think, children always have a role model that they follow … you know, they say, "I want to be like this person." When you sit a boy, a black boy, down in front of the television, who does he want to be like? There is no visible black role model on television so what he will repeat are the same models that are in his neighborhood, which is often marginal. We don't have a Will Smith or a Denzel Washington. And look, at the end of the day they are only media figures, but you still feel represented; you can identify. That's important.

Blacks are overwhelmingly represented in musical shows as well as athletic competitions that are featured on television. These stereotypical roles can serve as a way to overlook the lack of blacks in other programming and it can also reinforce the notion of blacks possessing talent only as musicians and athletes.[37] In fact, an activist who sought to increase awareness regarding black roles on television reported that in a meeting with a television station director, he was told that blacks did not need more roles in television because they

---

37. Although blacks are represented in televised musical performances, black or African derived music is heavily marginalized by state media. Musical forms such as rumba and hip-hop are rarely featured on television and rumba is not featured on musical shows that highlight Cuban traditional music, despite its roots in Cuba's musical and religious traditions. What is considered quintessentially Cuban often does not include black cultural forms.

already have their own channel: the sports channel. An eighty-three-year-old white artist and former actress said in response to a question regarding black representation on television:

> Sometimes my daughter and I are watching a movie and there will be a black person on there dancing and singing; when black people sing, it is marvelous. The majority sing better than us and oh, how they dance!!! In the arts I think that blacks have more or less the same space as whites. There are *mulatos*, blacks; I don't even think that there is a legitimately pure white person. We are a mix, from Africa, many Chinese. We have a mix so we are more or less equal. And here blacks aren't treated the way they are in other places. And I already told you that there are blacks in the Central Committee. *Black* blacks.

By emphasizing blacks' seeming innate ability to perform well, this interviewee can ignore the fact that in other areas, blacks are largely absent. She can further justify this absence through her opinion on representation based on a discourse of mestizaje,. If we are all a mix and whites have black ancestry as well, there is no need to focus on the details of representation. Nonetheless, as is prevalent in many interviews, there is still emphasis on racial difference by describing blacks as being black, *black* or so black that their skin looks blue, which is a common reference among all three racial groups in Cuba. In the meeting referenced above with the television director, the reason given for not having blacks in roles other than sports and the arts was that their skin is so dark they do not televise well.

Despite the previous interview, I found that many of my interviewees, of all three racial groups, did recognize that blacks did not appear often on the television. A forty-year-old *mulata* complained about the roles that blacks always play in Cuban programs:

> On the television the black man is always a musician, or an athlete, or a slave!! And from slavery the idea of the black man as strong or a worker with good physical attributes still remains. That was born in the mind of the Cuban and exists today.

A nineteen-year-old white male, although very open about the existence of racism, did not seem to think that the main problem was lack of access for blacks to enter into television:

INTERVIEWEE: In the soap operas here, look for a black person. Try to find one. If you do find one, he has to be a super actor. Put simply, they eliminate themselves.

INTERVIEWER: Is the problem that blacks do not seek the opportunity or are they being rejected by that sector?

INTERVIEWEE: It's both. There are also people that keep blacks out. It's clear that it has always been that way. And there are times when blacks themselves don't look for the job because they say, that is not my world. They say, 'I'm black; my thing is baseball, or I'm black; my thing is sports.' In professional terms they don't try to meet a goal. It's either their upbringing or their own racism. In a house where everyone is black they say, no, no, no let's not study, let's go beg for money or ride our bikes or let's go to the *malecón* [boardwalk] and we'll make money that way.

Here the interviewee moves from a discussion of blacks on television to a critique of blacks in general that suggests they are lazy, they do not want to work and that they go out and perform on the *malecón* (a popular spot for tourists) or beg for money instead. Thus, while there is recognition of racism that may exist within the mass media, his stereotypical views about blacks dominate his theory about their lack of representation and advancement.

There was a high awareness among black interviewees of the number of blacks in the Central Committee and sixteen out of the twenty black interviewees named the black members specifically and complained of the lack of representation in government. It was clear through the interviews that the topic of blacks in government and television was something discussed and thought about among them quite often. A sixty-six-year-old black male was not only bothered by the lack of black presence, but he also noted that the government tries to highlight a few token blacks during their programming to create a façade of diversity.

Right here in Cuba at the university the percentage of students with those majors that lead to good jobs are white. And the majority of the university is white. And the Central Committee has like four or five blacks. Almeida, Lazo, the one from the unions, that's it. Three! On television during political events or programs they direct the camera to the blacks that are present, boom, boom, boom, one, two, three so that they come out on the television. There! Three blacks!

Similarly, a member of UNEAC (Union of Cuban Writers and Artists) discussed that the topic arose in meetings of UNEAC by black artists that felt underrepresented.

> What bothers the black population the most in general, is that there are almost no blacks on television. It happens to us on soap operas, general programs, series, even though they have tried to change that problem recently. That topic has been debated a lot in UNEAC conferences and symposiums about the mass media. It comes up because there are people in UNEAC and other organizations that are black and they become upset and because they are on the inside, they protest about it. Why don't they select the black actors? They say that it is because there are no quality black actors. But black actors are just as good so why don't they do it? The level of participation should be equal.

UNEAC is the only mass organization that consistently addresses the problem of racism in Cuba. Color Cubano was founded by members of the union and their annual conferences often featured discussions on the topic of race. When Color Cubano was in existence, one of their main goals was to increase black representation on television and in the country's history books. The members that led the organization still continue to work toward this goal despite the dissolution of the group.

Education and Government

The black presence in the Cuban government has experienced periods of increase throughout the decades of the revolution, often followed by periods of decrease or stagnation.[38] During our interviews, white interviewees would cite the number of black members of the Central Committee with pride and black interviewees would describe the same number as evidence of racism. Although each province has a set of officials that are more racially representative than the national organs of power, most interviewees pointed to the lack of national black officials. Santiago de Cuba, for instance, has an equal racial make-up of blacks, *mulatos*, and whites among their elected officials, which more proportionally represents the majority black province than

---

38. Adams 2004.

what we find nationally.[39] National officials are of course more visible on state media and were more well known among interviewees than provincial officials. As Henley Adams has outlined, levels of nonwhite representation in both the national and provincial bodies have remained below population numbers since 1959.[40] When I was in the field from 2008 to 2010, the two most prominent black members of the Cuban national government were Juan Almeida, Vice President of the Council of the State and Esteban Lazo Hernandez, Vice President of the Council of the State.[41] At the time there were two other black members of the Council of Ministers, the President of the National Institute of Sports, Physical Education and Recreation, Julio Christian Jiménez Molina, and the Minister of Labor, Alfredo Morales Cartaya. As membership in the national organs overlaps considerably, vice presidents Lazo and Almeida were also members of the Politburo (Political Bureau).

Black representation within the government structure, has been discussed at Party Congresses but remains an issue that needs to be addressed more aggressively. A seventy-year-old housewife shared her views on the lack of blacks in government positions:

No one in the government talks about race because they say that there is equality but that's a lie. I think that they should talk about the issue because it's so important. Black people can be ambassadors, we can be politicians because there are blacks who have the potential and ability. But in the government you can count—we have Lazo and now we have one more new one. Everyone else is white, white and old already! When they die, I don't know what they are going to do. They are going to have to bring in old white people from who knows where . . . I get tired of it, so I laugh.

The frustration that she exhibits is clearly not something that arose because of our conversation about race. This interviewee, as well as many others, displayed a high level of concern with how many blacks were in government, and this seemed to be the proxy with which they viewed the government's

---

39. These numbers are for the year 2016.

40. Adams 2004.

41. Juan Esteban Lazo Hernandez is now the President of the National Assembly of People's Power. He has held that position since 2013.

commitment to racism. More nuanced views of the Central Committee pointed to which positions blacks were given:

> The minister of the unions has always been black, since I can remember. That is very interesting. The minister of sports is also black. Blacks are in certain positions. Lazo is a vice president and he's black, black so he is an exception but blacks do not hold the main government positions in the provinces and the ministers are never black. What I mean is, there's great difficulty to gain access. They have always discriminated against blacks. *Always*. And history doesn't talk about that; it tells you that blacks haven't been discriminated against. But we have to continue the battle. That is clear. We have to continue the battle.

The provincial officials in Havana are primarily white and many of the black and *mulato* officials are, as the above interview suggests, not in prestigious positions. Similar to the previous interview, a thirty-seven-year-old security guard said:

> There's only one black person in the high levels of government, Lazo. Oh and the head of INDER as well is there.[42] And even Lazo, they get him to do anything that has to do with Africa. He's always traveling there or meeting an African delegation. The head of the workers is also black. But that's it. Why? There are blacks at the local level of government and those are important positions but they don't have any power and they don't make any decisions.

The problem of black representation exists at the local levels as well, but I did not have any interviewees who mentioned local government positions when they discussed issues of representation. When I asked about them, they did point to more blacks at that level, but they also noted that these officials never discussed the issue of race or racism. The number of blacks on the Central Committee and the Council of Ministers and who they are were of prime importance to my interviewees of all races.

---

42. INDER stands for National Institute of Sports, Physical Education, and Recreation.

Conclusion

Following the Special Period, the Cuban government changed their rhetoric regarding racism slightly, acknowledging that there may be some vestiges of racism left over from prerevolutionary times that they have not been able to eradicate. If the government is either correct, or successful in masking the presence of discrimination outside of individual, errant attitudes, then we should find few respondents that report having experienced racism. Moreover, respondents should attribute any experience with discrimination to individual attitudes or some legacy of prerevolutionary times such as housing or quality of life in poorer neighborhoods. We find that experiences of discrimination are quite common among blacks. Moreover, interview data shows that racist practices within the tourism industry systematically keep blacks out of the sector. In addition to tourism, there are many other areas where blacks recognize discrimination, often of an institutional nature. As I will discuss in the next chapters, the economic reforms of the Special Period, the increased surveillance of blacks, and the visible barriers for employment in certain sectors have produced a heightened racial consciousness among many. The economic crisis in Cuba has ended, yet the consequences of it remain—there is more visible racism at work that contradicts and may even threaten the racial ideology of the revolution. It is yet to be seen whether the government will act on the new forms of racism in Cuba or if it will continue a policy of silence.

8 UNCOVERING BLACKNESS AND THE UNDERGROUND

BLACK CONSCIOUSNESS

Days after Barack Obama's presidential win on November 4, 2008, the black Cuban poet and essayist Victor Fowler wrote, "I still feel alarm in my chest. Tears of pride are pooling in my eyes from a profound relief. I hear Barack Obama . . . I look at my skin, I look at my children, I cry and I smile."[1] This sentiment, expressed by many others during my time in Havana in 2008 and 2009, is a testament to the presence of black consciousness in Cuba. His election, while happening in another country, elicited conversations throughout black circles in Cuba about black advancement and black pride. These conversations, what I term as underground critiques of racial ideology in Cuba, are ubiquitous throughout the black community. The experiences outlined in the last chapter are often impetuses to the conversations. This chapter uses survey data to examine the underground critique, revealing attitudes among blacks and how they view their racial identity in Cuba.

The data in the survey allows for an analysis of how components of Cuban racial ideology influence black consciousness and identity formation. I argue that although racial democracy has been successful in creating a perception of equality and decreased the saliency of race, black consciousness continues to exist and racial identity can be significant to blacks in their daily lives. This consciousness is not just based on skin color or heritage, but the presence of racism and perceptions of being undervalued in Cuban society. Discrimination in particular heightens the saliency of race and has a direct relationship to how blacks view their own identity

---

1. Vicent 2008.

and their connection to other blacks. At the same time, racial ideology and the norms outlined in this book are paramount to how blacks view social and political realities and their racial implications. We cannot separate ideology from identity; the former has great influence on the latter, even among those that reject the dominant racial ideology.

The dimensions of black consciousness are crucial in understanding black political attitudes and identity formation. In order to grasp racial attitudes and black political thought in Cuba we have to understand not just whether or not blacks are racially conscious, but what this consciousness looks like. The first section analyzes questions focusing on three categories: self-identification, racial significance, and representation. The second section discusses the relationship between experiences with discrimination and black consciousness.

Self-Identification

In chapter 1, I argued that while the racial democracy ideology does indeed negate the importance of race as a social cleavage and racism as a societal problem, it should be clarified that it does not generate silence on racial difference. Racial categories are well defined and are used to describe, emphasize, valorize, and denigrate physical difference. Using this logic, although blacks may not take race into consideration regarding their social relations, racial identification should still remain significant for blacks. The questions in the self-identification section are as follows: 1) being black is an important part of my self-image; 2) I am proud to be black; 3) I reject the fact that I am black; and 4) being black is more important to me than being Cuban.

A person's race and physical characteristics in Cuba are a large part of self-image, whether that image is negative or positive. Although social relations seem to be based less on race, the majority of blacks in the survey felt as though race was an important part of their identity. When asked whether being black is an important part of their self-image, 81.5 percent, either strongly agreed or agreed while only 9.5 percent disagreed or strongly disagreed (see Figure 8.1). These results are not surprising and connect with my argument regarding the importance of racial identity despite ideological rhetoric that suggests otherwise.

The second and third questions in this section should show that blacks are both proud to be black and do not reject that blackness. Despite the presence of the notion of black inferiority discussed in previous chapters, there is not a dominant discourse within black communities that rejects black pride.

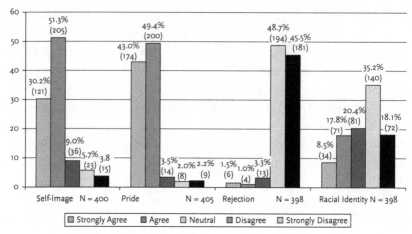

FIGURE 8.1 Self-Identification

Note: The questions read as follows. Self-Image: "Being black is an important part of my self-image." Pride: "I am proud to be black." Rejection: "I reject the fact that I am black." Racial Identity: "Being black is more important to me than being Cuban."

Rather, there seems to be among many a simultaneous pride in blackness and valorization of whiteness. Of course it should be noted that this valorization of whiteness is not something that is present among all communities or individuals. There were many in my interviews and interactions that reject Eurocentric notions completely and are prideful of black images and a black aesthetic. Thus for the second question, "I am proud to be black," 92.4 percent either agreed or strongly agreed. Similarly, 94.2 percent of the sample chose disagree or strongly disagree when given the statement "I reject being black." Responses to these particular questions are likely functions of social desirability: interviews and ethnographic research bore out more nuanced notions of self-identification, pride, and discourses of black inferiority as I have discussed throughout previous chapters.

The fourth question in this set deals with the relationship between nationalism and racial identity, which is a complex one. Racial democracy has been especially successful in creating high levels of nationalistic feelings among all races of a particular nation. Throughout Latin America racial democracy created national identities that did not include racial ties or differences.[2] In the United States the majority of blacks would be expected to place their racial identity above their national identity, due to the experience of racism and

2. Marx 1998.

the idea that that blacks have never enjoyed full citizenship as Americans.[3] Conversely, racial democracy has insisted that all races are part of the nation since the abolition of slavery. In a study conducted in Cuba, Puerto Rico, and the Dominican Republic in 2000, Sawyer et al. found that racial democracy is so entrenched that despite clear evidence of the awareness of racial hierarchies, all races in the three case studies consider themselves equal participants in the national project.[4] The article points to the role of nation building and nationalism in the dissemination of the racial democracy ideal. Taking this information into account, we would expect that few to no black Cubans would affirm their racial identity as primary to their national identity.

A similar survey conducted with ninety-six respondents in 1995 in Santa Clara, a city in the central region of the island, found that only 8 percent of blacks felt that their racial identity was more important than their Cuban identity.[5] The Sawyer et al. piece does not ask directly whether blacks place their racial or national identity first, but the high levels of patriotism among blacks suggests that national identity would take precedence or have equal importance as racial identity. While these surveys cannot claim to be representative of black Cubans as a whole, the results suggest that national identity is of high importance to blacks.

In order to test the importance of national identity versus racial identity, respondents were asked if being black was more important than being Cuban. The results were surprising in that 26.4 percent say that being black is more important than being Cuban, 20.3 percent were neutral, and 53.3 percent chose their Cuban identity as more important. Although this cannot be said for all respondents, many who chose the neutral answer expressed that to them, both identities were equally important. Thus, those that fall into the neutral category may differ on their reasons for choosing this answer and may in fact display strong measures of black consciousness.

Although a majority did respond that their national identity is more important, 26.4 percent consider their racial identity to be more important. The data suggest that racial consciousness among blacks surveyed exists at a high level for a sizable minority. We do not know how levels of consciousness may have changed due to the economic crisis, but these changes were still underway in 1995 when Hernandez conducted her survey and increased

---

3. Sawyer et al. 2004; Sidanius et al. 1997.

4. Sawyer et al. 2004.

5. Hernandez 1998.

levels of discrimination may have contributed to the higher finding in my data. Nonetheless, slightly more than a quarter of the sample is a meaningful number and beyond my original expectations considering the patterns of identity formation due to racial democracy.

Many black Cubans feel no less Cuban than white or mixed Cubans, and thus racial democracy has worked as a nationalist ideology that uses nation to trump racial identity. A black person can be aware of his or her less than equal standing in society but never connect that consciousness to being less of a citizen or separate from the Cuban nation. In other words, many blacks recognize the injustices within their country, but as the sample suggests, for the majority this does not allow racial identity to take precedence over feelings of nationalism.

Racial Significance

This section focuses on the significance of race and racism to blacks. The first two questions demonstrate the importance of knowledge of black culture and history. This particular grouping of questions serves to determine whether blacks see black history and black culture as something that is essential, particularly for their racial group. Do blacks feel especially connected to black history and culture or are they connected to Cuban culture as a whole without racial distinction? Respondents were presented with the statements 1) it is very important to me to teach my children the black/African cultural and spiritual traditions; and 2) for us (blacks) it is very important to know the role that blacks have played in the history of our country. Although there are many whites and *mulatos* that practice African religions in Cuba, they are still considered part of the black heritage. Thus, identification with the religions can be a source of racial consciousness among blacks. Both black history and spiritual traditions would be important to blacks as significant contributions to Cuban culture and history. Agreeing with both statements would not be against Cuban racial ideology, and it should follow that the majority of blacks would hold knowledge of their influence on the nation as important.

The majority of the sample, 67.1 percent, strongly agreed or agreed with the first statement showing the significance of the survival of African religions in Cuba to many blacks. For the second statement, regarding the black historical contribution, an overwhelming majority 93.1 percent strongly agreed or agreed. The significantly higher percentage that affirmed the second statement in comparison with the first is most likely due to the fact that the entire population in Cuba does not practice African-based religions, and thus it may not be important to them to pass this tradition on. The historical contributions of blacks are of much higher importance to a larger portion of respondents.

A different set of questions asked about racism in Cuba to address how blacks perceive the experiences of their group in relation to their own realities. These questions read: 1) the difficulties that blacks encounter because of racism affect me personally as well; and 2) blacks should be aware of racism in Cuban society. The first question demonstrates the level of group identity by linking the experiences of the racial group as a whole to individual experiences. In addition, the question points to a perception of racial identity as part of a unique group with a unique set of experiences. The second question addresses the existence of racism and whether blacks in particular should be aware of its existence. Those that adhere to the ideology of racial democracy in Cuba may not agree with these two statements, however those that identify with a unique black experience with racism would agree.

The first question regarding experience shows that 58.7 percent of the sample either strongly agreed or agreed while 27.2 percent either disagreed or strongly disagreed (see Figure 8.2). A majority of the sample identifies personally with their racial group and its experiences. This finding is particularly

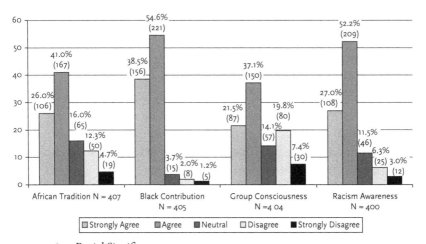

FIGURE 8.2 Racial Significance

Note: The questions read as follows. African Tradition: "It is very important to me to teach my children the African cultural and spiritual heritage." Black Contribution: "For us (blacks) it is very important to know the role that blacks have played in the history of our country." Group Consciousness: "The difficulties that blacks encounter because of racism affect me as an individual as well." Racism Awareness: "Blacks should be aware of racism in Cuban society."

important regarding racial consciousness. Although we identified that only 45% of the sample reported an experience with discrimination, there is a larger portion of the sample that is affected by racism regardless of their personal experiences because of membership in a marginalized racial group. A sense of linked fate among a majority of the sample could have important consequences for black public opinion and voting behavior should a political transition happen. Presently, it serves as evidence that a sense of black community exists because of disparate treatment of blacks in Cuba.

The second question in this section regarding awareness of racism in Cuba, resulted in 79.2 percent of the sample in agreement that blacks should be aware of the racism in Cuban society while only 9.3 percent disagreed or strongly disagreed. This finding shows that the level of awareness of racism in Cuba is quite high, which challenges the notion that the revolution had solved this problem. As a respondent shared with me while answering this particular question, "Every single black person knows about racism here in Cuba. There's no reason to have a meeting about that, everyone knows."

Representation

The issue of representation in Cuba was often discussed among both survey and interview participants as the most tangible and visible problem of racism in Cuba. Lack of black visibility in the tourism sector, on television, and in top professional positions are frequent examples given by blacks when discussing racism and how it manifests. This recognition is also juxtaposed with the ideas that 1) Cuba grants everyone equal opportunity, and 2) national identity should be emphasized over racial identity. There are conflicting messages about whether black Cubans are poorly represented, but the dominant ideology promotes the idea that all races constitute equal parts of the nation and have equal access. As a result, there are multiple discourses that travel among black circles and that constitute black public opinion. Some of these discourses reinforce the dominant racial ideology and some can discount the ideology as problematic because of the existence of racism. The questions in this section read: 1) we blacks have made notable advances; 2) we (blacks) are recognized as an important part of the culture and history of the country; 3) the African and Afro-Cuban ethical and cultural values have not been fully recognized by our society; 4) blacks should advance more in order to gain access and be visible in the different social and economic levels of the country; and 5) black representation in different levels of politics in the country is important.

The educational system in Cuba is universal but the material that students are taught often marginalizes black contributions. Blacks are largely absent from the history books and from national cultural promotion.[6] Black historical leaders, writers, and scholars are left out of the universal curriculum in schools and in particular, the Independent Party of Color is generally unknown among the Cuban population. Nonetheless, the few leaders that are highlighted in the educational system are also highlighted by the government as national heroes. Antonio Maceo, one of the heroes in the wars for independence, is one of the most featured heroes in Cuban history. Due to the national emphasis on few black figures and the invisibility of many, respondents may feel that blacks are adequately represented because there is no information to suggest that they are not. At the same time, there may also be a number of respondents that are aware of the lack of attention to many black historical figures, particularly those with higher levels of education that recognize that blacks are not properly represented. Without information about how blacks have advanced in Cuban society, we might imagine that the portion of the sample that attests to blacks' notable advances refers to only those few who are included in the historical narrative in Cuba: Antonio Maceo and Juan Gualberto Gomez, for example. As a young black artist aptly described in an interview,

The strategy has been first, trying to convince you that you haven't done anything; that blacks haven't done anything, or there are few blacks that have done something. That's the first step. When they convince you of that, which the system does with all of the young children here in the schools, you learn that the only ones that ever contributed to this country are Maceo, Gualberto Gomez, Quintín Banderas and *all* the rest are white. Second step: since you don't know that there are more, it becomes the truth and you think, "I'm represented." Between that and the media it creates a feeling of inferiority. All the cartoons are white. So you read the book, and there are four blacks that are noteworthy and ninety-six whites that are. Who do you want to be? You want to be like the ninety-six that are the majority. If there are no educational alternatives that can create some kind of conflict in the brains of young children, then everything will remain the same. And people will continue to think that they are represented.

6. Torres-Cuevas and Loyola Vega 2001.

Black invisibility is maintained with a rhetoric that promotes equality within the revolutionary and national projects so that black citizens have to look for black history rather than learn it through official channels. As a result, there are countless black writers, scholars, military leaders, and other historical heroes who are unknown to most Cubans.

Conversations that focused on racial representation in government produced responses similar to the above interviewee. A black historian expressed:

> It's as if there were a piece missing from the history. These are themes that we have to continue to analyze and work on and in some way introduce into the general curriculum. When we talk about the Republic, we talk about two or three blacks. First is Juan Gualberto Gómez and after that we don't talk about a black person until Jesús Meléndez.[7] Even after the national education policies that Fidel initiated in our revolution, there are no blacks that are emphasized. These were a set of policies that were initiated from the university. But how many black people studied at the university at that time? I believe that Almeida is the only person after the triumph of the revolution that is emphasized.[8]

In an interview with a thirty-six-year-old *mulato* truck driver, when asked about racism in Cuba the first thing that he said was,

> Our history is all white. When you learn about black people you learn about Maceo. That's it! They may put in two or three other black people and talk about slavery but we don't have any black history in our schools.

Although the survey data suggest that most blacks feel adequately represented in the country's history, there are those that disagree with that assessment. Furthermore, there were some black interviewees that recognized the lack of

---

7. Juan Gualberto Gómez was one of the foremost leaders of the struggle for black rights during the late 1800s and early 1900s. Founder of *La Fraternidad*, a newspaper dedicated to the advancement of Cubans of color, he also served as the president of the Central Directory of the *Sociedades de la Raza de Color*. Jesus Menéndez was a leading figure in the workers movement during the 1940s and served in government and as the director of the National Federation of Sugar Workers. He fought for the rights of sugar cane workers through the union and was a defender of the displacement and exploitation of farmers and workers in Cuba.

8. Juan Almeida Bosque was a prominent member of the Cuban government and part of the original expedition of men who began the military mission in the Sierra Maestra with Fidel Castro.

instruction on the Independent Party of Color. The problem is, as the first interviewee remarked, if you do not know who the major black figures are that are missing, you are not able to formulate an opinion that points to black invisibility. In a discussion with a black elementary school teacher, she said that she made a point to emphasize Antonio Maceo's role in the wars of independence because he was black, but she had never heard of the Independent Party of Color. There is a lack of awareness that drives the survey data results, such that most blacks feel adequately represented in Cuban history.

The next questions regarding black recognition contribute to evidence that when we analyze black consciousness, there is often a simultaneous recognition of racism and an acceptance of a good portion of ideological rhetoric coming from the government. The underground conversations can critique Cuban society and point to racist practices, but they also are influenced by racial democracy in many ways. A large majority of survey respondents felt that blacks were represented well by the country despite the fact that many of these respondents cited the existence of racism and discrimination. Of the sample, 81.2 percent thought that blacks in Cuba have achieved notable successes and 81.8 percent agreed that blacks are recognized as an important part of the culture and history of the country (see Figure 8.3). This second result was unexpected, as it would seem that a larger majority would recognize the

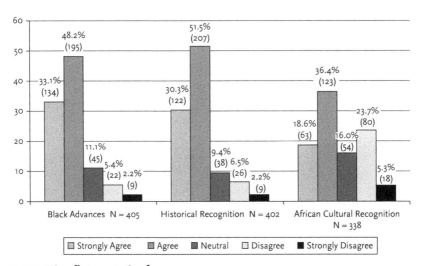

FIGURE 8.3 Representation I

Note: The questions read as follows. Black Advances: "We, blacks have made notable advances." Historical Recognition: "We (blacks) are recognized as an important part of the culture and history of the country." African Cultural Recognition: "The African and Afro-Cuban ethical and cultural values have not been fully recognized by our society."

absence of blacks in history. It suggests that the lack of alternative information leads blacks to believe that those that are highlighted are the only black historical figures that have advanced in Cuban history. Only 8.7 percent felt that blacks were not properly represented in the culture and history of the island, which points to one of the major successes of the revolution's racial rhetoric. Blacks surveyed overwhelmingly believe that they are given equal attention and are equal participants in the national project. The absence of blacks in the official history of Cuba creates ignorance about the black contribution but also creates a false sense that blacks, if not present in the history books, must not have done much (as the above interview argues). The question regarding Afro-Cuban culture produced a result where 55 percent reported Cuba does not recognize Afro-Cuban cultures and values, and 29 percent either disagreed or strongly disagreed with that statement. Cubans that practice Afro-Cuban religion should recognize that the religion does not receive the same support or attention that the Catholic Church receives in Cuba. There are no official spaces to practice the religion, only a recently created Association of Yoruba Culture, and I expected that the majority of the respondents would find that this religious tradition is not fully recognized.

The final questions regarding black representation show that almost the entire sample felt that economic and political representation was crucial for blacks in Cuba (see Figure 8.4). A large majority, 89.6 percent, thought that

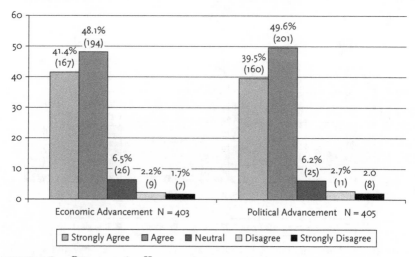

FIGURE 8.4 Representation II

Note: The questions read as follows. Economic Advancement: "Blacks should advance more and more in order to gain access and be visible in the different social and economic levels of the country." Political Advancement: "Black representation in different levels of politics in this country is important."

blacks should advance more in order to gain access and be visible in the different social and economic levels of the country. Similarly, 89.1 percent answered that the representation of black men and women in different levels of government in Cuba is important to them. The government has acknowledged that black representation in the government is an important goal and this finding supports an agreement with that goal. It also suggests that black advancement in particular is important to other blacks, showing a measure of solidarity.

Experience and Black Consciousness

In this section I analyze the correlation between racial consciousness among black Cubans and an experience of discrimination. My contention is that an experience with racism has a positive correlation with black political consciousness in Cuba. This becomes particularly true following the Special Period, as racial difference is brought to the forefront and experiences with racism increase. A considerable number of US scholars have done work on racial solidarity and consciousness rooted in experience, or the shared experience of oppression. In his book on black solidarity, Tommie Shelby calls for "a conception of solidarity based strictly on the shared experience of racial oppression and a joint commitment to resist it."[9] In his examination of US nineteenth-century racial politics, Eddie Glaude also links the commonality of experience and the marginalized position of blacks with racial solidarity that does not essentialize blackness.[10] While this project does not argue for a single black experience or political position, I contend, similar to Glaude, that black heterogeneity does not impede the solidarity built out of a shared second-class citizenship. Congruently, Michael Dawson writes, "Critical to the formation of social identity is the active process of comparing in-group and out-group members. The more differences that are perceived between the in-group and the out-group on the salient social dimensions, the stronger the group identity of in-group members."[11] The economic changes during the Special Period created racial explanations to disparities in access, widening the gap between blacks and whites. Differences in black and white opportunities, while always there, bubbled to the surface, thus making black group identity stronger as the saliency of race increased. William E. Nelson argues that black political consciousness "develops in response not only to positive

9. Shelby 2005, 11–12.

10. Glaude 2000.

11. Dawson 1994, 76.

stimuli, but negative stimuli as well. Under crisis conditions, black people will organize to challenge the main instruments of their oppression."[12] Whether or not this consciousness could develop into more than a shared group identity depends on a shared awareness of the problem and what may develop into a "crisis condition."

I do not suggest that racial consciousness arose only after the Special Period. Many markers that point to racial disparities have always been present such as the preponderance of blacks living in the poorest neighborhoods, the absence of blacks on television, and the domination of whites in high professional and leadership positions. As a noted Cuban author writes in reference to the existence of racism in Cuba,[13]

> As a black man myself, neighbor to an area next to Cayo Hueso, having lived very close to the so-called Canal del Cerro, walking through the city during my years as a bank messenger, having a son living in Veguita de Galo in Santiago de Cuba, sharing in the experiences of families and friends of my skin color, or for a thousand other reasons, despite the lack of statistics, I never had any doubt.[14]

Cuba has always operated under a system where whites control modes of access and occupy privileged positions.[15] There were always blacks that were aware of the existence of racial inequality who expressed a strong black identity before the Special Period. The economic crisis changed the scope of these privileged positions as they became the only way to thrive and possess hard currency, which determines purchasing power—a reality not seen during the revolution before this period.

As race became more salient through observed inequalities and personal experiences of discrimination, so did the importance of racial identity and the common experience among blacks. As discrimination and unequal treatment of blacks becomes a norm, grievances take on clear racial explanations and consciousness and solidarity are built through conversations of recognition. In this way, the Special Period served to further cement feelings of solidarity

---

12. Nelson 2002, 86.

13. Fowler Calzada 2009.

14. Cayo Hueso and Canal de Cerro are two of the poorest neighborhoods in Havana and are inhabited largely by black Cubans. Veguita de Galo is a similar neighborhood in the city of Santiago de Cuba in the Eastern province of the island.

15. Adams 2004.

among Afro-Cubans. The lack of available data on previous levels of consciousness and solidarity among blacks bars the possibility of an empirical analysis of the effects of the Special Period on black attitudes. Authors, within and outside of Cuba, have agreed that race came to the forefront after the economic crisis,[16] creating enough attention that leaders began to address the issue, albeit sporadically.[17] Evidence in the previous chapter suggest that this is the case as experiences of racial profiling, lack of access to jobs in tourism, and denied access to tourist spaces are all experiences that both affected blacks' notions of race and arose after the Special Period. Based on my interviews as well as the arrival of activism, art, and dialogue that express high levels of consciousness after the Special Period, I argue that a positive, affirming black identity is strengthening. The positive correlation between an experience of discrimination and notions of black consciousness serves as evidence for the changing racial dynamic influencing identity. In addition, the increasing presence of dialogue on this issue, particularly through the work of the hip-hop movement, has created a heightened awareness about the importance of black consciousness. Blacks identify a unique experience among each other and often turn to each other to reinforce this idea, which conflicts with the racial democratic notion that all Cubans are equal.

My analysis of experience does not discount the role of phenotype or heritage and ancestry—what Shelby terms *thin blackness*[18]—as religion, history, and feelings of common ancestry do factor into solidarity.[19] The common experience, the new relevance of race that has changed the meaning of blackness in Cuba, has created a stronger, more politicized identity that heritage would be unable to capture. As Manning Marable argued, racial inequalities and different experiences based on race cause blacks and whites to "perceive social reality in dramatically different ways" even in close social interactions with each other.[20] Whites can choose to see a racial democracy or a lack of discrimination due to their social position and personal experiences that lack a racial component. Conversely, it is increasingly difficult for blacks to ignore the meaning of their race by attributing experiences of exclusion to factors

---

16. Sawyer 2006; Espina Prieto and Rodríguez Ruiz 2006.

17. De la Fuente 2001c.

18. Shelby 2005.

19. Ancestry does in fact factor into Cuban conceptions of blackness more than in the United States (the focus of Shelby's study) due to the ability of black Cubans to retain the Yoruba language and religion brought over during the slave trade.

20. Marable 1995, 678.

other than race, as is common under racial democracy. As a male engineer expressed,

> There are whites that are drug dealers, that have been arrested, and that don't do anything with their lives. That shouldn't be my problem, but it is; because a black person, more than being a thief, is a black thief. A white thief is just a thief, but a black thief is always the *black* thief or the *black* man who punched someone, not just the person who punched someone. White people don't realize this and some black people don't either; the marginalization of blacks and lack of education about race produce these realities.

Whites often have a raceless character, whereas blacks are racialized against negative stereotypes. This racialization is performed by both blacks and whites and as the interviewee points out, many do not realize it simply because the topic of race is not often substantively discussed. Being black leaves many vulnerable to certain things: obstacles to job entrance in lucrative sectors, targeting by the police, being stereotyped and profiled in tourist areas. Many interviewees pointed to the racialization of black people as well as the lack of black representation in certain sectors or top positions. These testimonies often cited these examples not as personal opinions, but as something that is understood among blacks. They are part of the "hidden transcript" that circulates throughout black communities that point to the distinct black experience due to racist practices, particularly following the Special Period.

The role of experience is crucial not only in creating a different reality for blacks and whites, but in evaluating one's opinions about the meaning of race in Cuba. An experience of discrimination can often cause someone who may have ignored race in the past to begin to process its relevance in their lives and the lives of other blacks as well. In her study of black college students in the United States, Andrea Y. Simpson finds that the experience of discrimination or memories of one's first realization of racial difference "are crucial in the processing of the meaning of race in the students' individual lives and in the lives of others."[21] While conducting field research in Cuba, a Cuban of mixed descent expressed interest in filling out one of my surveys. I told him that the survey analyzes black consciousness. His response was, "Well, I'm black." When I asked him if he considered *mulatos* to be black, he responded yes.

---

21. Simpson 1998, 26.

He told me that when he would date white or lighter women in the past, he would always run into problems with the woman's parents because they never accepted him. He then told a story of traveling hundreds of miles across the island from Havana to Camaguey to visit a girlfriend who had a recent operation. When he got to the house, his girlfriend's mother asked who he was and he said that he was the girl's boyfriend. She insisted that he could not be and said that he was going to have to leave or she would call the police because her daughter doesn't have a boyfriend. When he insisted for a second time that he was her boyfriend, she said that she didn't want any black people in her house. She then sent him off to hitch a ride home with suitcase in hand. He shared that it was this experience that convinced him he was indeed black and that the separation of a mixed-race category meant little to whites. This man's repeated experiences with discrimination, the one told above being the first and most disturbing to him, reinforced his feelings of black identity and increased his cognizance of racial meanings in Cuba.[22]

Experience and Black Consciousness: Survey Data

While some find that experiences with discrimination strengthen group identity, others have found that the reverse is true: perceptions of discrimination are higher when a person identifies strongly with their racial group.[23] Sellers et al. suggest that there is probably a cyclical relationship in the United States where both can be true. I designed my model with the argument that experiences shape identity, so that those in Cuba that have direct experiences with discrimination are more likely to have high levels of racial consciousness and group identity. While I do not discount the reverse, those that have higher levels of racial consciousness are more likely to be aware of racial discrimination, the model focuses on discrimination as the independent variable because of societal changes that made experiences with discrimination more common in Cuba, a context that is much different than the United States. There were some interviewees, particularly in the hip-hop community, who pointed to consciousness raising moments that were produced through

---

22. I do not suggest here that all *mulatos*, or even blacks, embrace a black identity or develop strong consciousness because of an experience with discrimination. In the case of *mulatos*, there are some that indeed embrace a black identity and some that try to move as far away from blackness as they can. I do want to argue that experience does have an effect on how one perceives race and one's own identity.

23. Sellers et al. 1998.

alternative sources of education. The majority of my black and *mulato* interviewees, however, pointed to experiences of discrimination, particularly after the Special Period, that led them to think about what it means to be nonwhite in Cuba much more than before. The increased experience of discrimination that came with the Special Period as well as the increased saliency of race due to economic reforms, created a dialogue on race that changed the way that people view race. The new importance of blackness in people's daily lives and observances challenged the rhetoric in a way that had not happened in the previous decades of the revolution and produced new ways of perceiving race among blacks.

I have used four questions to analyze racial consciousness and group identity. The questions read: 1) black people should be aware of racism in our society; 2) the difficulties that blacks experience because of racism affect me as an individual as well; 3) being black is more important to me than being Cuban; and 4) socially, blacks should organize. The nature of the questions do not allow for the construction of a scale, as they test different components of black consciousness and would not correlate as a measure together. In other words, while there may be a significant number of black Cubans who feel that blacks should be aware of the racism in their country, few would place their black identity in front of their Cuban identity. Both are measures of black consciousness, but in different ways, or different levels. This phenomenon is due to the workings of the racial democracy ideology and the revolution in creating a single unifying identity—Cubanness—that overrides any racial affiliations.

The relationship between discrimination and group consciousness was examined using multinomial logistic regression with the four questions listed above under the assumption that the data behave as a random sample. I did not use ordinal logistic regression on this analysis because the proportional odds assumption that corresponds with using ordinal logistic regression did not hold. As shown in the previous section, the tests of group consciousness have positive results. In the analysis of racial consciousness and group identity, the survey showed that 58.66 percent of the sample felt that racism against blacks in general affects them as individuals (see Figure 8.2). We can glean from this result that not only are blacks conscious of racism affecting their racial group, but that a majority of the respondents show solidarity with other blacks as well. Respondents also displayed significant levels of consciousness in the results for the second question, where 79.25 percent of the sample answered that they strongly agree or agree with the statement "Black people should be aware of racism in our society." A respondent personally affected by negative treatment of their racial group suggests a higher level of consciousness than just displaying awareness of such treatment; however, both measures are indicative of black attitudes toward anti-black racism. Together the results show a majority of blacks in the sample possess clear feelings of black consciousness and solidarity because of racist treatment against their group.

I expect that there will be a relationship between an individual's racial consciousness or sense of racial group identity and having an experience of discrimination; as these variables should reinforce each other. Blacks would in fact feel connected to other blacks because of a common experience of racism and the distinct reality that they live in comparison to whites. To test whether an experience with discrimination is correlated to racial consciousness, I explore the following:

H1: There is a positive relationship between experiences of discrimination and feelings of group identity.

The visibility of racism after the economic crisis should reinforce the perception of different social realities due to the increase in racism in Cuba. Regardless of the number of people that display the different levels of consciousness that I have listed through the four questions, I expect to find that all four will have some significance when analyzed with an experience of discrimination. In other words, although there is a low percentage of Cubans that place their racial identity before their national identity, I still expect that an experience with discrimination has a significant relationship to this strong level of group consciousness.

In order to analyze the question "Blacks should be aware of the racism in this society," cross tabulations are shown in Table 8.1. The relationship between discrimination and the question "Blacks should be aware of racism in this society" indicates significance (p = 0.00) in that 91 percent of those that experienced discrimination either agreed or strongly agreed with this statement. All but four of the respondents that disagreed had no experience with discrimination. While the majority of the sample agreed with the statement that blacks should be aware of the racism in Cuban society, there is a clear and statistically significant pattern indicating a relationship with discrimination and the importance of awareness of racism.

Multinomial logistic regressions were done to analyze the three stronger measures of group identity: 1) the difficulties that blacks encounter because of racism affect me as an individual as well; 2) being black is more important to me than being Cuban; and 3) socially, blacks should organize. The survey

Table 8.1 Racial Consciousness and Experience with Discrimination

Blacks should be aware of racism in Cuban society	Experience with Discrimination	
	Yes	No
Strongly Agree	37.7% (65)	18% (38)
Agree	52.3% (90)	53.5% (113)
Neutral	6.4% (11)	14.7% (31)
Disagree	2.3% (4)	9.5% (20)
Strongly Disagree	1.3% (2)	4.3% (9)
Total	100% (172)	100% (211)

Pearson chi2(4) = 30.68; p = 0.00; N = 383

results examining the relationship between the first question and an experience with discrimination are significant. Table 8.2 shows that an experience with discrimination increases the likelihood of agreeing with the statement "The difficulties that blacks encounter because of racism affect me personally as well." Respondents who had an experience with discrimination are 4.90 times more likely to strongly agree with the statement and are 3.80 times more likely to agree with the statement than those with no experience with discrimination. Level of education also shows significance, with those who have a high school education or some college more likely to strongly agree or agree with the statement than those who do not have a high school diploma. Other control variables do not seem to be driving the results: occupation, gender, and age all show to be insignificant, with the exception of one age group (those in the category of thirty-five to fifty years of age) more likely to choose neutral. These results suggest that a personal experience with discrimination is connected to a sense that other blacks are affected by similar realities. In addition to that awareness, what happens to individual blacks with such an experience is joined by a sense of group identity such that they consider what happens to the group as a whole as having an effect on them as individuals.

The second question, "Being black is more important to me than being Cuban," when regressed with an experience with discrimination gives results that are insignificant. The bivariate relationship between these two variables does hold and we can thus determine that the relationship is significant because the controls in the regression analysis are not significant. As seen

Table 8.2 Relationship Between an Experience with Discrimimation and Group Consciousness

Group Consciousness	SA/SD	A/SD	N/SD	D/SD
Discrimination	4.90***	3.82**	1.40	0.55
High School	7.91**	5.43**	12.39	3.84
Some College	6.46**	4.13*	4.43	2.10
College Grad	5.60*	2.85	8.6**	1.57
Occupation	0.54	0.43	0.65	0.39
Gender	1.40	1.95	1.18	1.12
Age Group 2	1.14	0.60	0.63	0.45
Age Group 3	0.34	0.36	0.13*	0.23
Age Group 4	1.09	0.85	0.65	0.79

Note: Entries are odds ratios from a multinomial logistic regression on a categorical variable with responses of strongly agree (SA), agree (A), neutral (N), disagree (D), and strongly disagree (SD); strongly disagree is the base category. The measure of group consciousness reads, "The difficulties that blacks encounter because of racism affect me as an individual as well." A value of 1 indicates there is no predicted difference based on the independent variable. The first significant coefficient under the SA/SD column, for example, may be interpreted to mean that those with an experience with discrimination are 4.90 times more likely to respond SA to the question than those that did not have an experience with discrimination. The dummy variables for age are as follows: age group 2 = ages 25–35; age group 3 = 36–50; age group 4 = 51+.

Model χ^2 (20) = 79.51***

N = 335

*** p < 0.01, ** p<0.05, * p<0.10

in Table 8.3, 31 percent of those who answered no to an experience of discrimination also placed their national identity before their racial identity. Of those who did have an experience with discrimination, only 21 percent placed their nationality above their racial identity. Thus, the data show the common experience of discrimination to be a factor in an individual's sense of national versus racial group identity.

For the final question, the relationship between an experience with discrimination and whether blacks should organize, was analyzed with logistic multinomial regression analysis. The results were insignificant and, contrary to expectations, the desire to organize based on race does not seem to have any relationship to whether a person has experienced discrimination or not. The bivariate relationship was insignificant as well.

Table 8.3 Relationship Between Experience
with Discrimination and Group Identity

Being black is more important than being Cuban	Discrimination		
	Yes	No	Total
Strongly Agree	6.3%	2.4%	8.7%
	(24)	(9)	(33)
Agree	9.2%	9.2%	18.4%
	(35)	(35)	(70)
Neutral	8.1%	12.9%	21%
	(31)	(49)	(80)
Disagree	12.9%	22%	34.9%
	(49)	(84)	(133)
Strongly Disagree	8.1%	8.9%	17.1%
	(31)	(34)	(65)
Total	44.6%	55.4%	100%
	(170)	(211)	(381)

Pearson chi2(4) = 15.9903   p = 0.003

Conclusion

Racial democracy has an influence over the majority and affects racial atti-tudes significantly, but the awareness of racism and racial inequality pro-duces feelings of racial consciousness among blacks that simultaneously challenge the ideology. Respondents perceive that race bears little mean-ing in their social relations and despite evidence that suggests otherwise, a large majority of those surveyed feel that they are equally represented relative to whites in the history and image of the nation. This is particu-larly revealing considering the relative youth and higher level of education within this sample. Despite this finding, there are complexities in ideolog-ical influence on blacks. While relationships are seen to be colorblind by a large majority of respondents, they also recognize that race is a consid-eration for whites in their relationships with blacks. There are clear con-tradictions in how race is believed to affect personal relationships where the presence of racism is recognized among individuals alongside a general perception of racial harmony.

Respondents do not, as a majority, place their racial identity before their national identity. The overwhelming tendency to feel Cuban is more important than being black (53 percent versus 27 percent, with 20 percent choosing neutral) evidences the influence of racial ideology in Cuba over identity formation. Racial ideology has succeeded in reinforcing national identity over racial identity so that for most blacks, nation trumps race. Respondents who were surveyed represent on balance a somewhat younger and more educated segment of the Cuban population. The survey disproportionally captures Cubans who were born after the revolution and those under thirty-five years of age, and thus grew up during the Special Period. The exposure of this younger cohort to the revolution has been much different when compared to those over thirty-five. One would expect that their vision of revolution would also differ due to the economic crisis, the increase in inequalities, and the economic difficulties that Cubans experience due to the dual currency. Despite this difference, there is still a large majority of the sample that holds national identity before racial identity and that sees themselves as equal participants in the revolution and as equally represented by the nation. The dominant ideology regarding race is clearly still powerful among the younger population.

Nevertheless, there is evidence in the sample that a sizeable percentage of blacks do regard racial identity as most important in their lives. Through responses about experiences with discrimination, my research shows that while blacks continue to be victims of harassment by the police while they continue to be shunned from jobs in the lucrative emerging sector, and while there are significantly low levels of black representation in high positions both within the government and throughout different employment sectors, they see their race as an impediment to their own individual opportunity and advancement. The importance of how Cuban society has changed for blacks following the economic crisis cannot be understated. There is limited data to test levels of consciousness prior to the Special Period, but my interviews, conversations, and observations with blacks suggest that the meaning of race, and in turn identity and consciousness, has indeed increased during the last two decades creating a common experience of blackness in Cuba.

The Special Period did not debunk the ideology of racial democracy; rather, based on this data, I would argue that its legitimacy has been challenged by the part of society that identifies its fallacies. The norms that guide racial democracy continue to strengthen the ideology despite the presence of racism: respondents can acknowledge the existence of racism and display high levels of consciousness, but still believe that racism is only a matter of individual attitudes, or that their race has no affect on their social relations or experiences. There are clear contradictions in how blacks view race and politics that are driven by the differences in ideology and reality. The chapter shows that ideology can be challenged and embraced simultaneously and in the case of Cuba, racial consciousness cannot be defined in dichotomous terms. There are many gray areas where racial democracy is infused into racial attitudes producing distinct representations of consciousness and solidarity.

9 THE SEEDS OF A BLACK MOVEMENT?

RACIAL ORGANIZING AND THE ABOVE-GROUND MOVEMENT

A black scholar shared with me, in 2008, that the Special Period was the best and the worst thing to happen to black Cubans. He said this because while it is true that the crisis hit blacks the hardest, the political opening offered a space for dialogue on the problem of racism, a space that was virtually prohibited before this period. In addition, the opening allowed for the practice of Afro-Cuban religions, a cornerstone of black culture, expression, and solidarity in Cuba. The racial inequalities, most visible due to lack of access for blacks to work in the new emerging sectors, quickly became apparent to many and uncovered the racial problems that laid dormant in Cuba since the start of the revolution. This chapter will show that alongside the worsening of racial inequalities and the experience of racism for black Cubans in particular, a new black politics has emerged in Cuba. The "worst" consequence of the crisis, as the scholar termed it, has allowed for the best: racial consciousness and solidarity among artists, scholars, and activists that serves, albeit gradually, as a challenge to the previous approach to racism in Cuba carried out by the state.

The opening that has been offered by the state for racial dialogue has been a careful one that includes only those elites already linked to mass organizations or unions. Confining the above-ground critique and expression to a select few ensured that the growth of civil society would not undercut state legitimacy or provide a catalyst for a strong anti-racism movement. Among those that have been granted a space for expression, objectives that call for emphasis on racial inequality and representation continue to be communicated within the revolutionary framework. In other words, those who do not seek to alter the socialist system but rather to support and improve it have communicated much of the criticism that has been introduced in Cuba, especially pertaining to race and racial discrimination. Members of the communist party often author academic works that have called for more democratic representation, less inequality, and a more open dialogue concerning disparities.[1]

In addition to academic and artistic production, these same actors have begun to formally organize, often convening to discuss issues of race and possible courses of action to increase national dialogue on racism and black representation. Groups calling for an end to racial discrimination and an emphasis on black representation and culture have gained considerable legitimacy with the Cuban government.[2] The first such group, Color Cubano, arose out of debates concerning racial issues among members of the state-sponsored Unión de Escritores y Artistas de Cuba (UNEAC). A second group, La Cofradia de la Negritud,[3] was founded in 1998 and was revived in 2009 when scholars that had formerly been involved with Color Cubano joined the organization.[4] A third configuration, the Cuban chapter of Alianza Regional Afrodescendientes para América y el Caribe (ARAAC), stems from work across the African Diaspora. Until now these groups and other activist efforts have had a space to meet and debate, but have either not made specific recommendations to the government or, if they have, their recommendations have not been recognized or implemented. It remains to be seen whether future recommendations or proposals will 1) include demands regarding structural inequalities rather than a plan to combat racial prejudice, and 2) will be given serious consideration by the state.

This chapter highlights what I term the above-ground component of racial activism and consciousness in Cuba. I discuss three of the organizations that have emerged out of the political opening and the increased tolerance of a discussion of racism. The organizations highlighted operate in La Habana and represent three different configurations at various points in time since the Special Period, but membership in these organizations has been similar. There is a consistent group of academics, writers, and artists that can be found

---

1. See Hernandez 2003 and Morales 2007.

2. It could be argued that this legitimacy is predicated on the fact that these organizations are not mass organizations and their debates do not leave the confines of their meeting spaces. Thus should they try to expand the dialogue, they would most likely be rebuked by the government.

3. The group's name translates to Fraternity or Brotherhood of Blackness.

4. Color Cubano ceased to exist in 2009, although its founding members continue to work on the issue of racism in Cuba.

in the leadership and membership of each of these organizations; racial activism in La Habana constitutes a fairly small set of actors.[5] In addition to elite activism, the hip-hop movement has been at the forefront of racial expression and continues to promote messages of black pride and racial consciousness. Their attention to these issues allows for the dialogue to move beyond elite circles and reach a wider audience. They occupy a critical space in the production of racial messages and consciousness raising in Cuba. Finally, I will discuss public opinion on racial organization in Cuba, arguing that there is great potential in Cuba for a civil rights organization. Survey and interview data suggest that should there be an opportunity given for ordinary citizens to act collectively against racial discrimination, many blacks would participate in and support such an endeavor.

Organizational Activity

In 1993, members of the Union of Cuban Writers and Artists began to critically discuss the representation of Afro-Cubans in the mass media in Cuba. The complaints of the group dealt with both the stereotypical portrayal of blacks as domestic workers, entertainers, or criminals as well as the more typical absence of blacks in most Cuban television shows and movies. The group of intellectuals then moved beyond just representation and began to discuss issues of discrimination and unequal access barring Afro-Cubans from positions enjoyed by whites. Out of these debates grew the group Color Cubano, initially a forum created to discuss members' concerns regarding racial disparities. The group's stated purpose was to open a dialogue surrounding racial identity and racial discrimination that according to a founder, Gisela Arandia, should begin within the academic circle. More specifically, the organization's intention was to "to carry out an intelligent debate in present-day Cuban society regarding the manifestations of racism to the degree that they constitute a factor that impedes the complete (or full) consolidation of determinant factors of social equality."[6] Their projects included the only affirmative action project in Cuba's history to address the issue of housing disparities; a push to increase positive representation of Afro-Cubans in Cuban television

---

5. In 2016, after a series of incidents dealing with racism on the island and following President Obama's visit to Cuba, these actors have expressed the need to create concrete proposals that would have an effect on the population as a whole and that seek to address racial inequality more comprehensively (Abreu Arcia 2016).

6. Arandia 2005.

and cinema; and, lastly, an articulation of the need to transform primary and secondary school texts and materials to reflect not only Afro-Cuban culture and history, but the topic of race as well. Although the organization no longer exists, its leadership continues to work on these issues with the Cuban government, albeit with limited success and attention by government officials.

The first project put forth by the organization, named Project California, dealt with the housing dilemma in Cuba. The poorest housing developments in Cuba, *solares*, are occupied primarily by Afro-Cubans and house many Cuban families at once, often in decrepit conditions with community bathrooms and kitchens. Gisela Arandia, the leader of Color Cubano, chose the *solar* named California as a pilot project of what she called affirmative action. Funds were acquired from the government to renovate the *solar* so that each housing unit received its own kitchen and bathroom. In addition to the renovations, programs focusing on health care, black cultural awareness, computer programming, and job training were also implemented for the residents. The project has proved successful; however, the process to acquire resources was complicated by the government's slow response and willingness to fund the project. State responsiveness to these projects is crucial and will determine whether other similar projects can be carried out.[7] Strategically, the Cuban government should easily accept an endeavor such as Project California as the focus is not directly on race, but rather on housing, an issue that Fidel Castro has spoken about publicly.

The Cofradía de la Negritud declares itself to be an organization dedicated to social activism with the goals of increasing consciousness among civil society and the state of the growing racial inequality in Cuba. They also seek to promote the advancement of black Cubans both economically and spiritually within Cuban society and to work to ensure attention to the defense of black civil rights in Cuba. The group points to the strong racial component that is associated with the increase in economic inequality brought on by the Special Period in that blacks more often occupy the group of have-nots, whereas those with more access to hard currency are predominantly white. La Cofradia also points to the lack of action that the government has taken on the matter of racial discrimination and inequality and argue that the lack of attention to the problem since 1959 has caused black Cubans to lose too much time. The group's goal is to give a voice to blacks that have had the common experience of discrimination or have been blocked from their personal

---

7. As of 2015, there have been no advances on a similar project.

aspirations because of the color of their skin.[8] While it remains to be seen what space the group will be given by the state, the group has recently written letters to government officials outlining their goals and requesting attention to the matters listed in the group's official documents.

The Regional Alliance of Afrodescendants in the Americas and the Caribbean was founded on May 20, 2013, the same day of the protest of the Partido Independiente de Color that led to their massacre in 1912. The Cuba chapter of the organization arose after various meetings and exchanges with members of ARAAC throughout Latin America. Although much of the organizational activity that has occurred in Cuba was after the political opening of the Special Period, the timing should not be separated from the overall increase of Afro-Latin American activism in the last years of the twentieth century until the present. The ideas and inspiration for many of these groups in Latin America are drawn from each other in important transnational exchanges about blackness, civil rights, and racism in the region. In Cuba, ARAAC has organized various debates, events and panel discussions on the issue of racism.

The organizations dedicated to the issue of racism have indeed advanced the dialogue regarding racial disparities and discrimination, yet they also represent only a small sector of the island, the intelligentsia. Membership has not been extended to the general public, and although they are welcome, ordinary citizens are generally not present during their forums and meetings are not widely advertised. It can also be speculated that the group receives the support (or tolerance) that they do from the state because their grievances have not been widely publicized and they have not grown into a large-scale organization. One of the scholars who write on racial discrimination in Cuba expressed a similar concern for the effectiveness of scholarship and debate:

What happens in Cuba, and all over, is that we get frustrated as scientists because above all, when we produce these studies we meet with party officials. We are trying to get them to become familiar with our results and what we are doing on a daily basis but they don't care to read any of it, study the results, or take any kind of action. There are a million things that can be done, but it's not in our hands. We can continue to work and debate and make small community contributions

---

8. Taken from documents distributed by the Cofradia de la Negritud in 2008.

but the results are very small. There needs to be a policy that addresses the problems of racism and changes how our children are educated.

Many of those that organize in Cuba express the sentiment that the revolutionary government is in a unique position to create policy that can attack this problem directly, as they have done with many other social problems. The battle of ideas as a set of campaigns to address societal issues has never focused on the subject of racism and discrimination. The structure of the political system in Cuba allows the government to control the information that is disseminated to citizens, and the state largely defines which issues are of national importance. State control of the media and its intimate connection to organizational activities provide for a unique opportunity to promote a racial debate and policy initiative not found in other countries in the region. Nonetheless, the dialogue among this small group of actors continues with the hope that eventually there will be some action taken.

It is difficult to overstate the importance of the freedom of an organization to make claims regarding racism while remaining in the government's good graces. Prior to the Special Period and the subsequent political opening, a group making such declarations did not and could not exist. These organizations are not only a vehicle for dialogue and action, but serve as a voice for the Afro-Cuban communities. As one of its members shared with me,

> You ask me what I want (and I know that there are black people that agree with me), what I want is to empower. How are we going to organize the participation and the empowerment of the black population? Anything else doesn't interest me. When I go to the Central Committee I don't want the black person there to be the one at the door or the one serving tea. When I go to an office I want black people to be there too. I want to see black people in the companies, the ministries. We have to empower each other because that is the only thing in the path toward community strength. Power won't be given to anyone.

The elites that are part of this black counterpublic speak for an underrepresented space, advocating for a sector of the population that has been previously subsumed into other spaces. At the start of the revolution, various sectors were given representation in order to communicate their needs and work to improve conditions within their own communities. Organizations such as the Confederation of Cuban Workers, the Federation of Cuban Women, and the Federation of Cuban Students all represent sectors of the population which have specific needs, purposes and demands. Afro-Cubans have all been members within each federation, but have not been given an outlet for the pursuit of their own progress as a group. While it is difficult to obtain evidence regarding possible discrimination against blacks within the state federations, any claims based on racial identity are stifled. Therefore while no organization can represent all of the black community, these groups are communicating a new voice and lifting the silence regarding race.

Hip-Hop

The musical pioneers of racial expression in Cuba can be found within the hip-hop movement. Rappers have taken on racism and black consciousness in their songs, making hip-hop a form of resistance and a significant part of the above-ground critique of racial ideology in Cuba. Those who are part of the movement are representative of all races, but the majority (as well as the majority of its followers) are black, and the music, while not racially exclusive, is considered in Cuba—as in the rest of the world—to be black music. Rap groups take on many of the social ills that Cubans experience and often serve as a voice to the marginalized embodying the early hip-hop in the United States that served as a way to raise consciousness about such issues in its expression of blackness and the experience of poverty.[9] Cuban hip-hop does not enjoy the following that US hip-hop has garnered throughout the world and is a small movement as compared to other musical forms in Cuba that have national recognition such as salsa, rumba, and lately, reggaetón. Nonetheless, its presence as a strong critique of racial ideology in Cuba is a crucial one.

Hip-hop in Cuba is unique in its position because it operates with the support of the state, yet often its lyrics contradict state ideologies, particularly regarding race. It is perhaps because of this that the state has tried to downplay the draw of hip-hop among blacks. Although hip-hop is seen as a black cultural form in Cuba, state support of the music can lead to a different characterization. In honor of the Rap Festival in Havana in 2003, *Granma* published a piece titled *Todo Sea por el Mestizaje* ("Everything Will Be for *Mestizaje*"), which implied that mestizaje was a fundamental value of the movement. The author declares the goal of rap to represent Cuba's racial mix, rather than issues of marginalization or something that is primarily black or Afro-Cuban. The article goes on to say that "today we talk about

---

9. Ards 2004.

Latin Jazz, because the meeting between that African-American musical form and Cuban music was founded based on a dialogue of borrowing and interrelationships. Soon, I am sure that we will talk about Cuban rap with the same force insofar as we know how to protect the diversity of our *mestizo* (mixed race) profile."[10] De la Hoz is explicitly moving away from blackness when discussing the image of hip-hop and imposing the dominant ideology of Cuban mestizaje. Like Latin jazz, Cuban rap comes from a black musical tradition. Despite these characterizations or the work of ideology to mute black affirmation, hip-hop continues to be a musical form that both expresses and attracts black consciousness.

The state supports hip-hop music through the Agencia Cubana de Rap (the Cuban Rap Agency), created in 2002 as an umbrella organization to promote and provide an official affiliation for rap groups on the island, as well as the Asociacion Hermanos Saiz (AHS). The Cuban Rap Agency was created as rap gained more popularity and drew significant crowds for their concerts, and serves to support the movement and grant them space to flourish and perform. The role of both institutions is important in that they provide a space and equipment to perform, a resource that is not only significant for the music's visibility but because without institutional affiliation or support, groups cannot go on stage or organize in public spaces. The agency is currently run by those who are involved directly with the movement; however, its beginnings have been criticized heavily as its leadership was made up of people who had no previous knowledge of the music or the movement. The agency gives the space to groups to hold regular concerts, produce music, and provide other support in the professionalization of these groups. Their annual event, the Hip-hop Symposium, is attended by rap groups and artists from all over the island and hosts international participants as well. The symposium is made up of workshops, panels, and performances and with the leadership in the late 2000s, also held a workshop on racism and other issues of race and identity. The race workshop in particular gave participants a chance to both hear activists speak about racism and identity in Cuba and discuss it through stories and commentaries on the issue. The workshop served as a space to share opinions and increase awareness among the symposium's participants. In addition to those who work with the hip-hop movement, artists were invited who work on racial issues and the two concepts, rap and race, were closely linked throughout the symposium.

---

10. De la Hoz 2003.

What is unique and surprising about many of the hip-hop artists is their collaboration with many of the academics who are currently involved with racial issues. In many of the debates that I attended sponsored by Color Cubano, rappers and hip-hop producers were also in attendance to both listen and speak on their role in creating dialogue and awareness about race. In this sense they are very much in tune to the challenges that the possibility of racial policy confronts in the face of racial democracy. Thus their message is a clearly a political one, as communicated by a hip-hop artist:

First, I am. After being me, I project myself. I recognize myself as Cuban. I'm Cuban, very much Cuban, but I am very much black. And I'm black first in order to be Cuban. Racial democracy definitely affects consciousness. It also has to do a bit with the opportunities that came at the start of the revolution—black people experienced a betterment of their lives. So many like my parents see through the eyes of the revolution. I understand that. I am also very revolutionary. But perhaps we are more critical when it comes to analyzing certain things because I do not think that being a revolutionary and being passionate means being blind. The revolution is a process and you have to revise it every day.

Through this quote, one of the members of the hip-hop movement recognizes that in order to be politically effective, one has to be both critical and racially conscious. Here, much like in the United States, racial consciousness is connected to political ideology and how one views the role of race in relation to blacks as a group.[11] The notion of prioritizing racial identity over national identity is not a common one; it is one that may have growing popularity, however, particularly among the hip-hop movement and its supporters.

Hip-hop's role as a voice for black identity has a similar role to hip-hop in other parts of the world in its contribution to battle black invisibility. On hip-hop in the United States, Bakari Kitwana writes, "Rap marked a turning point, a shift from practically no public voice for young Blacks—or at best an extremely marginalized one—to black youth culture as the rage in mainstream popular culture."[12] Black Cuban artists have the task to bring to light continued black marginalization, pride in black culture and the

---

11. Dawson 1994.

12. Kitwana 2004, 27.

importance of consciousness. The artists navigate a sensitive political terrain, but many express themselves as revolutionaries wanting to expand the national image and the national discussion on identity. Roberto Zurbano, a scholar intimately involved with the hip-hop movement in Cuba, writes that hip-hop artists express themselves "assuming the emancipatory tradition of the Cuban Revolution and critically evaluating reality, including an analysis of and emphasis on race in Cuba's historical and cultural discourse."[13] In their treatment of black identity, they are essentially pushing a discourse that seeks black inclusion. The invisibility that black cultural expression and the black historical contribution have in the dominant Cuban narrative extends to the colloquial image of race as well. As Tanya Saunders argues, hip-hop groups have "contributed to the reemergence of black identity politics in Cuba" and they have consciously taken on the role of consciousness raising among black youth on the island.[14] The group Obsesión, for example, released a song titled "Calle G" that called for the destruction of the monument of former president, José Miguel Gómez, calling him an assassin for his leadership role in the massacre of 1912.[15] The song sought to not only protest the monument, but to raise awareness regarding the Partido Independiente de Color and their violent eradication in the early 1900s.

Rappers are pushing the discussion of racism and the relevance of black identity. Even more than being placed in an inferior position, blacks are often left out of the narrative completely and issues of race do not arise.[16] As such, black issues remain invisible and as rappers uncover these issues, they are raising consciousness among blacks. As Tricia Rose argues in *Black Noise: Rap Music and Black Culture in Contemporary America*, the process of creating a counternarrative for hip-hop is "about a carving out of more social space, more identity space. This is critical to political organizing. It's critical to political consciousness."[17] At a hip-hop concert in Cuba the typical audience is a

---

13. Zurbano 2009.

14. Saunders 2012, 43.

15. Calle G, or G Street, is also called Avenida de los Presidentes and features monuments of prominent presidents such as Salvador Allende and Simón Bolivar. The song that the Obsesión wrote states, "What happened to this country's memory? I don't know about you, but we are not represented! For me it's clear that racism is being glorified." Later they say, "Knock it down! It's Urgent! For the Independientes!" The song ushered a debate among activists in Cuba and produced an important public conversation regarding symbolism, history, and racism.

16. Mills 1998.

17. Rose 1994, 314.

young, black audience that follows the music not just for music's sake, but as a political statement as well. As the artists make statements about black pride, audience members raise their fists in the air, identifying with the message. Many rappers wear clothing that highlight global black leaders and contain messages of black liberation.[18] In this way rappers are creating and reinforcing a consciousness among a critical group of Cubans. The then associate director of the Cuban Rap Agency expressed,

> There were people talking about the issue of racism before the rap movement, but no one ever said the things that the rap movement did in the way that we did. No one had been as effective in communicating this issue. Academics have done work on this but it stays in a very small circle of intellectuals. The rapper talks to the people the way the people understand it. We speak the language of the street. We learned from these intellectuals, but then we translated it for everyone else. Now there are more people talking about the problem, mostly young people. When the exchange began with the hip-hop movement and young people it was like we were educating people, making them literate.

Although hip-hop in Cuba has not reached the popularity that it has in the United States, it has reached a core group of young people that are responding to their message of black pride and unity. Their following evidences a need among the black communities of Cuba to both speak about the black experience and challenge the dominant ideologies regarding race in Cuba.

By becoming part of the Cuban Rap Agency, Cuban hip-hop groups have negotiated (or have been granted) an official space, although they still occupy a marginalized cultural position. Despite the support of the state, blacks still are not part of the public sphere because they are not recognized as a cleavage within the Cuban nation that may have a special set or sets of interests. They are not afforded the space that other organizations are afforded because racial affirmation has been dismissed as divisive in the past. Moreover, there is still considerable difficulty to garner the resources to record a CD for all hip-hop artists.[19] Their relationship with the state, for this and many other reasons, has varied throughout the existence of a hip-hop movement in Cuba. While

---

18. Saunders 2012.

19. A significant accomplishment of the movement was the publication of the magazine *Movimiento*.

some would argue that hip-hop's affiliation with state organizations represents government cooptation, there is reason to believe that there is more nuance here.[20] In an interview with a hip-hop artist, she shared with me that indeed there have been several times where government officials have asked for the group's lyrics before they perform, but she has always denied the request. In addition, there are several hip-hop artists who were in leadership positions at the Cuban Rap Agency during my time in Cuba from 2008 to 2010. It can be argued, however, that different institutions tolerate different levels of state critique. During a trip in 2010, the group Los Aldeanos performed in Havana under the support of the AHS. The performance was a groundbreaking one for Cuba because Los Aldeanos were particularly critical of the Cuban government, so much so that they were not afforded official spaces to perform in Cuba until that concert. Thus the relationship between the state and hip-hop music is complex and ever-changing. What can be argued for the purposes of this book is that many of the artists, regardless of their level of critique of the Cuban government, are carving a space not only for the black voice, but for black existence. They argue for the relevance of the black voice as opposed to just the Cuban voice and challenge notions that have always been dominant within the public sphere and in this way serve to change the discourse.[21] The groups are part of the break in the silence so they are negotiating a new place within these dominant channels by saying that it is necessary to talk about blackness, debate about it, and reaffirm it.

Elites who are writing about and debating racial issues cannot get their message to the masses, and consequently hip-hop artists are occupying a privileged space. In addition to their shows, groups have begun to appear on television recently, albeit sporadically. A hip-hop music video for the song "Los Pelos" ("Our Hair") by the group Obsesión, for example, was shown on Cuban state television for the first time in 2010. The song says,

> *Pelo suelto y carretera, mira,*
> *¡No hay desriz!*
> *Me di cuenta que pa' que*
> *Si yo no naci así*
> *El hombre que me quiere me quiere como yo soy*
> *Llevo el Afro adonde quiera que voy*

---

20. Baker 2005.

21. Pough 2004; Neal 2004; Pardue 2008.

Hoy mi naturaleza rompe patrón de belleza
Que no me vengan con esas de que pa' lucir más fina
¿Hay que plancharse la cabeza pa' verse más femenina?
Óyeme, no, nananina mis códigos determinan
Coro: Pa' arriba los pelos, que crezcan los drelos.
Al que le guste bien y al que no, también.

Hair loose, I hit the streets
Look, there's no perm!
I realized for what?
If I wasn't born that way
The man who loves me loves me the way I am
I wear my afro wherever I go

Today my naturalness breaks the norms of beauty
Don't come at me saying I need to look more refined
You have to iron your hair to look more feminine?
Listen to me, no, my codes determine
Chorus: Let's celebrate our hair, let the dreadlocks grow
whether they like it or not

It should be noted that such a message has never appeared on Cuban state television and although its presence may have been an isolated choice by television personnel, it does not discount the importance of what the video represents—a chasm with mainstream programming and rhetoric. Obsesión's emphasis on hair challenges the Euro-dominant aesthetic that is shown clearly in previous chapters, and represents a new discourse in Cuba that highlights African Diasporic pride.[22] As Derek Pardue writes, "Hip-hop is a process of developing often for the first time, and empowered sense of self . . . a radical break from a dominant logic, that is the system. In this manner, hip-hop is a discourse of hegemonic critique."[23] Many of these groups see it as their responsibility to bring this dialogue out into the open and although they describe themselves as revolutionaries, they also acknowledge the lack of attention the government has given this issue.

---

22. Zurbano 2009; Fernandez Robaina 2005.

23. Pardue 2008, 27.

In an interview with World Focus, the hip-hop group Anónimo Consejo expressed that,

> The social and political connotation in hip-hop lyrics and the confrontation within our society can bother or offend some. But I believe that there are things that have to be faced and stated no matter how uncomfortable.

They go on to say that,

> We're protesting this because something is happening. Sometimes people hide it saying that there's no racism in Cuba or there is racial prejudice in Cuba. As people we have suffered racism in our lives; we've been discriminated against for being black, we've entered places and we aren't attended to, or in the street the police bother us more than they would a white person because of our way of walking, talking and dressing.[24]

Although they no longer perform together, Anónimo Consejo was one of the first to talk publicly about the Independent Party of Color in Cuba, and their themes were centered on the black experience and black affirmation.

Hip-hop promotes an image and form of expression that acts counter to what is accepted in the mainstream not only through music, but through other cultural markers as well.[25] In Cuba hair, dress, and overall image express a certain kind of message that is not new to hip-hop, but is new to Cuba. The use of the afro and dreadlocks and clothing that is associated with hip-hop all speak to the message of blackness, something that is not widely celebrated as an acceptable image.[26] As Sujatha Fernandes writes, "For Cuban rappers these styles are also a way of exhibiting their cross-national identifications, of asserting a collective sense of black identity in contrast to the racially integrative program of the Cuban state.[27] Yet more than that, donning markers of blackness in Cuba is a risk in that it makes you a target of negativity and anti-black stereotypes. As one young black male Cuban said,

---

24. World Focus 2009.

25. Rose 1994.

26. Saunders 2015.

27. Fernandes 2006, 128.

Black expressions, a beard, an afro, dreadlocks, you see a little bit more of that because of the artists, but it is still looked at negatively here. When I first started wearing an afro people would stare at me and call me crazy on the street. When I get on the bus, people look at me strangely.

Many blacks express their politics through dress and more so, through hair. Afros and dreadlocks are a marker of black politics and diasporic solidarity, even as these styles are marginalized, stereotyped and targeted by authorities such as police officers. Thus it's not only an expression of blackness, it's a direct affront to the norms of Cuban society. Blacks, through their very appearance, take social risks that are both purposeful and political.

Hip-hop, the small organizations that I have discussed, scholars, and artists constitute the majority of the above-ground dialogue regarding racism and black consciousness in Cuba. The following section discusses the potential for an organization based on race in Cuba based on interview and survey data.

Organization: Survey Data and Interview Data

There are countless examples of places and events where one can observe clear evidence of black consciousness in Cuba. Yet if hip-hop, art galleries, and elites spaces are the only public expressions of blackness and the problems of racism, we cannot make any assumptions about public opinion regarding potential mass organizations that would address such issues. The absence of institutional support for the struggle against racial inequality coupled with the taboo nature of discussing racism may have a particular influence on how Cubans view organizing on the basis of race. Moreover, the lack of a black movement in response to racism and racial inequalities can be used as evidence of low levels of black consciousness in Cuba and in Latin America in general. It can be argued that if race is not a salient factor in black lives, there would be little need to form any organization based on racial identity. Moreover, an organization based on race has been framed by the government as unnecessary at best and divisive at worst. Two questions on racial organizing were asked to determine how blacks view the possibility of a black organization. The first statement asked respondents to give their opinions on the statement, "Socially blacks should organize." The adjective "socially" was used rather than "politically" as the revolution bans any organization based on race, and thus opinions on political organizing would be influenced by possible consequences by the government. In other words, it would be impossible to parse out those who disagree with the statement based on their feelings of about race and identity and those who do not want to face any state persecution. Moreover, some would disagree with a statement about political organizing only on the basis of its illegality, rather than their personal opinions on the need for it in Cuba. The second question reads "Black people in support of a black organization would be just as racist as whites that exclude blacks."

As seen in Figure 9.1, 60 percent of respondents say that blacks should organize, 29 percent are neutral, and 21 percent say that they should not organize. These results demonstrate that blacks find that race is salient in their lives and that they would benefit from an organization that is based on race. An important majority of the sample see potential and purpose in a black organization. This is contrary to racial ideology in Cuba, which has suggested—and implemented through the prohibition of race-based organizations—that such an organization would be against national unity. These results are both surprising and exciting concerning the potential for black mobilization in the future.

The support among blacks for an organization that represents them is not the entire story. The second question in the survey regarding organizing stated that "black people in support of a black organization would be just as racist as whites that exclude blacks." Here we find that 59.2 percent either strongly agree or agree with this statement while only 27.6 percent say

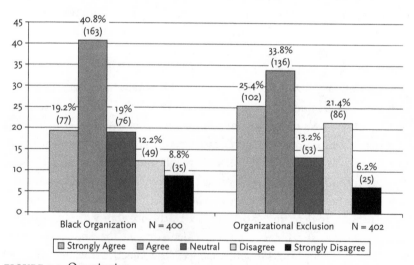

FIGURE 9.1 Organization

Note: The questions read as follows. Black Organization: "Socially, blacks should organize." Organizational Exclusion: "Black people in support of a black organization would be just as racist as whites that exclude blacks."

disagree or strongly disagree (13.2 percent are neutral). This question determines whether blacks that were surveyed buy into one of the main components of racial democracy that suggests that any racial organizing would be "racist". We find that although blacks see the value in organizing, many still find that racial organizations are racist and are influenced by government rhetoric. The results are quite contradictory (see Table 9.1), and of the 240 respondents who thought blacks should organize, 124 of them, or 51.7 percent, also thought that a black organization would be racist and eighty-one (33.7 percent of those that agreed with black organizing) thought that such an organization would not be racist. Not surprisingly, as two conflicting ideologies (the dominant and the counterideology) join, they produce incongruity in the contours of black thought. There are perhaps those that agree with some kind of organizing effort, but are conflicted about whether a black organization would be exclusionary.

Interview data revealed that while some blacks may be in favor of a black organization, most whites and *mulatos* felt that an organization based on race

Table 9.1 Relationship Between Racial Organizing and Perceptions of a Black Organization

Black organizations are racist	Blacks should organize					
	Strongly Agree	Agree	Neutral	Disagree	Strongly Disagree	Total
Strongly Agree	5.3% (23)	2.3% (9)	3.8% (15)	4.5% (18)	3% (12)	19.5% (77)
Agree	4.3% (17)	19% (75)	4.5% (18)	10.9% (43)	2% (8)	40.8% (161)
Neutral	6.6% (26)	7.3% (29)	3% (12)	1.5% (6)	0% (0)	18.5% (73)
Disagree	2.8% (11)	4.3% (17)	1.3% (5)	3.3% (13)	0.8% (3)	12.4% (49)
Strongly Disagree	5.3% (21)	1% (4)	0.8% (3)	1.3% (5)	0.5% (2)	8.8% 35
Total	24.8% (98)	33.9% (134)	13.4% (53)	21.5% (85)	6.3% (25)	100% (395)

Pearson chi2(16) = 89.0664   p = 0.00

would have no relevance in Cuba. Among those interviewed, only three out of twenty blacks were opposed to a race-based organization with all ten whites and nine out of eleven *mulatos* also opposing. The fundamental disagreement between whites and nonwhites about both the presence of racism (as shown throughout chapter 5) and the need for an organization to address this presence creates real obstacles toward challenging racial inequality. As Juliet Hooker writes, "whites tend not to recognize such inequalities as problems of justice and therefore to perceive the demands of nonwhites for redress as the main threats to solidarity. This, in a nutshell, is the problem of the racialized politics of solidarity.[28] "*Todos somos cubanos*" loses its legitimacy as a tool of unity or political solidarity because whites are both unwilling to engage in a fight for equality and tend to not support nonwhites efforts to do so. A white Cuban actress said that she did not see the need for any black organization yet she did see the need for the Federation of Cuban Women (FMC).

> The women's struggle, as Fidel said, was a revolution within a revolution, which is the same as blacks, a revolution within a revolution. Since at the start of the revolution the barriers to exclusive clubs that were for the white elite were removed and so many things were done at the time to get rid of racism, I don't think that a black organization or federation would have been necessary because really that was fought on a daily basis. Within the country there were many manifestations, racial as well, that went into creating the revolution. The Conjunto Folkorico was created,[29] there's a culture of racial mixing where Spain is present, China is present, the Cuban race is present, just like a great mix; we are all Cuban.

Her mention of Conjunto Folkorico, which has no political or economic, purpose, suggests that as long as blacks can express themselves culturally, they are well represented. Expressing support for the FMC but not for a similar civil rights organization for nonwhites was common among my interviewees, and reflects 1) the differences in attitudes regarding gender and race; and 2) the ideological discourse from the state that promotes the idea that Cubans can organize and fight against gender inequality and sexism, but not racism. The difficulty in discussing race versus gender is not

---

28. Hooker 2009, 11.

29. The Conjunto Folkorico is a dance and cultural group that was created in the early 1960s to promote Afro-Cuban dance and music.

unique to Cuba; support for affirmative action in the United States, for example, has been found to be viewed more negatively for blacks than for women.[30] Women's rights and gender inequality seem to be more comfortable topics to talk about among men and women, while racism is something that is often only discussed among those that are marginalized. Debates on affirmative action, racial organizations, and even the existence of racism tend to be contentious in any country, and governments and citizens throughout the Western Hemisphere often prefer to ignore the problem entirely.[31] The Cuban government takes this pattern a step further by prohibiting organization entirely among blacks for the acquisition of their civil rights and equality of opportunity.

This is not to deny the existence of nonwhites who follow the dominant ideology that promotes political solidarity. Black interviewees that were opposed to the development of black civil rights organizations often did so in accordance with their beliefs about the revolution. A black member of UNEAC shared with me why he was against the creation of any black organization in Cuba:

If you are looking for there to be no differences and that I be accepted as I am, then you are not creating your vision. You are differentiating yourself from the rest. Our constitution doesn't consider race. I know that in television you can count the black people on one hand, but we are still working.

For the interviewee, constitutional equality is seen as the same as racial equality in practice. Although he acknowledges racial disparities in the media, he does not consider organizing that points to a solution to the problem. Aside from those who did not separate their revolutionary beliefs with their beliefs on race, the majority of blacks that were interviewed did believe that the black communities would benefit from organizing.

Of course blacks should organize and I think it should begin from the foundation, which I consider to be the family. Family is the principal social organization in society and black families lack that network.

---

30. Eberhardt and Fiske 1994.

31. In the United States, for example, this trend can be seen as politicians, and Barack Obama in particular, shy away from national discussions on race and racial inequality (Harris 2012).

There should be organization in all aspects of black life in order to achieve their rights, social and political.

A black bellhop expressed the need for the government to acknowledge racism in order to raise awareness about the problem. When asked if he thought there should be an organization to fight against racism he said,

> Yes. We have to promote that. At the moment I think that there is a lot of will to do it. After a long time, we have achieved a day against homophobia. What I mean is that little by little the country has progressed. But in order to take steps like that, the government has to accept that there is racism; workers, teachers have to accept it. We need workshops about race and civil rights just as we have about gender. If the police stop you to ask for your ID, you should know how to react. We need tools and workshops. The topic of blackness is hardly discussed. When that begins, people will say, "Oh! That's the way it is here?" because racism exists.

The topic of mobilization also arose in some of the interviews. Many of the black interviewees that felt the need to mobilize on the issue also acknowledged that it would be a difficult task because racial consciousness is not present among many blacks. A hip-hop artist discussed the issue of complacency and lack of awareness of racism among blacks.

> You have to mobilize . . . I'm sure that in order to get there we need a crisis. Everyone has his or her ration card, everyone eats and that's the end of it. When people don't have that card, and blacks realize that they don't have the job that the white person has and they can't eat, then we'll have a crisis. But the thing is right now, you always end up eating; maybe worse than the white person because of history, but you eat. People resign themselves to that.

The bellhop that I interviewed said:

> I would say we are fifty-fifty on the issue of black solidarity. Because there are those that say, "No, no that doesn't interest me." I wish that we could mobilize. Right now I don't see the intention or inspiration to do so; maybe my children, my grandchildren, my *great*-grandchildren. You have to be proud to be black. And there are those

that aren't even proud. If we carry that politics with us, we can progress. I am absolutely sure that without that, things are not going to get better for us.

He expresses the need to mobilize in order to achieve rights but the dominant ideology has a strong influence on many in the population and as a result the issue of race is not seen as relevant to them. In addition, because the topic is prohibited from discussion, this further impedes people's will to discuss, organize, and mobilize. What is clear is that those that do express a sense of racial consciousness and feel strongly about the role of race in black lives recognize that 1) without consciousness blacks will not be able to organize on this issue; and 2) without organization, progress will not be made.

Conclusion

Scholars, writers, and artists have been at the forefront of the new racial activism in Cuba. Their work demonstrates the willingness of the Cuban government to allow the issue of racism to be discussed publicly, a significant change in policy as compared to the first decades of the revolution. State tolerance has led to important scholarly contributions on the Special Period and its effect on racism, the continued presence of anti-black prejudice in Cuba, and the need for a wider dialogue. Any personal contact with organizations dedicated to diminishing the effects of racism reveals the passion and urgency that these activists have in promoting the visibility of the role that race plays in Cuba. Racism is no longer a taboo topic in intellectual and artistic circles, and many who are invested in racial dialogue continue to push the boundaries of language previously set by the government. In a conference to discuss the subject in 2009, a member of the Communist Party stated that the revolution's triumph remains to be seen until we can combat racism in our society. Statements such as these suggest that among the elite there are brave, critical debates. Artists and musicians have also moved a discussion about racial identity and openly promote the importance of black pride and racial affirmation. We can also count the blogosphere as one of the sites of black activism in Cuba, where actors in and outside of Cuba are disseminating information, ideas, and opinions regarding racism, blackness and identity.[32] As access to

---

32. Blogs such as Negra Cubana Tenía Que Ser and Afromodernidades are adding to the information void that previously existed regarding such topics. In addition, writers and activists are increasingly able to respond to events, debates, and incidents in real time to a wide audience.

the Internet grows, which is currently happening with increased access and freedoms, social media will no doubt change the scope of racial consciousness, linking the underground with the above-ground in essential ways. Indeed the political environment has changed for all of these groups and the state, albeit reluctantly, is listening.

The strides that have been made by elites in Cuba are crucial for the possibility of policy that addresses racial inequalities, but they remain insufficient for a national debate to arise. While the state is listening, they are not promoting the expansion of established ideas about race among the citizenry. It is clear that race is significant to blacks and that organization is an aspiration among a portion of black Cubans, but state limits have continued to stifle the subject. As long as the debate remains confined, conventional wisdom may continue to see a racial organization as counterrevolutionary or exclusionary, despite the desire to vocalize racial concerns. The state could easily promote a change in thought that points to the relevance of civil rights activism, but it is unlikely that this would happen. There is great potential for a union of elites, the hip-hop community, and the general citizenry to participate in meaningful activism, particularly based on the interview and survey results presented in the last two chapters. As the discourse stands today, the focus on only prejudice, the lack of a formal organization, and the static rhetoric that negates structural racism will allow for only minor changes to occur.

CONCLUSION

The influence that racial ideology has on racial attitudes and racial consciousness in Cuba is shown throughout this project to be significant. Racial democracy in Cuba combines with socialist ideology to form a powerful racial ideology that is distinct to other Latin American societies that operate under the ideology of racial democracy. Throughout the decades of the revolution Fidel and Raúl Castro and the Cuban government have united belief in the revolution with belief in racial democracy, and as a result support of the revolution often correlates with the notion that racism is not a considerable problem in Cuba. State rhetoric and policy have promoted national identity and unity as supreme over racial identity, while claiming to have solved the problem of racism through socialist policies. The state also created a set of norms and an institutional framework that did not allow for the proliferation of alternate racial ideologies or information, barred the creation of any institution or organization that addressed race, and by creating institutions that addressed the needs of women, youth, and others created the philosophy that race was not a cleavage that mattered in revolutionary Cuba. Despite the ideological and political measures executed by the government, the presence of racism in Cuba cannot be denied and has, as supported by the data throughout this book, contributed to feelings of racial consciousness among black and *mulato* citizens. It has also produced activism and artistic expression that point to the need for renewed attention to racism. There are black conversations and collectives that reject racial democracy and exist throughout Cuba. They are vital to the national conversation about race and equality and have great potential for growth and change.

Cuban Racial Ideology

The start of the Cuban Revolution brought high levels of economic equality, which also created levels of racial equality that had not been seen in Cuban history. By dismantling informal segregation and increasing equality of opportunity for nonwhites, the Cuban government could claim that Cuba was a racial democracy more than any other country in the hemisphere at the time. This was particularly true because of the anti-racist philosophy that was created so that those who considered themselves to be revolutionary could not exhibit racist attitudes or conduct discriminatory practices. Racism, both individual and structural, was deemed a thing of the past and any policy enacted to prevent racial inequality was considered unnecessary. As a result, black representation in high government positions, the media, and in managerial positions in Cuba remained low throughout the decades of the revolutionary regime. The lack of action to address racism in Cuba left the advances for nonwhites at the onset of the revolution vulnerable.

The economic crisis revealed these vulnerabilities and racial inequality became visible. Racial ideology promoted by the government remained true to its foundation but because of increasing racial inequality, the Cuban government began to change their rhetoric to reflect the changes in Cuban society. Racism was still addressed as a remnant from the past, but disparities in housing and black representation in government was also recognized as something that should be tackled. This shift in rhetoric represented the changing role of race in Cuba but without any policy to accompany it, did not constitute any change in the dominant ideology that racism is not a problem in the country. In other words, racial ideology in Cuba did not experience any tactical shift and retained its components from the start of the revolution.

The effect of racial ideology at the individual level is nuanced, but it has a strong influence that causes it to shape all Cubans' views of race, albeit in different degrees. Most people see that there is racism in Cuba. Whether they define that racism as individual acts, vestiges from Cuban society before the revolution, or structural racism depends on the individual. Belief in the revolutionary government's accuracy in explaining Cuban racial realities depends highly on their views of the revolution as well as racial consciousness. At the same time, racial consciousness and partial adherence to the dominant racial ideology can occur together. There are a number of people in Cuba who believe in the revolution and thus do not believe that it can produce racial inequalities or a racist structure, but even these people will acknowledge that there are whites with racial prejudice. Conversely, there are blacks who possess a strong concept of racial consciousness and reject many of the elements of racial democracy by recognizing a racist structure and the need for an aggressive policy to open up opportunities for blacks and combat racial inequality. Nonetheless, those who possess such consciousness are influenced by racial democracy in some way. Most often this influence comes in people's definitions of racism as an individual phenomenon that cannot be attributed to government action or lack of action on the issue. It is this component of the ideology that largely maintains its survival. If racist attitudes only manifest with certain individuals, attention or awareness on the issue remains nonpolitical and even unnecessary.

Black Consciousness

Despite the power of racial ideology and revolutionary ideals, a significant group of blacks who were surveyed and interviewed express dissenting or alternative ideologies that respond to the existence of racial discrimination and inequality. The economic crisis changed Cuban society dramatically as levels of economic inequality and poverty increased. Afro-Cubans were hit particularly hard, largely due to the racial component of hiring in the lucrative emergent sector and their lack of access to remittances. During the Special Period employment discrimination became visible, racial profiling by the police increased, and blacks were regularly excluded from tourist spaces. Discrimination became a much more common experience among blacks, and consequently the policies and reforms of the Special Period increased the salience of race for blacks markedly. The increase in the saliency of race and experience with discrimination make the effects of the Special Period particularly important for racial consciousness among blacks. What it means to be black in Cuba changed for many during the Special Period, and out of these changes arose common experiences that were connected to race. Nonetheless, the survey sample shows that many of those that grew up during the Special Period still do adhere to revolutionary ideology regarding race.

Black political thought in Cuba is characterized by everyday conversations and racial recognition that point to blacks' relative position in society as well as their life chances. The increased role of racism is correlated to an increased feeling of racial solidarity that challenges the dominant racial ideology. Moreover, the political opening that was created during the crisis brought scholarly works on race, elite organizations that openly debated the question of racism and inequality in Cuba, and a rise in artistic and musical production that addressed the topics of race and racial consciousness. The role of black consciousness and spaces that promote it, such as hip-hop, are vital for an examination of racial ideology in Cuba and what its effects are. How blacks perceive race and how they perceive the ideology that is espoused by the state lends insight into what constitutes black thought.

The Future of Racial Politics in Cuba

Although all blacks do not possess a strong racial consciousness and many accept the dominant racial ideology as truth, this does not diminish the importance of those who do. As Michael Hanchard argues, "Black political thought, like most forms of political thought, often presents a vision of political community or of the world at large that generates little or no support at the moment of its initial presentation."[1] Hanchard cites the urgency of the civil rights movement that led the black liberation struggle based on ideas that were "not popularly held." In the case of Cuba, someone who considers black agency to be exclusionary, or even racist as some have expressed, may not agree with the ideas of activists and intellectuals leading the discussion on race in Cuba. What may unite disparate ideologies among blacks is the similarity of their grievances. In my interviews with some who expressed concerns that a black organization would be racist, issues of representation and equality of opportunity were of equal concern to those who favored racial organization or mobilization. The future of racial politics in Cuba lies in the ability of leaders to communicate these ideas publicly within a revolutionary framework and create spaces for these conversations to leave the home and enter into the national debate.[2] Whether the space will be granted

---

1. Hanchard 2006, 8.

2. Robert Gooding-Williams (2006) argues that public opinion regarding racism and the possibility for collective political mobilization among blacks in the United States is complicated by differing opinions on the significance, scope, and nature of anti-black racism, including the issue of whether it even exists. While he argues that significant variations in black public opinion are further complicated by class differences and competing identities, Cuba presents a case where class differences are muted and thus do not present an obstacle to racial solidarity and the potential for political action. As he states, "racial solidarity will be more plausibly interpreted as a function of politics, where the political speech and action of African Americans moves them to embrace the belief that they share certain problems and to act accordingly" (116). In Cuba the work of consciousness raising to challenge not only racial democracy, but the idea that racism should be interpreted as individual prejudice, is essential to strengthen racial solidarity and a build a larger consensus toward action. If leaders can effectively communicate the scope of racism and identify racist practices, the data in this project suggest that there would be considerable interest in a black movement that reaches beyond the current limited circles.

depends on the willingness of the Cuban government to give racism new consideration.

The Seventh Annual Congress of the Cuban Communist Party took place in April of 2016, just weeks before the completion of this book. In Raúl Castro's Central Report given at the opening of the Congress, he said,

> The promotion of women, young people, black and mixed-race Cubans to senior positions has progressively and steadily increased, on the basis of merit in their gradual transition through different responsibilities and personal qualifications. However, we are not satisfied with the results achieved, as old habits and prejudices persist which conspire against Party cadre policy.
>
> The fight against any trace of racism that impedes or halts the rise to leadership roles of black and mixed-race Cubans, the number of whom in the total Cuban population has continued to rise in census after census, must continue without respite. To consolidate the results in this important and just policy of the revolution, we must work systematically, with foresight and intentionality. A matter of this importance cannot be at the mercy of spontaneity or improvisation.

This was not the first party congress or speech where black and mestizo representation has been discussed by the president. Indeed, it is significant that the point was made; however, following the above mention of racism and prejudice, the president talked more specifically regarding the representation of women, the percentage of women in the labor force, and in leadership positions as well as their potential to lead in general. Thus it is not clear whether the discussion of racism will again be a symbolic gesture or if, like women's rights, race will be given a more substantive treatment in the coming years by the government. This treatment, of course, should include a public reckoning of the scope of inequality both in the labor force and the government—just as it is given for gender inequality—followed by policy prescriptions and an organization to monitor and prescribe such a set of policies. If the government should indeed promote a public battle against racism, this would be a new and welcomed path for Cuba, particularly among those who have fought for such a goal for decades.

The recent increase in black officials in the top organs of Cuban government and the slight increase in attention to racial issues introduces issues of descriptive versus substantive representation as well. In an interview with a top racial scholar in Cuba, he stated that he did not believe in higher black representation in government if that representation would reinforce the racial status quo. Survey results showed that an overwhelming majority of respondents believed that increased representation in government by blacks was important. It is unclear whether these respondents thought that black presence in government is important only symbolically or descriptively, or, if substantively, they believed that something would change for blacks as a result of black presence. Will these officials have any effect on policymaking efforts or attention to racial issues? An answer to such an inquiry would be speculative, but history would suggest that under the current regime, racial politics would not experience a real change. Government officials do not have any commitment to a particular constituency or community and even in the face of economic crisis and a sharp increase in visible racism on the island, the dominant ideology has remained the same. The earlier mention of race in the 2016 Central Report was communicated alongside the rhetoric from Fidel Castro that racial discrimination was eradicated at the onset the revolution. Changes that have occurred thus far: increase in representation in the Central Committee, an event commemorating the centennial of the Independientes de Color and a slight opening of artistic and scholarly expression, are largely symbolic and do not suggest a change in policy on race. Moreover, high-ranking members of government and the Communist Party continue to have a commitment to represent the dominant racial ideology.

The newest organization created within UNEAC is the Aponte Commission, named after the black activist who rebelled against the institution of slavery in the early nineteenth century. The commission has taken the place of Color Cubano and rather than promote a debate regarding inequality, it has declared its mission to fight racial prejudice in Cuba and promote debate regarding these prejudices that, according to the commission, reside only in the conscience of the people. The commission has promised to work closely with the government to monitor and prevent discrimination, collect grievances, and promote debate and research.[3] In a 2013 article in *Granma*, the leader of the commission cited a meeting with the Ministry of Education that should lead to the inclusion of more substantive black history in the national curriculum.[4] The commission is careful to highlight that Cuba is no longer a racist country as it was in 1959, and today, because of the essence of the revolution coupled with its support and political relationship with Africa, could

---

3. Eighth UNEAC Congress 2013 (Unión de Escritores y Artistas de Cuba 2013).
4. Delis 2013.

not be considered racist. The Aponte Commission's rhetoric falls in line with the leadership in claiming racism is only present in people's modes of thinking, and avoiding issues of representation or racial inequality. In fact, the commission has lauded the level of black representation within the government's structures. The commission's rhetoric evidences that the government will not promote comprehensive change in the near future and organizations that are aligned with the state will not veer far from the dominant racial ideology.

Brazil offers an interesting comparison to Cuba, in that great policy strides have been made to increase racial equality and debunk the myth of racial democracy. In Brazil, democratization, coupled with an increase in black representation in national government, led to a change in racial policy almost immediately. Within slightly over a decade the black movement gained traction, black representatives created a black political caucus, and plans for affirmative action policies were under way.[5] The black movement in Brazil was successful in putting pressure on the government to enact policies focused on reducing racial inequality, but the movement still has not been able to convince many black Brazilians that race should be a basis for organization.[6] Nonetheless, the example that Brazil shows is that without freedom of speech that allows for criticism of the government and expression of alternative racial ideologies and policy ideas, change within the government remains elusive. Members of Congress in Brazil were able to hold office, introduce legislation, and promote a national dialogue only after democratization.[7]

Without the possibility of a mass movement or the freedom within government to communicate opposing ideas, racial inequality will likely remain as it is in Cuba. As long as politicians can only follow the script written in 1959 and a review of racism is relegated to a commission of few that only makes recommendations to the state, we cannot imagine a move toward racial justice. I agree with the scholar in Havana who argued that the revolution cannot fully triumph without that move, and its realization would require the participation of many. While many black Cubans would like to see race cease to be one of the primary ways that society and opportunity are organized, their involvement will not be elicited.

Racial activism that remains within the ideals of the Cuban revolution is not only possible, but it seems essential in a time when support of the

---

5. Da Silva Martins et al. 2004.

6. Caldwell 2007; Telles 2004.

7. Johnson 2006.

revolution is waning, particularly among young people. If the revolution were to publicly fight for black rights and black advancement and discredit systemic practices that serve to limit progress toward equality, the government would be able to move away from predictable propaganda and once again be a leader in the fight for social justice, both within and outside of Cuba. This was the way that the revolution gained the support of blacks and *mulatos* at the start of the revolution and it would hold similar inspirational value to a new generation that, despite the silence, is well aware that racism still operates in Cuban society. A genuine, democratic critique of the revolution has to include all groups within it, and an anti-racist movement that encourages participation from all races has the potential to change public opinion in a country that is, despite the census numbers, predominantly nonwhite. If this movement is bolstered by activism that seeks to dismantle ideas of black inferiority and if the Cuban racial *ajiaco* can claim a space for black pride rather than try to erase it, then we will see revolutionary change in Cuba that would serve democracy well in the future.

APPENDIX

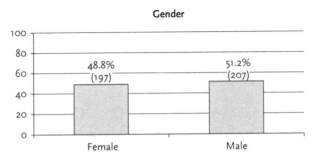

FIGURE A.1 Gender Distribution of Survey Respondents

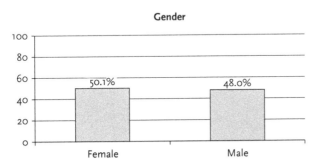

FIGURE A.2 Gender Distribution in Cuba
Source: Cuban Office of National Statistics, 2009.

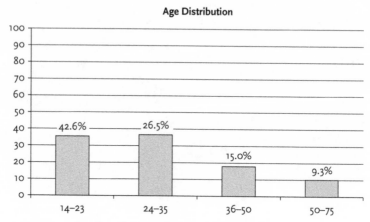

FIGURE A.3 Age Distribution of Survey Respondents

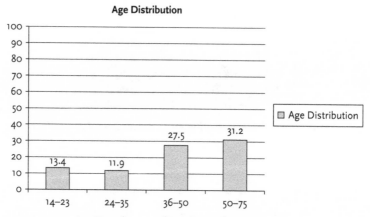

FIGURE A.4 Age Distribution of Residents of Havana
Source: National Office of Cuban Statistics, 2009.

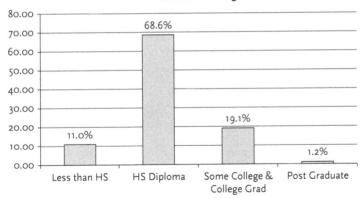

FIGURE A.5 Level of Schooling of Survey Respondents

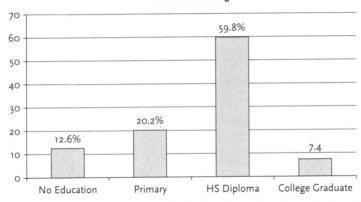

FIGURE A.6 Completed Level of Schooling for Cubans Over the Age of Eleven

Source: Cuban Census, 2002.

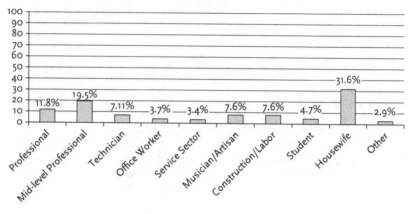

FIGURE A.7 Occupations of Survey Respondents

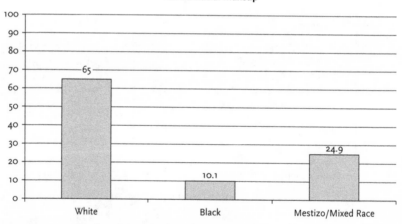

FIGURE A.8 Racial Make-Up of Cuba

Source: National Office of Cuban Statistics, Census 2002.

REFERENCES

Abreu Arcia, Alberto. 2016. Un II Coloquio que recién comienza. *Afromodernidades*. https://afromodernidades.wordpress.com.

Adams, Henley C. 2004. Fighting an Uphill Battle: Race, Politics, Power and Institutionalization in Cuba. *Latin American Research Review* 39.1: 168–182.

AFP, La Habana. 2010. Cubano estrella del Royal Ballet llama a "erradicar" racismo en la danza. *La Prensa Grafica*. April 22.

Allen, Jarafi S. 2011. *¡Venceremos? The Erotics of Black Self-Making in Cuba*. Durham: Duke University Press.

Alves, Jaime. 2014. On Mules and Bodies: Black Captivities in the Brazilian Racial Democracy. *Critical Sociology* 42.2: 229–248.

Althusser, Louis. 1994. Ideology and Ideological State Apparatuses (Notes toward an Investigation). In *Mapping ideology*. Zizek, Slavoj, Ed. London: Verso, 100–140.

Alvarado Ramos, Juan Antonio. 1996. Relaciones raciales en Cuba: notas de investigación. *Temas* 7: 37–43.

Arandia, Gisela. 2005. Somos o no somos. *La Gaceta de Cuba*. January/February: 59.

Ards, Angela. 2004. Organizing the Hip-Hop Generation. In *That's the Joint!: The Hip-Hop Studies Reader*. Forman, Murray, and Mark Anthony Neal, Eds. New York: Routledge, 311–324.

Arredondo, Gutiérrez Alberto. 1939. *El negro en Cuba, ensayo*. La Habana: Editorial Alfa.

Bailey, Stanley R. 2009. *Legacies of Race: Identities, Attitudes, and Politics in Brazil*. Redwood City, CA: Stanford University Press.

Baker, Geoffrey. 2005. ¡Hip Hop, Revolución! Nationalizing Rap in Cuba. *Ethnomusicology* 49.3: 368–402.

Banks, Ingrid. 2000. *Hair Matters: Beauty Power and Black Women's Consciousness*. New York: New York University Press.

Blanco, Tomás. 1942. *El prejuicio racial en Puerto Rico, Apuntes boricuas*. San Juan de Puerto Rico: Editorial Biblioteca de Autores Puertorriqueños.

Blue, Sarah A. 2007. The Erosion of Racial Equality in the Context of Cuba's Dual Economy. *Latin American Politics and Society* 49: 35–68.

Bobo, Lawrence. 2004. Inequalities That Endure? Racial Ideology, American Politics, and the Peculiar Role of the Social Sciences. In *The Changing Terrain of Race and Ethnicity*. Krysan, Maria, and Amanda E. Lewis, Eds. New York: Russell Sage Foundation.

Bonilla-Silva, Eduardo. 1997. Rethinking Racism: Toward a Structural Interpretation. *American Sociological Review* 62.3: 465–480

Bonilla-Silva, Eduardo. 2001. *White Supremacy and Racism in the Post-Civil Rights Era*. Boulder, CO: Lynne Reinner.

Bonilla-Silva, Eduardo. 2014. *Racism Without Racists: Color-Blind Racism and the Persistence of Racial Inequality in the United States*. 4th ed. Lanham, MD: Rowman & Littlefield Publishers.

Borjes, Esther. 2007. Batalla de ideas: una actitud ante la vida. Editorial Digital. *El Tiempo 21*. July 10, 2007.

Brown, Michael K., Martin Carnoy, Elliott Currie, Troy Duster, David B. Oppenheimer, Marjorie M. Shultz, and David Wellman. 2003. *Whitewashing Race: The Myth of a Color-Blind Society*. Berkeley: University of California Press.

Brodkin, Karen. 1998. *How Jews Became White Folks and What That Says About Race in America*. New Brunswick, NJ: Rutgers University Press.

Caldwell, Kia. 2007. *Negras in Brazil: Re-envisioning Black Women, Citizenship and the Politics of Identity*. New Brunswick, NJ: Rutgers University Press.

Caribbean Tourism Organization. *Latest Statistics 2014*. Caribbean Tourism Organization. June 19, 2015.

Cashmore, Ellis. 2001. The Experiences of Ethnic Minority Police Officers in Britain: Under-Recruitment and Racial Profiling in a Performance Culture. *Ethnic and Racial Studies* 24:4: 642–659.

Castro, Fidel. 1959. *1959 Speech at Havana Labor Rally*. Havana, Cuba.

Castro, Fidel. 1960. *8th Anniversary Speech of the Events of the 26th of July*. Havana, Cuba.

Castro, Fidel. 1961. *1961 Speech on the Second Anniversary of the Revolution*. Havana, Cuba.

Castro, Fidel. 2000. *War, Racism and Economic Injustice: The Global Ravages of Capitalism*. Alexandra Keeble, Ed. Melbourne: Ocean Press.

Castro, Fidel, and Michael Taber. *Fidel Castro Speeches. Volume II*. 1981. New York: Pathfinder.

Castro Ruz, Raul. Año del 50 Aniversario del Triunfo de la Revolución. Closing Session of the National Assembly of People's Power. Havana, Cuba. December 20, 2009.

Cialdini, Robert, Carl A. Kallgren, and Raymond R. Reno. 1991. A Focus Theory of Normative Conduct: A Theoretical Refinement and Reevaluation of the Role of Norms in Human Behavior. In *Advances in Experimental Social Psychology*. Mark P. Zanna, Ed. San Diego: Academic Press, 201–234.

Collins, Patricia Hill. 1998. *Fighting Words: Black Women and the Search for Justice*. Minneapolis: University of Minnesota Press.

Comaroff, John L. 1998. Reflections on the Colonial State, in South Africa and Elsewhere: Factions, Fragments, Facts and Fictions. *Social Identities* 4.3: 321–361.

Daniel, G. Reginald. 2005. White into Black: Race and National Identity in Contemporary Brazil. In *Race and Nation: Ethnic Systems in the Modern World*. Paul Spickard, Ed. New York: Routledge, 87–103.

Davenport, Christian, Sarah A. Soule, and David A. Armstrong II. 2011. Protesting While Black?: The Differential Policing of American Activism, 1960 to 1990. *American Sociological Review* 76: 152–178.

Davis, Darren W. 1997. The Direction of Race of Interviewer Effects among African-Americans: Donning the Black Mask. *American Journal of Political Science* 41.1: 309–322.

Dawson, Michael C. 1994. *Behind the Mule: Race and Class in African-American Politics*. Princeton, NJ: Princeton University Press.

Dawson, Michael C. 2001. *Black Visions: The Roots of Contemporary African-American Political Ideologies*. Chicago: University of Chicago Press.

Delis, Livia Rodriguez. 2013. Comision Jose A. Aponte: Defender lo conquistado. *Granma Internacional*. June 28, 2013.

Dilla Alfonso, Haroldo. 2002. Cuba: The Changing Scenarios of Governability. *Boundary 2*. 29.2: 55–75.

Domínguez, Jorge I. 1978. *Cuba: Order and Revolution*. Cambridge, MA: Belknap Press of Harvard University Press.

Domínguez, Jorge I. 2012. Introduction. In *Cuban Economic and Social Development: Policy Reforms and Challenges in the 21st Century*. Domínguez, Jorge, Everleny Pérez, Omar , Espina Prieto, Mayra, and Barberia, Lorena, Eds. Cambridge: Harvard University Press.

Duharte Jiménez, Rafael, and Elsa Santos García. 1997. *El Fantasma de la Esclavitud: Prejuicios raciales en Cuba y América Latina*. Bonn: Pahl-Rugenstein.

Dulitzky, Ariel E. 2005. A Region in Denial: Racial Discrimination and Racism in Latin America. In *Neither Enemies Nor Friends: Latinos, Blacks, Afro-Latinos*. Dzidzienyo, A., and S. Oboler, Eds. New York: Palgrave Macmillan, 42–50.

Eagleton, Terry. 1991. *Ideology: An Introduction*. London: Verso.

Eagleton, Terry. 1994. *Ideology*. London: Longman.

Eberhardt, Jennifer, and Susan Fiske. 1994. Affirmative Action in Theory and Practice: Issues of Power, Ambiguity, and Gender Versus Race. *Basic and Applied Social Psychology* 15.1: 201–220.

Eckstein, Susan. 2003. *Back from the Future: Cuba Under Castro*. 2nd Edition. New York: Routledge.

Espina Prieto, Rodrigo, and Pablo Rodríguez Ruiz. 2006. Raza y desigualdad en la Cuba actual. *Temas* 45.1: 44–54.

Federación de Mujeres Cubanas. 2009. Informe Central. 8vo Congreso de la FMC.

Fernandes, Sujatha. 2006. *Cuba Represent!: Cuban Arts, State Power, and the Making of New Revolutionary Cultures*. Durham, NC: Duke University Press.

Fernandez, Nadine. 1996. The Color of Love: Young Interracial Couples in Cuba. *Latin American Perspectives* 23.1: 99–117.

Fernandez, Nadine. 2001. The Changing Discourse on Race in Contemporary Cuba. *Qualitative Studies in Education* 14.2: 117–132.

Fernández, Nadine. 2010. *Revolutionizing Romance: Interracial Couples in Contemporary Cuba*. New Brunswick: Rutgers University Press.

Fernandez Robaina, Tomas. 2005. Las identidades afrocubanas dentro del Movimento Hip Hop. *Movimiento* 5: 21–22.

Fernandez Robaina, Tomas. 2009. *Identidad afrocubana, cultura y nacionalidad*. Santiago de Cuba: Editorial Oriente.

Fernández Robaina, Tomás. 2007. *Cuba Racial: Personalidades en el debate*. La Habana: Editorial de Ciencias Sociales.

Ferrer, Ada. 1999. Cuba, 1898: Rethinkng Race, Nation, and Empire. *Radical History Review* 73.1: 22–46.

Ferrer, Ada. 2000. Rethinking Race and Nation in Cuba. In *Cuba, the Elusive Nation: Interpretations of National Identity*. Fernández, Damian J., and Madeline Cámara, Eds. Gainesville: University Press of Florida, 60–78.

Finkel, Stephen E., Thomas M. Guterbock, and Marian J. Borg. 1991. Race of Interviewer Effects in a Preelection Poll, Virginia 1989. *Public Opinion Quarterly* 55.3: 313–330.

Forman, Murray, and Mark Anthony Neal. 2004. *That's the Joint!: The Hip-Hop Studies Reader*. New York: Routledge.

Forman, Tyrone A. 2004. Color-Blind Racism and Racial Indifference: The Role of Racial Apathy in Facilitating Enduring Inequalities. In *The Changing Terrain of Race and Ethnicity*. Krysan, Maria, and Amanda E. Lewis, Eds. New York: Russell Sage Foundation, 43–66.

Foucault, Michel. 2003. *Society Must Be Defended: Lectures at the College de France. 1975–1976*. New York: Picador.

Fowler Calzada, Victor. 2009. Contra el argumento racista. *Revista Encuentro* 53/54.

Frankenberg, Ruth. 1993. *White Women, Race Matters: The Social Construction of Whiteness*. Minneapolis: University of Minnesota Press.

De la Fuente, Alejandro. 2001a. *A Nation for All: Race, Inequality and Politics in Twentieth-Century Cuba*. Chapel Hill: University of North Carolina Press.

De la Fuente, Alejandro. 2001b. The Resurgence of Racism in Cuba. *NACLA Report on the Americas* 34.6: 25–30.

De la Fuente, Alejandro. 2001c. Recreating Racism: Race and Discrimination in Cuba's "Special Period." *Socialism and Democracy* 15.1: 65–91.

De la Fuente, Alejandro. 2008. The New Afro-Cuban Cultural Movement and the Debate on Race in Contemporary Cuba. *Journal of Latin American Studies* 40.4: 697–720.

De la Fuente, Alejandro and Laurence Glasco. 1997. "Are Blacks 'Getting out of Control'? Racial Attitudes, Revolution and Political Transition in Cuba." In

Toward a New Cuba? Legacies of a Revolution. Centeno, Miguel Angel, and Font, Mauricio, Eds. .Bouldner, CO: Lynne Reiner Publishing.

Gilroy, Paul. 1987. *There Ain't No Black in the Union Jack: The Cultural Politics of Race and Nation.* London: Hutchinson.

Glaude, Eddie. 2000. *Exodus! Religion, Race and Nation in Early Nineteenth-Century Black America.* Chicago: University of Chicago Press.

Glynn, Carol. 1996. Public Opinion as a Normative Opinion Process. In *Communication Yearbook 20.* Burleson, Brant, Ed. Thousand Oaks, CA: Sage Publications, 157–183.

Glynn, Carol, Susan Herbst, Garrett J. OKeefe, Robert Y. Shapiro, and Mark Lindeman. 2004. *Public Opinion.* 2nd Edition. Boulder, CO: Westview.

Godreau, Isar. 2015. *Scripts of Blackness: Race, Cultural Nationalism, and U.S. Colonialism in Puerto Rico.* Urbana: University of Illinois Press.

Godreau, Isar, Hilda Llorens, and Carlos Vargas-Ramos. 2010. Colonial Incongruence at Work: Employing US Census Racial Categories in Puerto Rico. *Anthropology News* 51.5: 11–12.

Goffman, Erving. 1986. *Frame Analysis: An Essay on the Organization of Experience.* Boston: Northeastern University Press.

Golash-Boza, Tanya, and Christina A. Sue. 2013. It was Only a Joke: How Racial Humor Fuels Color-Blind Ideologies in Mexico and Peru. *Ethnic and Racial Studies* 36.10: 1582–1598.

Goldberg, David Theo. 2002. *The Racial State.* Malden, MA: Blackwell Publishers.

Goldberg, David Theo. 2009. *The Threat of Race: Reflections on Racial Neoliberalism.* Malden, MA: Blackwell Publishers.

Gooding-Williams, Robert. 2006. *Look, a Negro! Philosophical Essays on Race, Culture and Politics.* New York: Routledge.

Guerra, Lillian. 2012. Visions of Power in Cuba: Revolution, Redemption, and Resistance, 1959–1971. Chapel Hill: University of North Carolina Press.

Gurin, Patricia, Arthur H. Miller, and Gerald Gurin. 1980. Stratum Identification and Consciousness. *Social Psychology Quarterly* 43.1: 30–47.

Guanche Pérez, Jesús. 1996. Etnicidad y racialidad en la Cuba actual. *Temas* 7.3: 51–57.

Harris, Frederick. 2012. *The Price of the Ticket: Barack Obama and the Rise and Decline of Black Politics.* New York: Oxford University Press.

Harris-Lacewell, Melissa Victoria. 2004. *Barbershops, Bibles and BET: Everyday Talk and Black Political Thought.* Princeton, NJ: Princeton University Press.

Hanchard, Michael George. 1994. *Orpheus and Power: The Movimento Negro of Rio de Janeiro and São Paulo, Brazil, 1945–1988.* Princeton, NJ: Princeton University Press.

Hanchard, Michael George, Ed. 1999. *Racial Politics in Contemporary Brazil.* Durham, NC: Duke University Press.

Hanchard, Michael George. 2006. *Party/Politics: Horizons in Black Political Thought.* New York: Oxford University Press.

Hanchard, Michael George, and Michael Dawson. 2006. Ideology and Political Culture in Black. In *Party/Politics: Horizons in Black Political Thought*. Hanchard, Michael, Eds. New York: Oxford University Press.

Helg, Aline. 1995. *Our Rightful Share: The Afro-Cuban Struggle for Equality, 1886–1912*. Chapel Hill: University of North Carolina Press.

Hernandez, Daniela. 1998. Raza y prejuicio racial en Santa Clara: un reporte de investigación. *América Negra* 15.1: 75–86.

Hernandez, Rafael. 2003. *Looking at Cuba: Essays on Culture and Civil Society*. Gainesville: University Press of Florida.

Hochschild, Jennifer L. 1995. *Race, Class and the Soul of the Nation: Facing Up to the American Dream*. Princeton, NJ: Princeton University Press.

Hogg, Michael A., and Scott A. Reid. 2006. Social Identity, Self-Categorization and the Communication of Group Norms. *Communication Theory* 16.1: 7–30.

Holt, Thomas C. 2000. *The Problem of Race in the Twenty-First Century*. Cambridge, MA: Harvard University Press.

Hooker, Juliet. 2009. *Race and the Politics of Solidarity*. New York: Oxford Unviersity Press.

Horkheimer, Max. 1972. *Critical Theory: Selected Essays*. New York: Herder and Herder.

Hostetter, Martha. 2001. *Cuba*. New York: H. W. Wilson.

De la Hoz, Pedro. 2003. Todo sea por el mestizaje. *Granma*. http://www.archivocu-bano.org/rap.html.

Jackman, Mary R. 1994. *The Velvet Glove: Paternalism and Conflict in Gender, Class, and Race Relations*. Berkeley: University of California Press.

Jiménez Román, Miriam. 1996. Un hombre (negro) del pueblo: José Celso Barbosa and the Puerto Rican "Race" Toward Whiteness. *CENTRO* 8.1: 8–29.

Johnson III, Ollie A. 2006. Locating Blacks in Brazilian Politics: Afro-Brazilian Activism, New Political Parties, and Pro-Black Public Policies. *International Journal of Africana Studies* 12.2: 170–193.

Johnson III, Ollie A. 2007. Black Politics in Latin America: An Analysis of National and Transnational Politics. In *African American Perspectives on Political Science*. Rich, Wilbur C., Ed. Philadelphia: Temple University Press.

Kelley, Robin D. G. 1994. *Race Rebels: Culture, Politics and the Black Working Class*. New York: The Free Press.

Kessler, R. C., K. D. Mickelson, and D. R. Williams. 1999. The Prevalence, Distribution and Mental Health Correlates of Perceived Discrimination in the United States. *Journal of Health and Social Behavior* 40: 208–230.

Kitwana, Bakari. 2004. The Challenge of Rap Music from Cultural Movement to Political Power. In *That's the Joint!: The Hip-Hop Studies Reader*. Forman, Murray, and Mark Anthony Neal, Eds. New York: Routledge.

Krysan, Maria. 1998. Privacy and the Expression of White Racial Attitudes: A Comparison Across Three Contexts. *The Public Opinion Quarterly* 62.4: 506–544.

Krysan, Maria, and Lewis, Amanda E. 2006. *The Changing Terrain of Race and Ethnicity*. New York: Russell Sage Foundation.

LeoGrande, William. 2000. Cuba: The Shape of Things to Come. In *Cuba: The Contours of Change*. Kaufman Purcell, Susan, and David Rothkopf, Eds. Boulder, CO: Lynne Rienner, 1–12.

Mannheim, Karl. 1991. *Ideology and Utopia: An Introduction to the Sociology of Knowledge*. London: Routledge.

Marable, Manning. 1995. History and Black Consciousness. In *Walkin' the Talk: An Anthology of African American Studies*. Lyne, Bill, and Vernon Damani Johnson, Eds. Upper Saddle River, NJ: Prentice Hall.

Martí, José. 1963–1966. *Obras completas*. La Habana: Editora Nacional de Cuba.

Martínez-Echazábal, Lourdes. 1998. Mestizaje and the discourse of national/cultural identity in Latin America, 1845–1959. *Latin American Perspectives* 25.3: 21–42.

Martínez Heredia, Fernando. 2009. Fundación del Partido Independiente de Color. In *Raza/Racismo: Antología de Caminos*. La Habana: Editorial Caminos.

Marx, Anthony W. 1998. *Making Race and Nation: A Comparison of South Africa, the United States, and Brazil*. Cambridge: Cambridge University Press.

Marx, Karl, and Engels, Frederick. 1970. *The German Ideology*. New York: International Publishers.

McAdam, Doug. 1982. *Political Process and the Development of Black Insurgency, 1930–1970*. 2nd Edition. Chicago: University of Chicago Press.

Merino-Falú, Aixa. 2004. *Raza, género, y clase social: el discrimen contra las mujeres afropuertorriqueñas*. San Juan: Oficina de la Procuradora de las Mujeres.

Mesa Redonda. Racismo en Cuba. January 22, 2010. Web.

Miller, Arthur H., Patrica Gurin, Gerald Gurin, and Oksana Malanchuk. 1981. Group Consciousness and Political Participation. *American Journal of Political Science* 25.3: 494–511.

Mills, Charles W. 1998. *Blackness Visible: Essays on Philosophy and Race*. Ithaca, NY: Cornell University Press.

Montejo, Arrechea Carmen. 2004. *Sociedades negras en Cuba, 1878-1960*. La Habana: Editorial de Ciencias Sociales.

Moore, Carlos. 1988. *Castro, the Blacks, and Africa: Afro-American Culture and Society, v. 8*. Los Angeles: Center for Afro-American Studies, University of California.

Moore, Robin. 1997. *Nationalizing Blackness: Afrocubanismo and Artistic Revolution in Havana, 1920–1940*. Pittsburgh: University of Pittsburgh Press.

Morales Domínguez, Esteban. 2007. *Los desafíos de la problemática racial*. La Habana: Fundación Fernando Ortiz.

Morejón, Nancy. 1993. Race and Nation. In *AfroCuba: An Anthology of Cuban Writing on Race, Politics and Culture*. Pérez, Sarduy Pedro, and Jean Stubbs, Eds. Melbourne: Ocean Press.

Moscovici, Serge. 1976. *Social Influence and Social Change*. London: Academic Press.

Mustelier, Zenobio. 1937. Contestando Nuestra Encuesta. *Adelante* 22. April, 1938.

Nascimento, Elisa Larkin. 2007. *The Sorcery of Color: Identity, Race, and Gender in Brazil*. Philadelphia: Temple University Press.

Neal, Mark Anthony. 2004. The Message: Rap, Politics, and Resistance. In *That's the Joint!: The Hip-Hop Studies Reader*. Forman, Murray, and Mark Anthony Neal, Eds. New York: Routledge.

Nelson, William E. 2002. Black Political Consciousness and Empowerment: The 20th Century Cognitive Basis of African American Politics. In *Black Identity in the 20th Century: Expressions of the US and UK African Diaspora*. Mark Christian, Ed. London: Hansib Publications Limited.

Neville, Helen, M. Nikki Coleman, Jameca Woody Falconer, and Deadre Holmes. 2005. Color-Blind Racial Ideology and Psychological False Consciousness among African Americans. *Journal of Black Psychology* 31.1: 27–45.

Nobles, Melissa. 2000. *Shades of Citizenship: Race and the Census in Modern Politics*. Redwood City, CA: Stanford University Press.

Ogbar, Jeffery O. G. 2004. *Black Power: Radical Politics and African American Identity*. Baltimore: Johns Hopkins University Press.

Omi, Michael and Howard Winant. 1994. Racial Formation in the United States: From the 1960s to the 1990s. 2nd Edition. New York: Routledge.

Pappademos, Melina. 2011. *Black Political Activism and the Cuban Republic*. Chapel Hill: University of North Carolina Press.

Pardue, Derek. 2008. *Ideologies of Marginality in Brazilian Hip Hop*. New York: Palgrave Macmillan.

Perera, Robbio, Alina, Julieta Garcia Rios, and Luis Lopez Viera. 2005. Vainilla y Chocolate: Y Que? *Juventud Rebelde*.

Pérez, Louis A. 2006. *Cuba: Between Reform and Revolution*. New York: Oxford University Press.

Perez-Stable, Marifeli. 2012. *The Cuban Revolution: Origins Course and Legacy*. 2nd Edition. New York: Oxford University Press.

Perry, Imani. 2011. *More Beautiful and More Terrible: The Embrace and Transcendence of Racial Inequality in the United States*. New York: New York University Press.

Pough, Gwendolyn D. 2004. *Check It While I Wreck It: Black Womanhood, Hip Hop Culture, and the Public Sphere*. Boston: Northeastern University Press.

Portuondo Linares, Serafín. 2002. *Los Independientes de Color: Historia del Partido Independiente de Color*. 2nd Edition. La Habana: Editorial Caminos.

Queeley, Andrea. 2015. *Rescuing our Roots: The African Ango-Caribbean Diaspora in Contemporary Cuba*. Gainesville: University Press of Florida.

Robinson, Cedric. 2000. *Black Marxism: The Making of the Black Radical Tradition*. Chapel Hill: University of North Carolina Press.

Ronquillo Bello, Ricardo. 2008. Risas Humillantes. *Juventud Rebelde*. April 20.

Rorty, Richard. 1994. Feminism, Ideology and Deconstruction: A Pragmatist View. In *Mapping Ideology*. Zizek, Slavoj, Ed. London: Verso.

Rose, Tricia. 1994. *Black Noise: Rap Music and Black Culture in Contemporary America.* Middletown, CT: Wesleyan University Press.

Sanders-Thompson V. 1996. Perceived Experiences of Racism as Stressful Life Events. *Community Mental Health Journal* 32.1: 223–233.

Saney, Isaac. 2004. *Cuba: A Revolution in Motion.* London: Zed Books.

Saunders, Tanya L. 2012. Black Thoughts, Black Activism: Cuban Underground Hip-hop and Afro-Latino Countercultures of Modernity. *Latin American Perspectives* 39.2: 42–60.

Saunders, Tanya L. 2015. *Cuban Underground Hip Hop: Black Thoughts, Black Revolution, Black Modernity.* Austin: University of Texas Press.

Sawyer, Mark. 2006. *Racial Politics in Post-Revolutionary Cuba.* Cambridge: Cambridge University Press.

Sawyer, Mark, Yesilernis Peña, and Sidanius Jim. 2004. Cuban Exceptionalism: Group-based Hierarchy and the Dynamics of Patriotism in Puerto Rico, the Dominican Republic and Cuba. *DuBois Review* 1.1: 93–113.

Schuman, Howard, Charlotte Steeh, Lawrence D. Bobo and maria Krysan. 1997. *Racial Attitudes in America: Trends and Interpretations.* Cambridge, MA: Harvard University Press.

Scott, James C. 1992. *Domination and the Arts of Resistance: Hidden Transcripts.* New Haven, CT: Yale University Press.

Sellers Robert M., Mia A Smith, J. Nicole Shelton, Stephanie A. J. Rowley and Tabbye M Chavous. 1998. Multidimensional Model of Racial Identity: A Reconceptualization of African American Racial Identity. *Personality & Social Psychology Review* 2.1: 18–39.

Sellers, Robert M., and J. Nicole Shelton. 2003. The Role of Racial Identity in Perceived Racial Discrimination. *Journal of Personality and Social Psychology* 84.5: 1079–1092.

Shelby, Tommie. 2005. *We Who Are Dark: The Philosophical Foundations of Black Solidarity.* Cambridge, MA: Belknap Press of Harvard University Press.

Sherif, Muzafer. 1936. *The Psychology of Social Norms.* New York: Harper and Brothers.

Sheriff, Robin E. 2001. *Dreaming Equality: Color, Race, and Racism in Urban Brazil.* New Brunswick, NJ: Rutgers University Press.

Sidanius, Jim, Seymour Feshbach, Shana Levin, and Felicia Pratto. 1997. The Interface Between Ethnic and National Attachment: Ethnic Pluralism or Ethnic Dominance? *Public Opinion Quarterly* 61.1: 103–133.

Simpson, Andrea Y. 1998. *The Tie That Binds: Identity and Political Attitudes in the Post-Civil Rights Generation.* New York: New York University Press.

Skidmore, Thomas E. 1993. *Black Into White: Race and Nationality in Brazilian Thought.* Durham, NC: Duke University Press.

Snow, David A. 2004. Framing Processes, Ideology and Discursive Fields. In *The Blackwell Companion to Social Movements.* David A. Snow, Sarah A. Soule and Hanspeter Kriesi., Eds. Malden, MA: Blackwell.

Spence Benson, Devyn. 2012. Owning the Revolution: Race, Revolution, and Politics form Havana to Miami, 1959–1963. *Transnational American Studies* 4.2.

Tajfel, Henri. 1974. Social and Intergroup Behavior. *Social Science Information* 13.2: 65–93.

Tate, Katherine. 1991. Black Political Participation in the 1984 and 1988 Presidential Elections. *The American Political Science Review* 85.4: 1159–1176.

Telles, Edward Eric. 2004. *Race in Another America: The Significance of Skin Color in Brazil*. Princeton, NJ: Princeton University Press.

Torres, Arlene. 1998. La Gran Familia Puertorriqueña e' Prieta de Beldá (The Great Puerto Rican Family is Really, Really Black). In *Blackness in Latin America and the Caribbean: Social Dynamics and Cultural Transformations*. Whitten, Norman E., and Arlene Torres, Eds. Bloomington: Indiana University Press.

Torres-Cuevas, Eduardo and Oscar Loyola Vega. 2001. *La Historia de Cuba 1492–1898*. La Habana: Editorial Pueblo y Educación.

Twine, France Winddance. 1998. *Racism in a Racial Democracy: The Maintenance of White Supremacy in Brazil*. New Brunswick, NJ: Rutgers University Press.

Unión de Escritores y Artistas Cubanos. 2013. Reporte del VIII Congreso.

Urrutia, Gustvo. 1937. El Nuevo Negro. *Adelante* 29.

Van Dijk, Teun Adrianus. 1996. *Discourse, Racism, and Ideology*. Tenerife, Spain: RCEI Ediciones.

Van Dijk, Teun Adrianus. 1998. *Ideology: A Multidisciplinary Approach*. London: Sage Publications.

Costa Vargas, João H. 2004. Hyperconsciousness of Race and Its Negation: The Dialectic of White Supremacy in Brazil. *Identities: Global Studies in Culture and Power* 11.4: 443–470.

Costa Vargas, João H. and Alves, Jaime Amparo. 2010. Geographies of Death: An Intersectional Analysis of Police Lethality and the Racialized Regimes of Citizenship in São Paulo. *Ethnic and Racial Studies* 33.4: 611–636.

Unión de Escritores y Artistas de Cuba. 2013. Informe Central. Octavo Congreso de la UNEAC.

Vicent, Mauricio. El 'efecto Obama' sacude la isla. *El Pais*. November 18, 2008.

Weitzer, Ronald John, and Tuch, Steven A. 2005. Racially Biased Policing: Determinants of Citizen Perceptions. *Social Forces* 83.3: 1009–1030.

Williams, Raymond. 1977. *Marxism and Literature*. New York: Oxford University Press.

Winant, Howard. 1994. *Racial Conditions: Politics, Theory, Comparisons*. Minneapolis: University of Minnesota Press.

Winant, Howard. 2000. Race and Race Theory. *Annual Review of Sociology* 26: 169–185.

World Focus. 2009. Interview with Anonimo Consejo. www.worldfocus.org.

Zurbano, Roberto. 2009. El Rap Cubano: Can't Stop Won't Stop the Movement! In *Cuba in the Special Period: Culture and Ideology in the 1990s*. New York: Palgrave Macmillan.

INDEX